WA 1275906 6

D1458901

NEW HORIZONS IN BRITISH URBAN POLICY

New Horizons in British Urban Policy

Perspectives on New Labour's Urban Renaissance

Edited by

CRAIG JOHNSTONE
Liverpool John Moores University, UK

MARK WHITEHEAD
University of Wales, Aberystwyth, UK

ASHGATE

Published by
Ashgate Publishing Limited
Gower House
Croft Road
Aldershot
Hants GU11 3HR
England

Ashgate Publishing Company
Suite 420
101 Cherry Street
Burlington, VT 05401-4405
USA

Ashgate website: http://www.ashgate.com

British Library Cataloguing in Publication Data
New horizons in British urban policy : perspectives on New Labour's urban renaissance
1.Urban policy - Great Britain 2. City planning - Great Britain 3.Inner cities - Great Britain
I.Johnstone, Craig II.Whitehead, Mark
307.1'216'0941

Library of Congress Cataloging-in-Publication Data
New horizons in British urban policy : perspectives on New Labour's urban renaissance / edited by Craig Johnstone and Mark Whitehead.
p. cm.
Includes bibliographical references and index.
ISBN 0-7546-3413-2
1. Urban policy--Great Britain. 2. Urban renewal--Great Britain. 3. Community development, Urban--Great Britain. 4. Sociology, Urban--Great Britain. 5. Labour Party (Great Britain) I. Johnstone, Craig, 1975- II. Whitehead, Mark, 1975-

HT133.N47 2004
307.76'0941--dc22

2004003995

ISBN 0 7546 3413 2

Printed and bound by Athenaeum Press, Ltd.,
Gateshead, Tyne & Wear.

Contents

PART 2: BEYOND THE RENAISSANCE – ISSUES FOR THE FUTURE OF BRITISH URBAN POLICY

List of Figures

List of Tables

List of Illustrations

List of Contributors

Franco Bianchini Reader in Cultural Planning and Policy and Director of the Cultural Planning Research Unit, De Montfort University, Leicester

Sue Brownill Principal Lecturer, School of Planning, Oxford Brookes University

Mark Goodwin Professor of Human Geography, School of Geography, Archaeology and Earth Resources, University of Exeter. Immediately prior to publication he was Professor of Political Geography, Institute of Geography and Earth Sciences, University of Wales, Aberystwyth

Patsy Healey Emeritus Professor of Town and Country Planning, School of Architecture, Planning and Landscape and Director of the Centre for Research on European Urban Environments, University of Newcastle-upon-Tyne

Gareth Hoskins Human Geography Tutor, Institute of Geography and Earth Sciences, University of Wales, Aberystwyth

Rob Imrie Professor of Human Geography, Department of Geography, Royal Holloway, University of London

Craig Johnstone Research Fellow, European Institute for Urban Affairs, Liverpool John Moores University

Martin Jones Reader in Human Geography, Institute of Geography and Earth Sciences, University of Wales, Aberystwyth

Michael Keith Professor of Sociology and Director of the Centre for Urban and Community Research, Goldsmiths College, University of London; Councillor, London Borough of Tower Hamlets; Chairman of Thames Gateway London Partnership.

Mike Raco Lecturer, Department of Geography, University of Reading

Andrew Tallon Lecturer, School of Housing and Urban Studies, University of the West of England, Bristol

Andy Thornley Reader in Urban Planning Studies, Department of Geography and Environment, London School of Economics

Ivan Turok Professor of Urban Economic Development, Department of Urban Studies, University of Glasgow

Kevin Ward Senior Lecturer, School of Geography, University of Manchester

Karen West Research Fellow, Department of Geography and Environment, London School of Economics

Mark Whitehead Lecturer, Institute of Geography and Earth Sciences, University of Wales, Aberystwyth

Preface

For a book primarily concerned with British urban policy, this edited volume has an unusual geographical point of origin. In fact, it was at the end of a trip to the USA to present papers at the Annual Meeting of the Association of American Geographers in 2000 that we had a conversation over a meal in Niagara Falls that sowed the seeds of this edited collection. Reflecting on our respective conference presentations on different aspects of British urban policy, we agreed that it was becoming increasingly difficult to 'keep-up with', and consequently to conceptualize, the urban policy landscape emerging in New Labour's Britain. Whether it be in our own specialist areas of neighbourhood governance or urban crime prevention or in related policy areas – health, education, social exclusion, economic development, devolution, community democracy, planning, housing, cultural policy and place-marketing – which all appeared to be having important impacts on urban areas, we both felt that too much was happening too fast for policy-makers and academics to fully understand, question and effectively inform the urban regeneration process in the UK.

Later that same year the New Labour government published its long-promised Urban White Paper, *Our Towns and Cities: The Future – Delivering an Urban Renaissance*, the first in 23 years. This ostensibly appeared to offer the sense of perspective on English (if not British) urban policy we were seeking. The purpose of this White Paper was to provide an integrating framework and ideological vision for urban policy development throughout England. At the heart of this document was the desire to instigate a social, cultural, economic, and political renaissance within English cities. While the White Paper only applied to English cities, we felt that the principles of *urban renaissance* it evoked under-girded a broader *Third Way* – one which sought to synthesize the economic rationales of neo-liberalism with the social concerns of the old Left – which appeared to be emerging in urban policy throughout Britain.

In response to our conversation in the USA and the publication of the Urban White Paper we decided to convene a conference session at the 2002 Annual Conference of the Royal Geographical Society (with the Institute of British Geography) in Belfast in which New Labour's urban renaissance project could be examined in more detail. The session, also entitled *New Horizons in British Urban Policy*, sought to bring together academics from a number of disciplines who, through their disparate interests and specialist knowledges, could help us make sense of the British urban policy landscape.

We found the conference session productive and felt it important to try and draw together the ideas and themes raised during our discussions in a publication. The result is this edited collection. Our intention was to produce a book which served three purposes: first, to provide an accessible insight into the changing form and function of British urban policy; second, to suggest innovative ways of conceptualizing and analysing urban policy; and third, to explore potential strategies through which contemporary urban policy could be reinvigorated and the process of urban renaissance made more inclusive. This book is not, therefore, simply a collection of conference papers. Presenters at our Belfast conference session have substantially re-written or produced new contributions to reflect both the aims of the book and the most recent policy developments. Their work is supplemented by that of additional authors who were invited to contribute chapters on other key issues within contemporary urban policy. But the Blair government's urban renaissance agenda touches on so many public policy spheres that it would be almost impossible to cover every issue in depth. Thus, it is our intention here to provide not a compendium of New Labour's urban policy but *perspectives* on it.

In order to provide the reader with a clear sense of the different objectives of this book, all of the chapters, with the exception of the introduction, are split across two sections. These chapters especially, although not exclusively, address the main aims of the book as described above. In this context, Part 1 of this book, entitled *Analysing New Labour's Urban Renaissance Project*, describes some of the key changes in British urban policy under New Labour and considers different ways in which these changes might be conceptualized. Chapters 2 and 3, for example, explore how British cities are being re-imaged as successful, vibrant communities of opportunities, and some of the consequences which success can bring to urban centres. Through a focus on newly emerging neighbourhood and crime-prevention policies, Chapters 4 and 5 consider how contemporary attempts to create more open, inclusive and safe cities, are in real danger of creating spaces of elitism, suspicion and exclusion in Britain. Focusing on the particular cases London and Scotland, Chapters 6 and 7 then consider the impacts which devolution, as key processes associated with the New Labour Movement, is having on the formation and implementation of urban policy. Chapters 8 and 9 draw this section to a close by exploring some conceptual frameworks through which the contemporary urban renaissance and its associated policy fields can be contextualized and analysed.

Part 2 explores a series of ways in which the role and operation of urban policy in Britain could be restructured. This section, which is called *Beyond the Renaissance – Issues for the Future of British Urban Policy*, discusses the role of planners in the formation of more inclusive city spaces; the importance of building political institutions which effectively integrate urban policy at a local, urban, regional and national level; the significance of gender issues for urban policy and regeneration; and strategies for generating urban spaces which reflect the multi-ethnic traditions of urban Britain.

Craig Johnstone and Mark Whitehead
Liverpool and Aberystwyth, June 2004

Acknowledgements

In completing this project we have become indebted to a large number of different people. Firstly, we would like to acknowledge the efforts and patience of all the contributors and thank them for supporting the idea of an edited collection and for their co-operation during its production. Secondly, we would like to state our appreciation to Ashgate for permitting us to write this book. We are grateful to all the Ashgate staff who assisted in the production of the book, but particular thanks go to Valerie Rose for her editorial guidance and Sarah Horsley for her work on the preparation of the final manuscript. Thirdly, our thanks to the two anonymous referees who considered the original proposal we put forward for this book. Their comments were both helpful and instructive. Fourthly, we would also like to express our gratitude to the Urban Geography and Political Geography Research Groups of the Royal Geographical Society (with the Institute of British Geographers). Their generous financial support for the conference session from which this book emerged was invaluable. Fifthly, we are indebted to Julie MacLeavy who provided invaluable assistance during the production of the final version of this book. Finally, our appreciation to our colleague Graham Gardner, Geographer and novelist, who was a third participant in our initial discussion over dinner in Niagara Falls about the policies and politics of New Labour.

Abbreviations and Acronyms

ASBO	Anti-Social Behaviour Order
BNP	British National Party
CABE	Commission for Architecture and the Built Environment
CAT	City Action Teams
CCT	Compulsory Competitive Tendering
CCTV	Closed Circuit Television
CDP	Community Development Projects
CLES	Centre for Local Economic Strategies
CURS	Centre for Urban and Regional Studies
DETR	Department of the Environment, Transport and the Regions
DfEE	Department for Education and Employment
DoE	Department of the Environment
DSS	Department of Social Services
DTI	Department of Trade and Industry
DTLR	Department of Transport, Local Government and the Regions
EIP	Examination in Public
ERDF	European Regional Development Fund
ESRC	Economic and Social Research Council
FEDS	Framework for Economic Development
GEAR	Glasgow Eastern Area Renewal
GLA	Greater London Authority
GLC	Greater London Council
GOL	Government Office for London
ICT	Information Communication Technology
LDA	London Development Agency
LEU	London Ecology Unit
LGIU	Local Government Information Unit
LPAC	London Planning Advisory Committee
LRC	London Research Centre
LSE	London School of Economics
LSP	Local Strategic Partnership
MBC	Metropolitan Borough Council
NDC	New Deal for Communities
ODPM	Office of the Deputy Prime Minister
PAT	Policy Action Team
PPA	Priority Partnership Areas
PPP	Public Private Partnerships
RBC	Reading Borough Council
RDA	Regional Development Agency

RGS/IBG	Royal Geographical Society with the Institute of British Geographers
SDA	Scottish Development Agency
SDS	Spatial Development Strategy
SEU	Social Exclusion Unit
SIP	Social Inclusion Partnership
SRB	Single Regeneration Budget
SRBCF	Single Regeneration Budget Challenge Fund
SSS	Smart Successful Scotland
SURI	Smaller Urban Renewal Initiative
SWPR	Schumperterian Workfare Postnational Regime
SYWDT	South Yorkshire Women's Development Trust
TEC	Training and Enterprise Council
TfL	Transport for London
UDC	Urban Development Corporation
UDP	Unitary Development Plan
UNESCO	United Nations Educational, Scientific and Cultural Organisation
URBED	Urban Economic Development Group
WCSP	West Central Scotland Plan
WDS	Women's Design Service
WMGRP	West Midlands Gender and Regeneration Project
YIP	Youth Inclusion Project/Partnership
YOT	Youth Offending Team

INTRODUCTION

Chapter 1

Horizons and Barriers in British Urban Policy

Craig Johnstone and Mark Whitehead

Introduction

In the autumn of 1968 Harold Wilson's Labour government initiated the first distinct urban policy framework in Britain. The birth of this explicitly urban branch of policy occurred with the launch of 'an urban programme of expenditure mainly on education, housing, health and welfare in areas of special social need [–] localized districts which bear the marks of multiple deprivation' (Home Office, 1968). Almost 30 years to the day later, Tony Blair visited the Holly Street estate in Hackney. Flanked by his Deputy, John Prescott, the Prime Minister was in east London to launch the government's £800 million New Deal for Communities. After fifteen months in power, this high-profile initiative was the Labour government's first attempt to make good on its promise to create a more equitable society by tackling the recalcitrant socio-economic problems of urban Britain.

Although the Urban Programme marked the beginning of three decades of continuous central government intervention in urban affairs, choices made in all areas of public policy, both before and after 1968, meant that the deprivation faced by some communities in 1998 was arguably more acute than it had ever been. But while the towns and cities of 1998 shared many of the same problems with those of 1968[1], in many respects they were also very different from those of that earlier era. The industrial restructuring instigated in the 1980s by Thatcher's Conservative government in response to the economic crisis of the 1970s destroyed thousands of blue-collar jobs and decimated the employment base of the old industrial towns and cities of the Midlands, northern England, South Wales and Scotland's Central Belt (see Hudson, 1989; Gamble, 1994). While some, more peripheral, towns are still struggling to come to terms with their changed circumstances, the larger cities have been better placed to embrace the switch to a service sector, consumption-based economy and are showing signs of recovery. Consequently, and for the first time in many years, Britain's cities are being viewed, by politicians, as spaces of hope rather than spaces of despair.

---

1 For a history of British urban policy pre-1997 see CDP, 1977; Lawless, 1979 and 1989; Rees and Lambert, 1985; Lawless and Brown, 1986; Robson, 1988; Parkinson, 1989; Deakin and Edwards, 1993; Atkinson and Moon, 1994; Imrie and Thomas, 1999.

This changing attitude towards cities is most clearly evident in New Labour's 'road map' for urban renewal: the first White Paper to be published on urban issues for 23 years, *Our Towns and Cities: The Future – Delivering an urban renaissance* (Department of Environment, Transport and the Regions (DETR), 2000a). Based on the report of the Urban Task Force (1999), it outlines a vision of towns and cities that are attractive, environmentally sustainable centres of economic growth and prosperity where citizens have access to good quality services and an active role in shaping the future of their communities. Rather than their problems, the document focuses on the opportunities provided by urban areas – the descriptions of inner city decline characteristic of previous urban policy statements replaced by evidence of successful regeneration. But while the White Paper is concerned with all quality of life issues, specific emphasis is placed on urban design and physical regeneration. Cognisant of the growing demand for housing in Britain, it advocates higher density living in attractively designed mixed-use developments located, as much as possible, on previously developed 'brownfield' land – in essence, a re-colonization of town and city centres by the middle classes (Smith, 2002).

The high profile afforded to *Our Towns and Cities: The Future* – both by the involvement of influential figures in its development and the 2002 Urban Summit in Birmingham, at which the urban regeneration elite restated their commitment to its central tenets – makes it all too easy to conflate New Labour's urban renaissance 'project' with the objectives set out within the pages of this document. But the government's urban policy agenda is much broader and issues of deprivation, which are largely marginalized within the White Paper, are dealt with in a parallel document, *A New Commitment to Neighbourhood Renewal* (SEU, 2001). This sets out a vision for long-term community regeneration to be delivered through the newly established Neighbourhood Renewal Unit. It builds on the work started by the volley of New Deal initiatives launched early in Blair's first term in office and the research undertaken by the 18 Policy Action Teams of the Labour-created Social Exclusion Unit (SEU).

As a consequence of the considerable changes in the nature, form, content and delivery of British urban policy that have taken place under New Labour, it has been very difficult for practitioners, academics and urban residents themselves to keep up with what has been happening. In light of these difficulties, this book attempts to make sense of what has been going on in the world of British urban policy since 1997. By carefully unpacking the different urban policy initiatives that collectively constitute the Blair government's urban programme, this book also provides a critical analysis of New Labour's renaissance vision and its potential as a long-term solution to the problems of urban Britain. In this chapter we begin this process by sketching out the main features of contemporary urban policy, exploring the political ideals upon which it is founded and identifying the principal challenges that must be overcome if New Labour is to deliver its urban renaissance. In so doing our intention is to provide a context within which subsequent chapters can be positioned and more clearly integrated.

From 'patchwork quilt' to 'bowl of spaghetti'

Urban policy initiatives have proliferated at such a rate since New Labour came to power that, early in 2003, the regeneration minister, Lord Rooker, admitted the resultant policy maze was as complex as 'a bowl of spaghetti' (*The Guardian*, 2003). The metaphor of spaghetti is a helpful way of illustrating the organization of contemporary urban policy. Its use is also revealing because it clearly resonates with the Audit Commission's depiction of urban policy in the late 1980s as a 'patchwork quilt' (Audit Commission, 1989). Significantly, the contemporary urban policy landscape is even more diverse and complicated than it was then (see Table 1.1). In this sense it is noteworthy that while the notion of a patchwork quilt effectively captured the spatial complexity of the different area-based initiatives that existed in the late 1980s, the metaphor of spaghetti denotes an altogether higher-order of urban policy complexity: a diverse landscape of strategies and initiatives that cross different spaces, scales and policy arenas. Collectively, it represents an attempt to generate what New Labour describes as a *renaissance* in urban economies, communities and metropolitan life.

Keeping track of urban policy developments has been made more difficult in recent years by the devolution of powers to the Scottish Parliament and Welsh Assembly. Scotland has long had different urban priorities and policies and in many respects the Scottish Executive is simply maintaining this tradition. However, the main proposals set out in *Building Better Cities: Delivering growth and opportunity* (Scottish Executive, 2003a) closely mirror those put forward in the English Urban White Paper and would seem to indicate a degree of cross-border policy transference, even though the two documents were based on separate pieces of research and the advice of different advisory panels[2] (see Turok, this volume). The situation in Wales is somewhat different, as only certain powers have been devolved from the centre and the Assembly does not have an urban policy in the same distinct way as England and Scotland. Nonetheless, the economic development, social exclusion and housing policies all now devised in Cardiff, impact strongly on urban Wales. The Assembly has, moreover, developed an *Index of Multiple Deprivation for Wales* (National Assembly for Wales, 2000) and in 2001 launched its Communities First initiative to tackle deprivation in the nation's most deprived wards (National Assembly for Wales, 2001).

To add to the confusion, increasing pressure is being placed on public service providers to tackle 'postcode' poverty and social disadvantage through the refocusing or 'bending' of their mainstream activities. This makes it difficult to work out where urban policy ends and other public policy sectors begin. Meanwhile, regional policy, with its focus on economic competitiveness and the links between cities and their wider regions, is also implicitly urban. Indeed, given that almost 90% of the British population live in towns and cities, it can be argued

---

2 The two strategy documents were under-girded, in England, by Robson, Parkinson, Boddy and Maclennan (2000) *The State of English Cities* and, in Scotland, Scottish Executive (2003b) *Review of Scotland's Cities – The Analysis*.

Table 1.1 Regeneration initiatives compared: 1989 and 2003

'Patchwork quilt' (1989)	'Bowl of spaghetti' (2003)	
• City Grant	• Action Team for Jobs	• Neighbourhood Management
• Derelict land grant	• Active Community Programme	• Neighbourhood Nursery Centres
• English Estates	• Capital Modernization Fund (small retailers)	• Neighbourhood Renewal Fund
• Enterprise allowance	• Children's Fund	• Neighbourhood Support Fund
• Enterprise Zones	• City Growth Strategies	• Neighbourhood Wardens
• Estate Action	• Coalfields Task Force	• New Deal for Communities
• Regional Selective Assistance	• Community Champions	• New Entrepreneur Scholarships
• Section 11	• Community Chest	• Playing Fields and Community Green Spaces
• Task Forces and CATs	• Community Empowerment Fund	• Positive Futures
• Technical and Vocational Education Initiative	• Community Legal Partnerships	• Regional Centres for Manufacturing Excellence
• Urban Development Corporations	• Creative Partnerships	• Safer Communities Initiative
• Urban Programme	• Crime Reduction Programme	• Single Regeneration Budget
• Welsh Development Agency	• Drug Action Teams	• Spaces for Sport and Arts
• Work-related NAFE	• Early Excellence Centres	• Sport Action Zones
	• Early Years Development and Childcare Partnerships	• StepUp
	• Education Action Zones	• Street Wardens
	• Employment Zones	• Sure Start
	• European Regional Development Fund	• Sure Start Plus
	• Excellence Challenge	• Urban Regeneration Companies
	• Excellence in Cities	• Youth Inclusion Programme
	• Fair Share	• Youth Music Action Zones
	• Framework for regional employment and skills action	
	• Health Action Zones	
	• Healthy Living Centres	
	• Healthy Schools Programme	

Source: *The Guardian*, 14th January 2003, based on data supplied by CURS, University of Birmingham.

that very little public policy is without an urban dimension. But while most public policies have implications for towns and cities, we would argue that the percentage embodying a clear vision of the urban and geared exclusively to achieving urban priorities remains very small. It is probable that *Our Towns and Cities: The Future* occupies a less central position within its policy field than did the last Urban White Paper, *Policy for the Inner Cities* (DoE, 1977), and yet it remains a useful distillation of a Labour government's thinking on contemporary urban issues. It not only indicates how New Labour perceives 'the urban' but also sets out a vision of what could best be described as *post-inner city urban policy* (Whitehead, 2001). In significant contrast to the 1977 document, which was largely obsolete inside two years following a change in government, the 2000 Urban White Paper provides a framework within which strategy continues to be developed (see ODPM, 2003; Scottish Executive, 2003a).

Positioning and interpreting the urban renaissance

Although this book focuses explicitly on contemporary expressions of British urban policy, it does not analyse urban policy for its own sake. In order to understand the particular way in which this book approaches urban policy, it is helpful to consider Peck's (1999) distinction between *shallow* and *deep* policy analysis. Peck argues that the analysis of policy can take two basic forms:

- *shallow policy analysis* – which approaches policy as a technical concern, to be assessed within the parameters of the policy community itself

- *deep policy analysis* – which understands the policy process as a zone within which political power, economic ideology and cultural values collide and are contested.

While concerned with the detailed workings of contemporary urban policy, this book uses urban policy as a basis for analysing the wider social, economic and political processes that are shaping the Britain of New Labour. Consequently, through the analysis of urban policy, this book contributes a new perspective to the growing literature on the New Labour project (cf. Hay, 1999; Driver and Martell, 2002). Crucially, we feel that the *newness* of the perspective offered by this book emerges out of its explicit concern not only for the social and economic logic of New Labourism, but its inter-related spatial dynamics. Understanding urban policy in this *deeper* sense, we argue that just as every previous era of urban regeneration in Britain reflected a particular set of political and economic beliefs and principles, New Labour's urban renaissance is under-girded by a newly emerging set of political and economic ideologies.

Much has already been written on the social, political and economic origins of the New Labour movement (cf. Budge et al, 1998; Driver and Martell, 1998; Giddens, 1998; Callinicos, 2001). Indeed, a whole series of names and ways of understanding New Labour's particular brand of politics have emerged over the recent years. These have included notions of a *Third Way* (Giddens, 1998), *Post-Thatcherism* (Driver and Martell, 1998), *a renewal of social democracy*, *Thatcherite Revisionism* (Hay, 1999), and even claims of *Crypto-Conservatism*

(Hall and Jacques, 1997). While we do not wish to begin a futile pursuit of New Labour's true political and historical origins, what now appears clear is that whatever New Labourism is, it represents both an acceptance and rejection of Thatcherism (Driver and Martell, 1998, pp.1-5). Beyond its contested Thatcherite antecedents, however, we argue that the politics of New Labour is a complex hybrid, forged out of the inter-related forces of global economic competition, British electoral politics, transatlantic policy transfer, and the modernization of the *old* British Labour Party. Despite representing a complex hybrid of political and economic forces, it has been argued that the philosophies and principles of the Third Way provide an, albeit limited, intellectual coherence and rationale for the New Labour movement (Giddens, 1998 and 2000; Hargreaves and Christie, 1998). While widely, criticized as a political model (cf. Hay, 1999; MacLeod and Goodwin, 1999; Callinicos, 2001), we claim that the idea of a *Third Way* provides important insights in to the logics of the New Labour movement.

The notion of a political Third Way is certainly not a discourse unique to the New Labour government in Britain. As Giddens (1998) recognizes, the idea of a political Third Way has been used many times before in a variety of different political situations. Despite its frequent political usage, the contemporary incarnation of Third Way politics has some specific connotations. Within the ideologies and rhetoric of the New Labour government, the phrase Third Way has become a code for a kind of middle politics, forged between the principles of Thatcherite neo-liberalism and more traditional brands of social democracy and welfarism[3]. Despite its vernacular utilization, it would, however, be wrong to think of contemporary Third Way politics as a uniquely British phenomenon. Indeed, many of its principles can be traced back to policies of the New Democrats in the USA (Callinicos, 2001) and various Scandinavian welfare regimes (Etherington and Jones, 2004). In this sense it has been suggested that the Third Way more closely resembles a case of *The West Wing* meeting *Yes Minister* than Old Labour meeting the New Right.

While perhaps characterized more by political pragmatism than ideological coherence, the Third Way is premised upon an acceptance, within prevailing global economic pressures, of tight controls on government spending and the promotion of a competitive market ethos throughout society. Allied to such neo-liberal orthodoxies, however, Third Way politics also suggest the need for a more *caring* brand of public policy, which while encouraging personal freedoms and individualism, addresses issues of social injustice and promotes the formation of a more inclusive and engaged social community (Giddens, 1998, p.65). The hybridized political principles engrained within the Third Way have been expressed in a variety of policy initiatives in Britain, from welfare-to-work, to devolution and from the modernization of the National Health Service to local government reform. Throughout the pages and chapters of this book, it is made evident that the urban renaissance represents an important component of New

---

3 For discussion of where Third Way politics fits onto the continuum separating neo-liberalism and traditional social democracy see Levitas, 1998, ch.5.

Labour's Third Way project. In this sense we interpret contemporary urban policy as an uneasy and problematic marriage of the large-scale anti-poverty programmes of the post-war social democratic state, with the economic imperatives of Thatcherite neo-liberal urban policy. In this context, this book explores how the varied initiatives contained within the urban renaissance are attempting to balance the need for economically competitive and socially inclusive urban spaces throughout Britain.

New Labour: new urban policy goals?

The inherent political tensions contained within the orthodoxies of the Third Way are clearly evident in New Labour's urban policy record. At one level, there has been a concerted attempt by the Labour government to maintain tight controls over public spending on urban policy (DETR, 1998a) – the initial retention of the Single Regeneration Budget Challenge Fund[4] by New Labour was indicative of a desire to continue with the Conservative penchant for competitive bidding within the urban policy process (DETR, 1998b). The competitive allocation of urban funds by New Labour has, however, been attenuated by a desire by the government to target urban funding on the most deprived urban areas. Using the newly devised *Index of Multiple Deprivation* (DETR, 1998c)[5], the New Labour government ring-fenced 80% of Single Regeneration Budget resources (the largest single source of special purpose grant funding for urban regeneration at that time), for the 50 most deprived areas in urban Britain (DETR, 1998b, p.4). It also launched New Deal for Communities, which targets social exclusion within small pockets of high deprivation (DETR, 1998d), and the Neighbourhood Renewal Fund, which is providing £900 million to the 88 most deprived boroughs in England during its first three years. The Scottish Parliament and the Welsh Assembly have adopted similar programmes, the latter, for example, distributing £83 million to its 88 most deprived communities between 2001/2 and 2004/5 through its Communities First initiative (National Assembly for Wales, 2001). We would argue that these developments within urban policy reveal just some of the many tensions that underscore a Third Way renaissance within urban regeneration.

In tackling urban deprivation New Labour has been careful to distance itself from the urban policies of previous Labour administrations. The eradication of inequality through redistributive taxation was a central feature of the post-war cross-party Keynesian political consensus, making the extension of this effort into deprived urban areas in the 1960s and 1970s uncontroversial. But 18 years of Tory rule has seen inequality repackaged as an essential feature of a successful market economy and the poor recast as generally undeserving of either sympathy or state assistance. Crucially, Will Hutton notes:

---

4 The designation of new SRB schemes ended in 2000, although funding for this last round will continue until 2007. 11 different funding streams received by the RDAs, of which the SRB Challenge Fund was one, are being merged to form a 'single pot'.

5 Replaced since by the updated *Index of Multiple Deprivation* (DETR, 2000b).

> The currents that have carried Britain, and indeed the western world, to their present pass are still running strongly from the right. We are asked to make obeisance at the shrine of deregulation, liberalism, privatization, low taxes and the minimal state. New Labour still feels it has to genuflect before these gods if it is to earn its legitimacy (Hutton 1998, p.2).

In response to this changed political climate, Labour has substituted the goal of equality for the less controversial 'equality of opportunity', has shifted its focus from supporting the deprived to tackling the causes of deprivation, has called for the efficient use of both additional and mainstream resources through the 'joining up' of the work of government agencies, and has placed an obligation on communities to help themselves.

A hallmark of New Labour's urban policy has been its emphasis on partnership and community engagement. Legislation has forced state agencies to collaborate as never before, generating new modes of governance for urban problems. In England, local authorities have been required to constitute Local Strategic Partnerships (LSPs) drawing together all the key players in the local public, private, voluntary and community sectors. A duty exists on each LSP to develop and implement a *Community Strategy* and, on the 88 most deprived boroughs in England, an additional *Neighbourhood Renewal Strategy* detailing the regeneration effort on which allocations from the Neighbourhood Renewal Fund will be spent. While the instituting of such partnership arrangements has been driven, at least in part, by New Labour's local government modernization agenda and also the need to overcome budgetary constraints created by the administration's self-imposed public spending curbs, their creation is also an acknowledgement that urban problems are complicated, cross institutional boundaries and cannot be solved by any one agency working in isolation.

Unlike Conservative urban policy of the 1980s and 1990s, which mostly viewed communities as an inconvenience (Goodwin, 1991; Brownill, 1993; Foster, 1999) and, even in later years, heavily circumscribed their involvement in regeneration (Ward, 1997), New Labour has placed great emphasis on community consultation, participation and cohesion (SEU, 2001; Lloyd, 2002). This engagement with the community is expressed most clearly in the New Deal for Communities. Unlike previous initiatives, this programme was designed to be community led from the outset, with local people not public agencies identifying local problems and local solutions (DETR, 1998d). While asking recipients of regeneration efforts what they view as priorities seems an eminently sensible way of increasing the likely success of urban policy, it is also indicative of the government's desire to rebuild the community and its institutions as the 'third leg' of society to complement the market and the state (see Levitas, 1998; Imrie and Raco, 2003). This Communitarian doctrine, which argues that individual rights must be earned through the acceptance of civic responsibilities, is evident across the spectrum of New Labour policy, and stands in stark contrast to the individualism promoted by Thatcher's Conservatives. From this perspective, urban renewal is no longer seen as something done to communities but a process with which members of communities have a duty to actively engage.

Some potential barriers to urban renaissance

New Labour's broad approach to urban renaissance has undoubtedly addressed some of the inherent weaknesses of policies of the recent past, but barriers to success still cast doubt on the government's ability to deliver lasting urban renewal. Some are deep-seated 'wicked issues' that have taunted governments for generations, some were created or at least exacerbated by urban and economic policies of the past, and some have been brought about by the actions of New Labour itself. While it would be premature – perhaps by 20 years – to draw any firm conclusions about the success or failure of Blairite urban policy, in this section we briefly sketch out our what we perceive to be the principal barriers to its success.

The first barrier is created by the scale and intensity of urban problems. Much has been done over the last 20 years to resurrect 'those inner cities' through physical regeneration schemes, but the gentrification of city centres, mass disposal of the highest quality council housing in the 1980s under 'right to buy', and more recent housing market failure has served to concentrate much metropolitan deprivation in the inner suburbs and peripheral council housing estates. While residualization of this nature makes 'problem' areas easier to identify, such concentrations of unemployment, benefit dependency, poor educational attainment, crime, poor health, and abandoned housing are very hard to tackle and the stigmas surrounding such areas almost impossible to remove. Crucially, inter-generational exclusion means this socially disadvantaged 'underclass' has become not only 'hard to reach' but also 'hard of hearing' (McLaughlin, 2002) – resistant to reintegration into mainstream society.

The most deprived neighbourhoods tend to be found in the big cities yet, in many respects, the problems faced by old industrial towns, particularly in northern England and South Wales, are more severe. While Birmingham, Cardiff, Glasgow, Leeds, Liverpool, Manchester, Newcastle and Sheffield have re-imaged themselves as European or even global centres for business, tourism, retailing and culture with some success, more peripheral towns have struggled to recover from the closure of their primary sources of employment, be they mining, textiles or related forms of manufacturing. Cities contain pockets of both deprivation and affluence whereas some towns are comprised of wards that nearly all score highly on indices of deprivation (DETR, 2000b; National Assembly for Wales, 2000). As more wealthy and mobile residents have moved away from such places, falling demand for accommodation has caused housing markets to fail. In some towns and cities, large tracts of publicly- and privately-owned dwellings stand empty[6]. To address this problem the government has set up nine Market Renewal Pathfinders. In each Pathfinder area housing stock will be reorganized through demolition and new building in an attempt to create more sustainable communities (ODPM, 2003). But while this move is not without merit it does little to address the essential

---

6 In Burnley, for example, it is estimated that 15% of properties are vacant (Burnley Task Force, 2002).

obsolescence of peripheral towns that developed around industries that no longer exist.

A second barrier is the community itself. Labour is eager to build cohesive, participative communities that take responsibility for their own future well-being (Levitas, 1998; SEU 2001) but it faces a number of challenges if it is to achieve this objective. In recent decades, the few serious urban riots witnessed in Britain have been catalysed by institutionalized police racism and deprivation (Lea and Young, 1982; Benyon, 1984; Scraton, 1985), with resulting violence targeted at state institutions, most notably the police. The disturbances that erupted in a number of England's northern towns in 2001 and in Wrexham in 2003 marked an altogether more worrying development in that they involved the white and ethnic minority members of the same deprived communities fighting against each other. Investigations into these violent episodes uncovered communities deeply divided along racial lines in which interaction between ethnic groups was minimal and distrust endemic. Each blamed the other for its poverty, with the white community accusing the government of favouritism towards the Asian community and asylum seekers in the allocation of regeneration resources (Cantle 2001; Burnley Task Force, 2002; *The Sunday Times*, 2003). The situation has since been further inflamed by the electoral successes of the British National Party in Burnley, Blackburn and Calderdale.

Even when tensions within communities are minimal, engaging residents in community regeneration initiatives is fraught with difficulties. Unlike welfare-to-work, which carries the threat of financial privation for non-participation, residents of deprived areas cannot be forced to participate in urban renewal. After years during which society has become more individualistic, the return to collective action is an alien concept to many. Others who would like to get involved simply do not have the capacity to participate effectively[7]. A much-discussed example of these problems is the Aston Pride New Deal for Communities Partnership in Birmingham. Recent research evaluating the efficacy of Labour's New Deal for Communities programme has shown that the creation of a community-based partnership in Aston has been fraught with difficulties (Cambridge Economic Associates, 2003). A purported lack of leadership in the Aston Pride Partnership has prevented a clear vision or programme of regeneration emerging for the area. This has meant that large quantities of state funding have remained unspent (ibid.). Aston Pride provides a salutary tale of urban community policy, which raises issues over residents' capacity to establish and effectively run multi-million pound urban regeneration programmes and New Labour's broader vision of a social inclusive democratic city.

The third barrier is growing regional inequality. While old industrial towns, particularly in the North of England, slide further into decline – the 2001 census (Office of National Statistics, 2003) recorded a net population reduction in both the

7 Experience has shown that community members often do not have the confidence or the basic skills – reading, writing, linguistic – to engage with regeneration practitioners. Those that do get involved often find themselves excluded by the technical language of practitioners.

Northeast and Northwest – housing and labour markets in Southeast England have overheated. Employers are struggling to fill jobs in parts of London and the Home Counties, but housing shortages, coupled with high levels of demand, have pushed the cost of the average home in this part of the country to levels beyond the reach of many. Concerned about the affect this is likely to have on key workers – nurses, teachers, bus drivers etc – many of whom are already unable to afford to live close to their place of work, and the negative impact the high cost of living could have on London's central position within the global economy, the government is to invest £446 million in the regeneration of the Thames Gateway – an area stretching for over 20 miles east from Docklands encompassing both the north and south shores of the River Thames – in the three years to 2006 and a further £164 million in the expansion of other strategic areas in Southeast England (ODPM, 2003). While the Thames Gateway is an area of brownfield land ripe for redevelopment and the issue of housing affordability must clearly be addressed, the concentration of new employment opportunities in the Southeast – 300,000 by 2031 in Thames Gateway alone – does little to redress the imbalance between here and the rest of Britain. The problem is exacerbated by the existence of the Regional Development Agencies (RDAs). Whereas central government once exercised control over industrial location to ensure equitable distribution across the country, the different English regions along with Wales and Scotland are now actively competing with each other for inward investment (see Goodwin, this volume). While the presence of European and other grant aid in some regions may increase their competitive advantage, they must constantly battle against the locational benefits offered by London and Southeast England.

The fourth barrier is the monumental complexity of Labour's urban policy. This is most notable in England, although the limited power of its Assembly means Wales must cope with policy emanating from both Cardiff and London. New Whitehall policy Units have layered strategy after strategy and initiative after initiative on top of each other and over those set up by the previous government. It is not uncommon for certain urban neighbourhoods to be the recipient of funding from various Single Regeneration Budget rounds, New Deal For Communities, the Neighbourhood Renewal Fund, Sure Start, the Children's Fund and many of the other initiatives listed in Table 1.1. The potential for replication is immense and, given that each must have its own Board and comes with its own targets, the drain on the time and energy of regeneration practitioners and community activists is enormous[8].

Different government departments have long been known to create policy independently of each other but most apparent since 1997 has been a lack of co-ordination between the various Units, often located within the same department, charged with delivering the urban renaissance. The problem is arguably one born of organizational structures and ministerial demands to deliver results. Initially the

---

8 At the time of writing the government's Regional Co-ordination Unit is starting to address this issue through the piloting of Single Local Management Centres – local management initiatives aimed at co-ordinating and rationalising regeneration programmes and cutting bureaucracy.

Social Exclusion Unit was located within the Cabinet Office while responsibility for urban policy rested with the Department of Environment, Transport and the Regions which itself was subsequently recast as the Department of Transport, Local Government and the Regions (DTLR). Further reorganization in 2002 led to the Office of the Deputy Prime Minister (ODPM) taking control of urban, regional and social inclusion policy. While this latest reorganization should aid co-ordination as it brings together all the department heads on the same Board, the Units that exist within the ODPM still answer to three different junior ministers: one responsible for local government and the regions, one for housing, planning and regeneration and the third for social exclusion, regional co-ordination and neighbourhood renewal. Not only do different arms of the ODPM machine have different political masters, the implementation of policy is driven and monitored by two separate regional bodies, which makes joining it all up on the ground very difficult. The programmes of the Neighbourhood Renewal Unit are managed through the regional Government Offices while the Urban Policy Unit, which has devolved more control over the allocation of regeneration funding to the regional level, is largely reliant on the Regional Development Agencies (RDAs) to deliver its programmes. However, as the RDAs were principally created to pursue an economic regeneration agenda, and have been under the aegis of the Department of Trade and Industry since June 2001, they have shown little interest in those aspects of urban renewal that do not obviously contribute to wealth creation and the raising of economic competitiveness (Greenhalgh and Shaw, 2002). As a consequence, English Partnerships, the other regeneration arm of ODPM, is being given a greater role than was originally intended in the preparation and redevelopment of brownfield land. Transport meanwhile, which is central to sustainable urban renaissance, is now in the hands of an entirely separate department.

One of the causes of what *The Guardian* (2001) described as 'initiativitus' in urban policy is the concern amongst ministers that they are seen to be doing something to address urban problems. Many of the flagship programmes introduced by Labour in the late 1990s, like New Deal for Communities, are long-term investments in renewal that may not deliver significant change for five or even ten years. But communities demand and the political cycle, with General Elections every four or five years, requires much more rapid change. Thus, government departments and policy units apply intense pressure on those running regeneration to deliver quick returns. Units also demonstrate their worth by churning out new initiatives with alarming regularity. Such 'fast policy' (Peck, 1999) permits the final achievements of long-running initiatives to be presented as inconsequential as, long before their completion, they will invariably have been sidelined by newer versions that are supposedly altogether better.

The fifth and final barrier is the managerial, performance indicator culture that New Labour has instituted. Despite promises to give those working 'on the ground' the freedom to respond to local conditions, strict accounting procedures and inflexible targets are at risk of making New Labour's urban policy as centralized and unresponsive to geographical variation as that of the Conservatives. Indeed, Crawford (2001, p.59) observes that under the Blair government, 'the managerialist urges to objective setting, performance measurement and output-fixation...has reached a new zenith'. Floor targets, league tables, regional Government Office auditing, independent evaluations, performance management regimes, edicts from programme-commissioning Units, and constant prodding from the Delivery Unit give public service providers and regeneration programme managers very little room for manoeuvre. In an era in which governments are increasingly reliant on multi-agency partnerships to deliver policy, such managerial techniques are designed to ensure that the renewal objectives articulated by ministers are not ignored locally. As government has given way to governance and the role of the central State has gradually shifted from Fixer of Problems to Director of Operations, maintaining control over complex networks of actors has become a key problematic. Over time local policy delivery regimes tend to become resistant to direction from the centre and it is through managerial techniques that New Labour is attempting to govern governance (Whitehead, 2003).

While a desire to measure progress is understandable and not without merit, and an interest in 'what works' fairly logical if rather reductionist, the micro-management of policy delivery from Whitehall threatens to pull apart the very joined-up governance structures the government has been so eager to promote. According to Crawford (2001, p.67):

> managerialist reforms are essentially hierarchical and as such antithetical to the management of complex networks: they emphasize inward-looking and myopic forms of performance management and output fixation which often work against holistic governance. As a consequence, they often fail to address 'wicked issues', focusing upon narrowly defined, measurable elements of a problem. They are simultaneously wide-angled but tunnelled vision.

The focus on certain centrally defined targets necessitated by performance indicator culture discourages public service providers from participating fully in partnerships whose objectives are peripheral to their own. Moreover, in order to produce satisfactory outputs it is possible that regeneration programmes, for example, will try to sidestep the more intractable socio-economic problems in the knowledge that their effort is unlikely to deliver significant measurable change.

Structure and content of the book

This book provides an integrated critical analysis of New Labour's urban renaissance programme. Understanding the *renaissance* not simply as the visions and pronouncements of Labour's Urban White Paper, but as the whole ensemble of urban policy initiatives devised since 1997, analysis combines detailed work on the internal workings of contemporary urban policy with sophisticated theoretical readings of the wider logics and ideologies of New Labourism. Reflecting on British urban policy, analysis questions whether it is possible to balance the dynamic capitalist urban economy, so coveted by the New Right, with the egalitarian city and community-based metropolis desired by the Old Left (cf. Callinicos, 2001, p.29). Within the multifarious initiatives and projects associated with Labour's urban renaissance, we claim it is possible to explore the economic ideologies and political practices of the New Labour government in new and interesting ways. In terms of urban policy, the creation of a more equitable society now seems to depend upon the creation of an *equality of opportunity* rather than more traditional programmes of income redistribution. This book explores whether such discourses and practices are enhancing or betraying egalitarianism in British cities (Callinicos, 2001, pp.45-6). In a similar way, this book also considers the urban renaissance's emphasis on community-oriented urban policy and the creation of a more open, democratic city. In many ways, the community focus of New Labour's urban renaissance appears to represent a clear response to the de-humanized, economic policies of Thatcherism. However, different chapters in this book question whether in the creation of space for public participation in urban life, New Labour has recreated a highly policed authoritarian populist city, as much as it has created a cosmopolitan metropolis (Callinicos, 2001, pp.55-67; DETR, 2000a). Such tensions between an old and a new politics, which are inscribed within contemporary urban policy, are a constant theme throughout this volume. Throughout such deliberations, however, we hope to combine a continued concern for the internal workings of British urban policy, with a constant awareness of the broader political and economic structures within which these policies are being devised and delivered.

The first two chapters in Part 1 of this book explore the ways in which British cities are being recast and remade as successful and exciting places in which to live and work. In Chapter 2, Hoskins and Tallon explore the promotion of an 'urban idyll' as part of New Labour's urban renaissance project. The authors maintain that the construction of an idyllic representation of city living, which is composed of seductive images of a vibrant metropolis made up of waterfront living, penthouses, coffee shops and designer stores, is a key component of the government's attempts to *repeople* cities. Comparing the idea of an urban idyll to its longer standing parallel, the rural idyll, this chapter shows that, just as in rural areas, the idea of an urban idyll is tending to produce a very exclusive and exclusionary vision of the city. Chapter 3 focuses upon the problems which a successful urban economy can create for towns and cities. In this chapter Raco argues that while much urban policy analysis focuses upon deprived or under achieving urban areas, if New Labour's urban renaissance is to be a success, it is important to be aware of the types of urban problems which can beset vibrant metropolitan centres. Drawing on the case of Reading, a purported governmental model of urban renaissance, Raco recounts the socio-environmental costs which can accompany rapid and lightly-regulated economic growth, and explores the potential of such growth to generate exclusive metropolitan areas as well as the inclusive sites envisaged by the Labour government.

Chapters 4 and 5 describe and analyse contemporary government policies which have been develop to create safer, democratic and more inclusive urban spaces in Britain. In the first of these chapters Whitehead charts the rediscovery and use of the neighbourhood by New Labour as a key spatial scale and site at which to deliver contemporary urban policies in Britain. Drawing on research carried out on neighbourhood democracy and New Deal for Communities schemes in Walsall, Whitehead suggests the ideal of the neighbourhood is being used not only as a new spatial target for urban spending, but also as a moral framework for combating urban social disintegration. While acknowledging the potential of neighbourhoods to act as new spaces of social inclusion, community participation and cosmopolitan belonging, Whitehead argues that, as they are currently being constructed, neighbourhoods are in danger of becoming exclusionary, *barricaded* spaces of urban isolationism. In Chapter 5, Johnstone explores the links that are emerging between crime, disorder and urban policies. The author claims that the government sees addressing issues of crime and anti-social behaviour as crucial pre-requisites to the formation of a more inclusive metropolitan society. Significantly, Johnstone shows that current attempts to promote social inclusion in British towns and cities are being undermined by the tendency for urban crime and disorder policies to manage social risk through the selective exclusion of disadvantaged groups from urban communities and public life.

The next two chapters in this section explore the impacts which devolution is having on urban policy. In chapter 6, Thornley and West describe the emergence of the Greater London Authority (GLA) and consider the impact that it has had on the formation and implementation of urban policy in the British capital. The authors argue that, as a devolved urban authority, the GLA reflects New Labour's broader desire to provide more strategic contexts for urban policy integration throughout Britain. But through their research on the internal workings of the GLA, Thornley and West show how hopes of policy integration can be difficult to achieve when strategic authorities are bound by short-term political ambitions, and lack power over key urban policy areas. In Chapter 7, Turok considers the impact which devolution in Scotland has had on the form and function of urban policy. He suggests that devolution has brought with it a greater sympathy towards urban social issues in Scotland, and a more open and transparent policymaking process. He does, however, warn that the proliferation of urban (and related) policy areas under the new Scottish Executive has created an uneven set of policy frameworks which must be more carefully integrated and harmonized in the future.

The final two chapters in Part 1 explore different theoretical contexts within which New Labour's urban renaissance project can be analysed. In Chapter 8, Imrie interprets the government's Urban White Paper for English towns and cities through the conceptual apparatus of governmentality. Drawing on the application of Foucault's notion of governmentality by political theorists, the author argues that New Labour's Urban White Paper can be conceived of as a governmental programme, or collection of political technologies, designed to manage urban citizens. Imrie uses this perspective to identify how urban policies like the White Paper are being used to disconnect urban problems from issues of socio-economic injustice, and to construct urban populations as enterprising economic actors who are responsible for their own successes and potential failures. In Chapter 9, Jones and Ward draw on theories of crisis to argue that contemporary Third Way policies for British cities have been designed to address the political crisis of urban policy formation rather than the socio-economic crises of cities themselves. Understanding the contemporary urban renaissance as a crisis of crisis-management, Jones and Ward claim that through the continual promotion of neo-liberal orthodoxies in urban policy New Labour is in danger of intensifying not attenuating contemporary urban problems.

Chapter 10 is the first in Part 2. Here Healey explores the role of planning in the creation of social democratic cities. The idea of a 're-invented social democracy' is central to New Labour's ideological agenda, yet the author argues that the government has produced no clear strategy to suggest how this vision can be delivered within the spaces and places of urban Britain. Healey claims that the formation of a social democratic city is dependent upon creating opportunities for *mixity* and diversity in city life, and argues that the recent publication of the Planning Green Paper, *Planning: Delivering a Fundamental Change*, provided a unique opportunity to harmonize planning structures with the desire to create more inclusive and socially vibrant spaces within the city. She concludes, however, by claiming that within the Planning Green Paper, the social dynamics of planning remain under-developed, with planning being presented as a largely technical process involving negotiations between economic development and environmental conservation.

In Chapter 11, Goodwin examines the multiple scales at which contemporary urban policy is being delivered. Comparing the present day links that are being forged between urban and regional policy with those of the urban/regional policy of Clement Atlee's 1945-51 Labour administration, the author argues that current forms of urban policy are unable to effectively deal with the kinds of uneven socio-economic development which cause urban social disadvantage. According to Goodwin this situation has arisen because, despite its name, current urban policy is rarely conceived of and implemented at an urban level. This makes it difficult to manage intra-urban competition. At the same time, he argues that contemporary urban policy is hindered by the absence of the types of national planning policies which served to discourage inter-urban competition in the immediate post-war era.

In Chapter 12, Keith charts the emergence of Local Strategic Partnerships as key institutional vehicles responsible for delivering an urban renaissance in the UK. He argues that although Local Strategic Partnerships offer the hope of a *reinvented* local state, they also embody many of the political contradictions associated with Third Way Labourism. Drawing on his experience of the Tower Hamlets Local Strategic Partnership, Keith reveals how these newly emerging political structures reflect local summations of national political tensions relating to representative and participatory democracy, co-ordination and accountability, strategic and consensual decision-making, social inclusion and service delivery and knowable and unknowable notions of the city.

Brownill uses Chapter 13 to develop a gender-based critique of British urban policy. At one level, the author commends New Labour's urban renaissance programme for recognizing the important relationships that exist between gender and urban regeneration. She is, however, critical of the type of links that are presently being constructed between gender and regeneration within contemporary British urban policy, arguing that urban gender policies focus on 'issues confronting women' rather than on developing a broader understanding of gender issues. Crucially, Brownill maintains that urban policy fails to confront the forms of gendered exploitation which are etched in to the spatial form of urban areas.

In the final chapter, Bianchini analyses the role of cultural policy in urban regeneration, arguing that culture is a vital asset within attempts to regenerate cities. He maintains, however, that contemporary cultural planning strategies for cities in Britain are focusing upon highly prescribed and narrowly conceived notions of culture. Drawing on examples of cultural planning experiments in European cities, Bianchini asserts that Britain needs to develop broader *intercultural* and *transcultural* projects which incorporate a much richer diversity of ethnic traditions into the remaking of cities. According to Bianchini such strategies offer hope not only for economic regeneration, but also of a more culturally inclusive and ethnically tolerant city.

References

Atkinson, R. and Moon, G. (1994), *Urban Policy in Britain*, Macmillan, Basingstoke.

Audit Commission (1989), *Urban Regeneration and Economic Development: The Local Government Dimension*, London: HMSO.

Benyon, J. (ed) (1984), *Scarman and After: Essays Reflecting on Lord Scarman's Report, the Riots and their Aftermath*, Pergamon Press, Oxford.

Brownill, S. (1993), *Developing London's Docklands: Another Great Planning Disaster?*, Chapman, London.

Budge, I., Crewe, I., McKay, D. and Newton, K. (1998), *The New British Politics*, Addison Wesley Longman, London.

Burnley Task Force (2002), *Burnley Speaks, Who Listens...? A summary of the Burnley Taskforce Report on the disturbances in Burnley in June 2001*, Burnley Task Force, Burnley.

Callinicos, A. (2001), *Against the Third Way*, Polity Press, Cambridge.

Cambridge Economic Associates (2003), *New Deal for Communities National Evaluation: Partnership Reports 2002/3*, Cambridge Economic Associates Ltd, Cambridge.

Cantle, E. (2001), *Community Cohesion: A report by the Independent Review Team, chaired by Ted Cantle*, Home Office, London.

Community Development Projects (1977), *Gilding the Ghetto: The State and the Poverty Experiments*, CDP Inter-project Editorial Team, London.

Crawford, A. (2001), 'Joined-up but fragmented: contradiction, ambiguity and ambivalence at the heart of New Labour's 'Third Way'', in R. Matthews and J. Pitts (eds), *Crime, Disorder and Community Safety*, Routledge, London.

Deakin, N. and Edwards, J. (1993), *The Enterprise Culture and the Inner City*, Routledge, London.

DETR (1998a), *DETR Annual Report 1998*, DETR, London.

DETR (1998b), *The Single Regeneration Budget: A Guide for Partnerships*, DETR, London.

DETR (1998c), *Index of Multiple Deprivation*, DETR, London.

DETR (1998d), *A New Deal for Communities*, DETR, London.

DETR (2000a), *Our Towns and Cities: the Future – Delivering an Urban Renaissance*, HMSO, London.

DETR (2000b), *Index of Multiple Deprivation*, DETR, London.

DoE (1977), *Policy for the Inner Cities*, HMSO, London.

Driver, S. and Martell, L. (1998), *New Labour – Politics After Thatcherism*, Polity Press, Cambridge.

Driver, S. and Martell, L. (2002), *Blair's Britain*, Polity Press, Cambridge.

Etherington, D. and Jones, M. (2004), 'Beyond contradictions of the Workfare State: Denmark, welfare-through-work, and the promise of job rotation', *Environment and Planning C: Government and Policy*, forthcoming.

Foster, J. (1999), *Docklands: Cultures in Conflict, World in Collision*, UCL Press, London.

Gamble, A. (1994), *The Free Economy and the Strong State: the Politics of Thatcherism*, Macmillan, Basingstoke.

Giddens, A. (1998), *The Third Way: The Renewal of Social Democracy*, Polity Press, Cambridge.

Giddens A. (2000), *The Third Way and its Critics*, Polity Press, Cambridge.

Goodwin, M. (1991), 'Replacing a surplus population: the politics of the LDDC', in J. Allen and C. Hamnett (eds), *Housing and Labour Markets*, Unwin Hyman, London.

Greenhalgh, P. and Shaw, K. (2002), 'Regional Development Agencies and physical regeneration: Can the RDAs actually deliver the Urban Renaissance', paper presented to the 3rd Regeneration Management Research Workshop – The Urban Renaissance in Question, University of Durham, 15th November 2002.

Hall, S. and Jacques. M. (1997), 'Blair: is he the Greatest Tory Since Thatcher?', *Observer*, 3rd April 1997.

Hargreaves, I. and Christie, I. (1998), *Tomorrow's Politics: the Third Way and Beyond*, Demos, London.

Hay, C. (1999), *The Political Economy of New Labour: Labouring under False Pretences*, Manchester University Press, Manchester.

Home Office (1968), *Urban Programme Circular No.1*, October 1968, Home Office, London.

Hudson, R. (1989), 'Rewriting history and reshaping geography: the nationalised industries and the political economy of Thatcherism', in J. Mohan (ed) *The Political Geography of Contemporary Britain*, Macmillan, Basingstoke.

Hutton, W. (1998), *The Stakeholding Society*, Polity Press, Cambridge.

Imrie, R. and Raco, M. (eds) (2003), *Urban Renaissance? New Labour, Community and Urban Policy*, The Policy Press, Bristol.

Imrie, R. and Thomas, H. (eds) (1999), *British Urban Policy: An Evaluation of the Urban Development Corporations*, Sage, London.

Lawless, P. (1979), *Urban Deprivation and Government Initiative*, Faber and Faber, London.

Lawless, P. (1989), *Britain's Inner Cities*, Chapman, London.

Lawless, P. and Brown, F. (1986), *Urban Growth and Change in Britain: An Introduction*, Harper and Row, London.

Lea, J. and Young, J. (1982), 'The riots in 1981: urban violence and political marginalisation', *Critical Social Policy*, vol. 1(3), pp. 59-69.

Levitas, R. (1998), *The Inclusive Society*, Macmillan, Basingstoke.

Lloyd, M.G. (2002), 'Urban regeneration and community development in Scotland: converging agendas for action', *Sustainable Development*, vol. 10, pp. 147-54

MacLeod, G. and Goodwin, M. (1999), 'Space, scale and state strategy: towards a rethinking of urban and regional governance', *Progress in Human Geography*, vol. 23(4), pp. 503-27.

McLaughlin, E. (2002), 'The crisis of the social and the political materialization of community safety', in G. Hughes, E. McLaughlin and J. Muncie (eds) *Crime Prevention and Community Safety: New Directions*, Sage, London.

National Assembly for Wales (2000), *Index of Multiple Deprivation for Wales*, National Assembly for Wales, Cardiff.

National Assembly for Wales (2001), *Communities First Guidance*, National Assembly for Wales, Cardiff.

ODPM (2003), *Sustainable Communities: Building for the Future*, ODPM, London.

Office of National Statistics (2003), *Census 2001*, accessed via www.statistics.gov.uk/census2001/default.asp

Parkinson, M. (1989), 'The Thatcher government's urban policy 1979-89', *Town Planning Review*, vol. 60, pp. 421-40

Peck, J. (1999) 'Grey Geography', *Transactions of the Institute of British Geographers*, Vol. 24, pp. 131-35.

Rees, G. and Lambert, J. (1985), *Cities in Crisis*, Arnold, London.

Robson, B. (1988), *Those Inner Cities*, Clarendon, London.

Robson, B., Parkinson, M., Boddy, M. and Maclennan, D. (2000), *The State of English Cities*, HMSO, London.

Scottish Executive (2003a), *Building Better Cities: Delivering Growth and Opportunities*, Scottish Executive, Edinburgh.

Scottish Executive (2003b), *Review of Scotland's Cities – The Analysis*, Scottish Executive, Edinburgh.

Scraton, P. (1985), *The State of the Police*, Pluto Press, London.

Smith, N. (2002), 'Gentrification generalised: from local anomaly to urban regeneration as global strategy', paper presented to Upward Neighbourhood Trajectories: gentrification in a new century conference, Glasgow, 26th and 27th September.

SEU (2001), *A New Commitment to Neighbourhood Renewal: National Strategy Action Plan*, Cabinet Office, London.

The Guardian (2001), 'Delivery to take priority over policy', 8th June.

The Guardian (2003), 'Maze of initiatives "like spaghetti"', Society section, 14th January.

The Sunday Times (2003), 'A lovely place for a riot', News Review, 29th June.

Urban Task Force (1999), *Final Report of the Urban Task Force*, E & F N Spon, London.

Ward, K. (1997), 'Coalitions in urban regeneration: a regime approach', *Environment and Planning A*, vol. 29, pp. 1493-1506.

Whitehead, M (2001), *The Politics of the Environmental City: State Intervention and the Regulation of Environmental Space in the West Midlands*, unpublished PhD thesis, University of Wales, Aberystwyth.

Whitehead, M. (2003), '"In the shadow of hierarchy": meta-governance, policy reform and urban regeneration in the West Midlands', *Area*, vol. 35, pp. 6-14.

PART 1

ANALYSING NEW LABOUR'S URBAN RENAISSANCE PROJECT

Chapter 2

Promoting the 'Urban Idyll': Policies for City Centre Living

Gareth Hoskins and Andrew Tallon

Imagine strolling through a dockland area digesting Friday's lunch one summer's afternoon. You cross paved walkways punctuated with illuminated water features and hear the liquid patter of a fountain's droplets overlaying the hum of a not-too-distant business district winding down for the week; you negotiate the clutter of plastic art planted sporadically in the concrete and circle a twelve-foot anchor drenched in treacle-like gloss paint; you approach an arcade and hear people conversing around brushed steel tables of coffee houses whose interiors invoke an impression of Latin-American Moderne. Drinking espresso, soy latte, or the finest bottled Belgian beer, these people are part of the new British metropolitan bohemia and while your cynicism compels its condescension you secretly fancy yourself as a member.

Introduction

A key strand of New Labour's urban policy in Britain involves promoting a vision of town and city centre living as a desirable alternative to suburban and rural life (Department of Environment, Transport and the Regions (DETR), 2000a, p.29). This chapter uses empirical research undertaken in Bristol and Swansea, supplemented by evidence from other British cities, to analyse repeopling strategies in metropolitan centres. We argue that the current form of urban regeneration in contemporary Britain is discursively underpinned by the construction of a seductive 'urban idyll' – an imagined geography instrumental in New Labour's urban renaissance project. We then go on to suggest that the selling and marketing of urban space as part of the contemporary urban renaissance is selective: advocating lifestyles subscribed and available to only a select few, while simultaneously rendering invisible many of the existing inner city inhabitants most in need. The chapter concludes by identifying the contradictions between New Labour's urban policy aim of generating a new version of urban living and the creation of a more socially inclusive city.

In advance of any coherent regenerative strategy, the British city centre has enjoyed a revival in recent years for certain kinds of people attracted to a particular kind of lifestyle. The expression of a wide array of complex factors, this revival has been widely understood as part of a global move towards flexible modes of capitalist accumulation (Harvey, 1989; Sassen, 1991; Dear, 2000), facilitating a shift from the city as locus of production (Leitner and Sheppard, 1989) to the city as cathedral of consumption (Goss, 1993 and 1999; Ritzer 1999).

Such mechanisms have encouraged rapid in-migration to the city centre, leading to the emergence of high-status residential landscapes fuelling economic polarization and social fragmentation. Seeking to transform the partiality of this mode of urban regeneration, New Labour's urban policy has encouraged moves to revalorize declining city centres by converting resources of cultural capital to economic capital (Valentine, 2001). In this way, cities are attempting to re-package themselves as global players, asserting a profile that demands involvement with international networks of capital. An important component of this re-packaging is the enticement of new residents to the city centre. This is not a novel phenomenon. Trends since the mid-1980s brought about by the growth of producer services and information industries that include law, finance, media and advertising, have cultivated a large group of well educated and highly paid professionals who choose to live in the city centre because of its proximity to the workplace and its cultural and leisure facilities (Hamnett, 1999 and 2000). Already this has had the effect of displacing residents in previously working-class metropolitan areas and is illustrative of 'a recolonization of the town and city centres by the middle classes' (Smith, 2002). While we acknowledge that gentrification within the city centre has been a relatively long experienced process (see for example, Zukin, 1982 and 1991; Ley, 1996; Smith, 1996; Butler, 1997; Hamnett, 2000), the concept of the 'urban idyll' seems particularly apt for application in the policies advocated by New Labour. Here, the 'joined-up thinking' between Whitehall departments and the culture industries have made possible a vision with a comprehensive consistency not previously encountered. Further, the influence and reach of these policies is likely to inform the shape of the urban environment in ways different to those made under earlier more *laissez-faire* planning regimes.

In this chapter we employ the term urban idyll to represent the idea of a vibrant city neighbourhood that is emerging as central to the commodification of urban space and implicit in New Labour's Urban White Paper (DETR, 2000a). We seek to explore the relations of power that construct the urban idyll as an imagined geography and question its social legitimacy by critiquing its metaphorical and material imposition on the landscape.

During the last two decades, a series of government documents have responded to calls within urban design schools to realize: compact, mixed use and sustainable cities (Department of the Environment (DoE), 1996a; DETR, 2001); vital and viable city centres (Comedia, 1991; Urban and Economic Development Group (URBED), 1994); and the city centre as 'a place for people' (DoE, 1995 and 1996b; DETR, 2000b). These aspirations are incorporated within Lord Rogers' Urban Task Force Report (1999b) and the Urban White Paper (DETR, 2000a), both of which aspire to achieve an 'urban renaissance' in British cities where city centre living is given a key role. In practice however, such places are difficult to create. While policy documents can point to the kind of urban neighbourhoods they wish to emulate, citing Bologna, Barcelona, Madrid, and Amsterdam as examples, translation within a British context is no easy task. Anonymous urban districts signposted as 'loft quarter', 'village', or 'ethnic-town' can often only be distinguished by the colour of the flags surrounding them and are thus more like low-cost attempts to increase land rent than any genuine reflection of an area's identity. Nonetheless, efforts to generate a sense of place are becoming more sophisticated employing strategies that involve street layout, building design, mixed-use designation and the recruiting of street performers to animate the space and self-consciously reflect an image of cosmopolitanism.

The rural idyll as heuristic device

Work within rural studies has long conceived of the rural as an affiliated set of socially constructed meanings rather than as a bounded geographical space (Cloke, 1999). The application of this perspective to the city can be useful particularly when exploring the articulation of the urban in government policy and other public discourses. The Urban White Paper and materials marketing inner-city housing, for instance, can be read as complimentary cultural texts that illustrate the way in which the city is reconceptualized.

It is well documented that the idea of the rural idyll has important consequences for the way the countryside is experienced (Mingay, 1989; Short, 1991; Bunce, 1994; Cloke, 1999; Halfacree, 2003). To understand its operation it is important to acknowledge its prolonged oppositional construction against the urban. Social myths, for instance, extol the stability of the countryside in relation to the dynamism of the city (Holloway and Hubbard, 2001). By extension, the rural then becomes allied to a number of positional goods including a sense of timelessness; an emphasis on traditional family values; harmonious relations between nature and culture; an absence of social problems; and the fostering of physical, spiritual and moral health (Holloway and Hubbard, 2001, p.154). The contemporary inner city, by contrast, has typically been imagined using dystopian mythologies as '...the dark underside of the city, a place of crime and disorder...' (Short, 1991, p.50). Associated with this relational existence, one particularly important caveat to come out of thinking about the rural idyll is its implication for social exclusion. In particular, its propensity to render invisible certain groups practices and issues not compatible with its bucolic picturesque image.

Since the rural and the urban have been defined in opposition to one another, it is not surprising that the current attempt for a new urban strategy seeks to undermine those entrenched binary divisions by appropriating themes usually associated with the rural. In both policy documents and urban design, several components more familiar when couched in terms of the countryside are being strategically associated with the city. We refer here to the ideas of community, nature and history, which while not of course spatially bound in the rural, are at least key tropes in our understanding of it.

Firstly, the notion of an urban community or city neighbourhood is repeatedly evoked in both policy and promotional literature to dent conceptions of the city as an incoherent and anonymous sprawl. The Urban White Paper in particular regards this as an achievable ideal to be encouraged through coherence of design and planning for mixed use. Interestingly, pro-urban myths are often juxtaposed with a regressive countryside stereotype of the 'ignorant and brutish yokel or "country bumpkin"' (Holloway and Hubbard, 2001, p.120) and against visions of a monotonous, dreary, sterile and socially repressive suburbia (see Ley, 1996). The city in this sense is mobilized to highlight the notion of a 'cultural "melting pot"...providing opportunities for variety, social mixing and vibrant encounters between very different social groups' (Holloway and Hubbard, 2001, p.121). In this sense, city centres can, like contemporary rural villages, be seen as ideological in that they selectively reflect and reproduce the interests of specific social classes, ages, genders, ethnicities and sexualities. It is clear today that traditional notions of the city centre as dystopian are outdated. Areas such as London's Docklands, Cardiff Bay, Manchester's Canal Street and Salford Quays, Bristol's Harbourside and Birmingham's Brindley Place (see Illustration 2.1) are very much the vanguard in the resettlement of the inner city, concretising a metaphorical reconstruction of the city in general following the urban idyll (Short, 1991; Crilley, 1992; Holcomb, 1994). The increasing withdrawal of new urban neighbourhoods behind fortifications, however, seems to test the viability of the notion of community in these locations.

Source: Mark Whitehead

Illustration 2.1 The new 'inner city': Brindley Place, Birmingham

The second set of rural imaginings to be discursively attached to the city revolves around its proximity to, or association with, nature (Whitehead, 2001). The Urban White Paper notes, 'Access to green spaces reduces stress and promotes well-being. Parks and open spaces are among the most valued features of the places people live' (DETR, 2000a, p.66). In addition, the insertion of a sustainable, environment-friendly agenda into development policy for the city must surely reflect the idea that nature, if not close by, then at least must be a central consideration in urban architectural design and planning. This appears to be leading to a situation whereby urban renewal is often 'uncritically being recast as a positive and necessary environmental strategy' (MacLeod and Ward, 2002, p.159).

The third set of meanings active in the construction of an urban idyll concerns history and heritage. Both private and public sector developers within the city centre have long been conscious of the value of the historical as a resource. Indeed, the Urban White Paper highlights the economic benefits of bringing history to the fore:

> Historic buildings, parks and open spaces make a great contribution to the character, diversity and sense of identity of urban areas. Small-scale improvements to the historic fabric of an area generate a market-led return to urban living, supporting existing communities and adding to the economic base (DETR, 2000a, p.72).

A number of programmes including Heritage Economic Regeneration Schemes, The Historic Environment Review, and the Townscape Heritage Initiative are identified in the Urban White Paper as important moves to exploit what English Heritage calls 'The Heritage Dividend' where 'refurbishment of the historic fabric can act as a catalyst for wider regeneration, tackling social exclusion and building communities' (ibid.). Discussion of the urban condition within academic literature has identified this preoccupation with history in contemporary design as a reaction to the hypermobile, transient and fragmented lifestyles of today's society (Harvey, 1989; Jameson, 1991; Sudjic, 1993). Typical landscapes informed by this reaction intentionally codify reference to a stable, homogenous, imagined past where the politics of inequality and displacement are aestheticized and hence go unchallenged (Mitchell, 2000). In this respect, many renovated dockland areas could be described as shallow parodies of their city's previous global role in trade and industry. A dry disused dockland by the 1970s, a key stage in the conversion of Swansea's Maritime Quarter for residential use was the dredging of the in-filled basins and the reintroduction of water. In Bristol's Harbourside abandoned industrial craft have been salvaged and transformed into exclusive bars and fashionable eateries for affluent residents in the plush apartments nearby.

Tim Edensor offers hope in comments recently about the 'veritable inarticulacy' of the stories told by such industrial relics when worked through the 'reified designs of planners and heritage marketeers' pointing out their potency in providing alternate readings of urbanity and progress not envisaged by the scene makers of this type of development (Edensor, 2003). Nevertheless, Swansea's Maritime Quarter and Bristol's Harbourside, self consciously aestheticize their earlier boom years with street furniture of heavily glossed cranes, chains and industrial machinery punctuating the walkways. Such relics – reified on plinths surrounded by iron balustrades – are not intended to communicate an obsolete industrial epoch but rather valorise the historical significance of the local area while simultaneously avoiding any engagement with the politics of their destruction. Hence encountering these objects allows us to appreciate the global role once played by these ports without contemplating the reasons for their demise. But of course, the urban idyll is something more than the appropriated associations with community, nature and history. The following section will elaborate on its characteristics with some empirical examples.

Characteristics of the urban idyll

Common themes used to market new city centre housing and the contemporary urban lifestyles associated with it are evident in diverse promotional material used in Britain. Cosmopolitan café society, images of the night-time city, spectacular urban scenery, waterfront settings and sexual imagery make frequent appearances. Together they represent clear attempts to comprehensively repackage our conceptions of the city along bohemian lines. In general, city authorities, property developers and estate agents are becoming more sophisticated in their marketing of city lifestyles, much of which clearly targets a young professional audience. Images are regularly portrayed in newspaper supplements and fully illustrated in the *Home* or *Property* sections of *The Daily Telegraph*, *The Sunday Times* and *The Observer* newspapers. In both Bristol and Swansea, there is an active promotion of city centre housing by public and private sectors utilizing a wide array of media including posters, banners, websites, newspapers, brochures and even beer mats. These materials provide an impression of the imagined geographies underpinning what is being sold and whom it is being sold to. Our analysis of city centre marketing material suggests that different images are mobilized to target a diverse community of prospective buyers. The emphasis however, is clearly focused on a limited number of common themes, images and texts.

In Bristol city centre for example, the housing created in the Harbourside and Old City districts is set in attractive waterfront landscapes; ideal for those urban professionals demanding a vibrant and cultured living environment while being close to their place of work. Marketing of housing in a city such as Bristol can project numerous, sometimes conflicting images of the city to different groups simultaneously. One promotional leaflet targeted at London club-goers, for instance, emphasizes the 'excitement and stylishness of the city' as a place to live. By contrast, another promotion aimed primarily at the elderly paints a picture of a 'cosy provincial city centre emphasising its solidity, history and access to the countryside' (Urban Task Force, 1999a, p.8). Thus Bristol can at the same time be 'a hotbed of youth culture' and 'a cosy provincial city' depending on who is being targeted (Urban Task Force, 1999a, p.13). Much private sector property publicity markets life on the waterfront with an emphasis on modern aesthetics, central locations, and 'well-priced' waterside apartments. The recently completed renovation and conversion of Avon House into over 100 apartments by the developer Redrow offered 'sophisticated, cosmopolitan and exciting living in the heart of the city centre' (www.5102.co.uk, 2001) while making much of the local area's architecture, heritage, buzzing nightlife and stylish contemporary design. *The Sunday Times* (2002) reported that waterfront developments and town houses in Bristol are marketed from around £150,000 up to £600,000, partly because of the location's popularity with professionals who wish to relocate from London. The average Bristol property price stood at £110,000 in 2002. At the time of writing, the house price boom in Bristol city centre is yet to be dented.

At the westward end of the M4, Swansea city centre's Maritime Quarter has been successful in attaching itself to ideas of a leisurely bohemian lifestyle. Two hundred yards from the central business district, its apartments sit above an emerging café, restaurant and nightclub hot spot. The attractions of waterfront and maritime living are highlighted with an emphasis placed on modern design and access to leisure facilities. Property prices in the Maritime Quarter rose sharply during the 1980s and 1990s, and by early 2003, they had reached a range of £75,000 to £200,000 (www.bayletting.com, 2003). Other examples of marketing within the private sector include Loft Co.'s 'exciting new lifestyle apartments'. Using the motif of Manhattan's loft living, this company aims to provide contemporary homes in the heart of Swansea at a cost of £175,000 (www.loft-co.com, 2001); particularly exclusive considering the average property price in Swansea was £69,000 in 2002 and average annual incomes under £20,000. One key way of marketing city centre living in Swansea has been through the *City Living* scheme run by the City and County of Swansea and Swansea Housing Association. This promotes living in the heart of the city centre, city culture and affordable housing for a range of groups, with lower status sections of the population explicitly targeted as potential city centre residents with rents of around £40-60 per week (www.city-living.org.uk, 2000; see also Illustration 2.2).

The marketing of city centre housing as a tool for regeneration can be traced back to the docklands and marina developments of the 1970s and 1980s (Brownill, 1994). Since the mid-1980s many have identified a growing industry involving the deliberate manipulation of place images, which are often associated with residential promotion (Appleby, 1990; Ward, 1998; Hall, 2001). This practice is exemplified by the London Docklands redevelopment that sought to attract people 'of the right sort' to take up residence (Burgess and Wood, 1988; Crilley, 1992 and 1993; Brownill, 1994). A range of innovative strategies and initiatives to market the city centre as a place to live have since been introduced in order to further the development of a 'living heart'. These methods are linked with practices of place promotion which have traditionally been the preserve of tourism and business (Page, 1995; Ward, 1998; Holcomb, 1999; Short and Kim, 1999).

The 2000 Urban White Paper, although proselytising the notion of a shared vision throughout its pages, is surprisingly shy on the details of its incarnation preferring instead to place the responsibility of design on those in the community and its development partners. A general, albeit illusive and aspirational model for design, is offered by Lord Rogers in his Urban Task Force Report (1999b, p.1). It calls on us to realize 'a new vision for urban regeneration founded on principles of design excellence, social well-being and environmental responsibility', suggesting:

> There is also a need to improve the quality of architecture in the English built environment. Our buildings, streets and public spaces should be beautiful, functional and flexible. We must rediscover the art of civic design to create urban neighbourhoods of lasting quality that work for the individual, family and wider community.

Source: Reproduced with kind permission of Swansea Housing Association

Illustration 2.2 Marketing affordable housing and lifestyle in central Swansea

Certainly design is central in the establishment of New Labour's urban renaissance and this is confirmed by Prime Minister Tony Blair's high profile association with the Commission for Architecture and the Built Environment (CABE) which monitors design quality across all projects from the ordinary and everyday building types such as schools and houses, to flagship developments and landmark buildings. The contribution made by architectural expertise to the new urban form, however, is being threatened by simple economics. Private finance initiatives and design-and-build schemes, for example, encourage individual projects that often undermine an architect's wider more holistic vision. Perhaps a more accurate expression of the urban idyll as envisaged by New Labour's urban policy can be found in the promotion of residential apartment blocks appearing in urban centres across Britain.

One confident embodiment of the urban idyll is the winner of the City Life Award in *Hot Property Magazine* (April 2003). The Visage, to be completed in 2005 in Swiss Cottage London, is a high-tech block of 170 apartments sold as 'the epitome of metropolitan cool'. It is clear from Barratt's electronic brochure that this is not just a house but also a membership card to a way of life with access to exclusive cultural capital.

> Further lifestyle enhancements include a twenty four hour concierge service, underground parking and you can even join a tailored lifestyle management scheme to look after your every need, whether it be booking theatre tickets or arranging catering and a butler for a special evening in your exclusive apartment.
> (www.barratthomes.co.uk, 2003)

Barratt advertizes other apartments throughout Central London in a similar way with gimmicks playing on affectations of opulence. The Exchange situated in the heart of London is, for instance, sold as 'a lifestyle package that will be the envy of many modern Londoners'. The website pinpoints its location on a map of central London and kindly identifies locations significant to prospective future residents such as the Royal Academy, The Victoria and Albert Museum, The British Museum, The National and Tate Galleries as well as Selfridges, Harrods and Harvey Nichols.

The promotion and marketing of new city centre housing must surely provoke questions relating to social fragmentation and exclusion commonly associated with gentrification. We maintain that the current form of gentrification, underwritten as it is by a New Labour backed vision of urban renaissance, can be distinguished from the earlier market-led process of gentrification since policy is now such a strong driver of the process (Wyly and Hammel, 1999; Lees, 2000 and 2003). In the 2000 White Paper, urban renaissance is sold as a cure for the ailing city, not the existing population. Rather than addressing the needs of residents, the residents are instead replaced with more affluent citizens who better fit the popular image of a cosmopolitan bohemia. MacLeod and Ward point out this very process noting with dismay:

> And while such fragrant media do all they can to invite the opportunity of mass gentrification, many of those investigating the possibility of life in the revived inner city can testify to the limited availability of such opportunity. Class difference and the stench of money power permeate every pore of the new political economy (MacLeod and Ward, 2002, p.158).

The entrenchment of the urban idyll in city centres promotes an exclusive vision as dominant. Marina developments – identifiers of the new landscape of leisure and affluence – allow a few to walk around the graveyard of an exterminated mercantile and industrial economy, to live within the houses of previously priced-out or evicted tenants, and most worryingly, to enjoy the space as a scene in which they themselves need not feel implicated.

It is crucial to emphasize here that geographies are never isolated. The landscape, at any one moment, is a node in a network of flows where decisions made effect and are dependant on things happening elsewhere. Hence, the production of a city centre landscape in the form of an urban idyll inevitably entails the constant reproduction of other landscapes in other places (Schein, 1997). In this respect, the victims of the realization of the urban idyll (displaced residents of city gentrification) become a force in the creation of landscapes elsewhere, adding to the housing pressures of adjacent local councils and contributing to their further decline. Alternatively, low-income residents residing in profitable locations ripe for development are moved en masse to housing on the margins of new suburban enclaves.

Issues of gentrification in the city will become more relevant as opportunities for new housing on brownfield sites decrease over time, making it more likely that the socio-economic upgrading of housing will spread to poor working class neighbourhoods causing widespread social tension between the haves and have nots and an exacerbated potential for urban unrest. This scenario is especially relevant in cities such as Leeds, Liverpool, Glasgow, Manchester, Bristol, Birmingham and Newcastle-upon-Tyne, all of which have witnessed a recent boom in city centre housing development while still enduring problems of long term unemployment and substandard housing. The London borough of Tower Hamlets provides an apposite example of displacement.

The biography of Keeling House within the Bethnal Green area of Tower Hamlets is a disturbing instance of the 2000 Urban White Paper's future hopes. Here the sanctioning of gentrification appears to legitimize the removal of poorer residents. Completed in 1957 by modernist architect Denys Lasdun, it was originally conceived as a vertical remedy to the city's post war housing shortage, but, hindered by a chronic lack of public investment, it came to embody the flaws of many similar solutions in vogue at the time. A decaying block of public flats until only a few years ago, by the late 1990s Keeling House's central location and unique design had created a rent-gap potential far too lucrative for developers to ignore. By 2000 renovation work transformed the block into a luxury set of apartments each selling at around £200,000 with penthouses that had been added to the top floor at £375,000 (www.bbc.co.uk/news, 2000). In a move very much in line with today's Urban White Paper's directives on valuing the historical, English

Heritage designated Keeling House a Grade Two listed building in 1993. Unfortunately, rather than 'acting as a catalyst for wider regeneration, tackling social exclusion and building communities' (DETR, 2000a), the expense of refurbishment increased significantly with listed building status, and council monies were funnelled to other properties in the borough. Consequently, residents in the decaying block were removed because the structure was deemed unsafe. This process, however, made way for private investors to serve the needs of those at the opposite end of the economic spectrum – providing the very best in city living with high-end perks such as a concierge service, a glass foyer, and interior waterfall designed by sculptor Anthony Donaldson (www.findaproperty.co.uk, 2001).

This story is a pertinent example of processes where council flats and public buildings such as hospitals and office blocks within the inner city are being reborn as trendy private apartments for the 21st century. Central London's poorer communities, in particular, have endured this exchange, with highly paid young childless professionals as the vanguard intensifying demand for such properties. Many of London's most neglected and deteriorating neighbourhoods have now become synonymous with sophisticated urban living. The average house price in 2001 in the borough of Tower Hamlets, for example, was £211,500, compared with the Greater London average of £205,800 (www.bbc.co.uk/news, 2001). In London's Covent Garden, 20-25% of property on the market is former council property and is becoming increasingly attractive due to its relative value compared with other now privately owned blocks (*The Sunday Times*, 2001).

The examples described above, however, may become less frequent. There is growing recognition amongst city authorities that a revitalized city centre is not best realized through the sole provision of high-rent property. Indeed, the Urban White Paper acknowledges this advocating mixed use and mixed community as a basic requirement for a neighbourhood's vitality. Owing to increased levels of public scrutiny and participation, new initiatives sensitive to existing communities allowing those with lower incomes to participate are to be commended. Swansea Housing Association's *City Living* programme utilizes much of the symbolism of the urban idyll vision while providing affordable housing for a range of low-income tenants. The importance of establishing a bohemian experience in Swansea's 'Café Quarter' remains central to the manufacture of central Swansea's urban idyll. Obligingly, the city living programme means that wages for necessary service workers are indirectly subsidized by the Housing Association in liaison with the City Council through the provision of low-rent city centre property.

Repeopling the city centre: an orchestrated change in membership

The Urban White Paper has forged an official version about what a new British city should be, what it should look like and whom it should serve. The implementation of this vision however means that many existing inhabitants (low income, elderly, homeless, immigrant populations) have been largely overlooked. One characteristic shared by many of the housing developments discussed above is their high level of security. This has prompted many commentators to caution against mirroring the trend of fortification associated with North America's gated communities (Blakely and Snyder, 1997; Webster, 2001). Indeed, MacLeod and Ward (2002) see the strong connection between utopian visions and a desire for isolation invoking the phrase 'privatopia' while commenting that:

> It seems indisputably the case that many efforts to contrive urban utopias are prompted by an intensifying concern on the part of individuals and families to insulate themselves from the threats to physical, financial and emotional security often associated with contemporary urban life (MacLeod and Ward, 2002, p.159).

A concierge service, electronic gates with codes, secure underground parking and visual intercom systems connected to the resident's television screen are all Orwellian expressions of growing fears about threats to personal security (see Illustration 2.3). The intensification of social and spatial control embodied in these fortified enclaves suggests that New Labour's avocation of the harmonized, socially mixed urban communities of the urban idyll is flawed. The mechanisms employed to improve the well being of the city's current population seem to entail generating wealth by introducing new affluent members to take their place. Thus, the notion of an urban renaissance is implicitly based on excluding certain 'undesirable' elements not least those already resident. Public portrayal of the city is tilted to attracting new development, high-class housing and leisure facilities for those who embody a cultured, sophisticated and cosmopolitan lifestyle. The image of the city, its brand, and the physical shape it takes in the future, will re-cast appropriate inhabitants and displace others in a reconstituted urban space (Smith and Williams, 1986; Smith, 1996); a 'spatial apartheid' (Judd, 1995) based on cool.

New Labour's championing of an urban renaissance is rapidly establishing pockets of development recognisable as the urban idyll, and this urban idyll is as much a technology of representation as it is a technology for renewal, reproducing guidelines for a favoured kind of urban citizenry, figuratively emplacing them in a landscape informed by a bohemian aesthetic while other residents are rhetorically and materially recast as 'outsiders'. Concerned by this, MacLeod and Ward have noted that 'the contemporary city now constitutes an intensely woven patchwork of utopian and dystopian spaces that are, to all intents and purposes, physically proximate but institutionally estranged' (MacLeod and Ward, 2002, p.153).

There have been successful examples of physical regeneration and social revitalization in many British urban landscapes which do indeed make positive contributions to more sustainable, liveable, vital and viable cities. We argue however that the future of 'Our Towns and Cities' as conceived by current urban policy rests on cultural competition enlisting images that provide the greatest return for capital investment in the short term where the rhetoric of inclusion is employed only to sugar the pill. With the encouragement of high-status, high-cost spectacle aesthetics, groups presently living in the city become further disenfranchised, written out of the plans, priced out of the market and prevented from attaching themselves to their own urban renaissance. The implications of this are profound. Unless such groups are included in the initial imagining of the

Source: Andrew Tallon

Illustration 2.3 Urban 'privatopia', Bristol city centre

redeveloped city; unless they are allowed to contribute more fully to envisioning policy, then these groups will at best continue to be displaced, and at worst be objectified, cast as extras in a scenography of the city adding colour and a little edge.

Concluding remarks

While interrogating the vision of urban renaissance within promotional and policy discourse, we have suggested that the embedding of idealistic saleable meanings and place imagery conceals other more fractured, diverse and multifarious ways of understanding the city which are crucial for the equitable deliverance of urban social justice. By way of illustration, we have identified the instrumentalization of an urban idyll and described its operation as an imagined vision mobilized to inform the production of residential geographies within the city centre. Clearly the design and promotion of the city centre is underpinned by a bohemian aesthetic to entice both investment and people to the centre. As such, the Urban White Paper's adherence to an imagined urban idyll is likely to have little beneficial impact on existing populations in the city centre but rather ensure their displacement and further disenfranchisement.

Appropriating themes drawn out in studies of the rural idyll helps us identify an emerging construction of the city that is similarly partial and hence exclusionary in many of the same ways. Importantly, the urban idyll does not represent the antithesis of its rural counterpart. It is better seen as more of a mirror tending to selectively appropriate tropes from its bucolic equivalent. Self-consciously codified in the urban context, a sense of community, an association with nature and an affinity with the historical increasingly emerge as identifiers of aspirational city lifestyles and positional goods targeted exclusively towards the well off. The dockland residential enclaves with their café and bar culture have for some time been the mainstay of this urban idyll where low cost land, proximity to the centre and malleable cultural backdrop can readily be converted by local growth coalitions for high profit. In an effort to regenerate the ailing inner city, New Labour's urban policy appears to represent the proliferation of such spaces, revealing the ideological tensions inherent within a third way political rationale that seeks social inclusion through an entrepreneurial mode of economic development.

References

Appleby, S. (1990), 'Crawley a space mythology', *New Formations*, vol. 11, pp. 19-44.

Blakely, E.J. and Snyder, M.G. (1997), *Fortress America: Gated Communities in the United States*, The Brookings Institution, Washington D.C.

Brownill, S. (1994), 'Selling the inner city: regeneration and place marketing in London Docklands', in J.R. Gold and S.V. Ward (eds), *Place Promotion: The Use of Publicity and Marketing to Sell Towns and Regions*, Wiley, Chichester.

Bunce, M. (1994), *The Countryside Ideal: Anglo-American Images of Landscape*, Routledge, London.

Burgess, J.A. and Wood, P. (1988), 'Decoding Docklands: place advertising and decision-making strategies of the small firm', in J. Eyles and D.M. Smith (eds), *Qualitative Methods in Human Geography*, Polity Press, Cambridge.

Butler, T. (1997), *Gentrification and the Middle Classes*, Ashgate, Aldershot.

Cloke, P. (1999), 'The country', in P. Cloke, P. Crang and M. Goodwin (eds), *Introducing Human Geographies*, Arnold, London.

Comedia (1991), *Out of Hours: A Study of the Economic and Social Life of Twelve Town Centres in the UK*, Gulbenkian Foundation, London.

Crilley, D. (1992), 'Remaking the image of the Docklands', in P. Ogden (ed), *London Docklands: The Challenge of Development*, Cambridge University Press, Cambridge.

Crilley, D. (1993), 'Architecture as advertising: constructing the image of redevelopment', in G. Kearns and C. Philo (eds), *Selling Places: The City as Cultural Capital, Past and Present*, Pergamon, Oxford.

Dear, M.J. (2000), *The Postmodern Urban Condition*, Blackwell, Oxford.

DETR (2000a), *Our Towns and Cities: The Future – Delivering an Urban Renaissance*, HMSO, London.

DETR (2000b), *Planning Policy Guidance 3: Housing*, HMSO, London.

DETR (2001), *Planning Policy Guidance 13: Transport*, HMSO, London.

DoE (1995), *Projection of Households in England to 2016*, HMSO, London.

DoE (1996a), *Planning Policy Guidance 6: Town Centres and Retail Development*, HMSO, London.

DoE (1996b), *Household Growth: Where Shall We Live*, HMSO, London.

Edensor, T. (2003), 'Industrial ruins and their ghosts', paper presented at the Annual Meeting of the Association of American Geographers, New Orleans, 5th-9th March.

Goss, J. (1993), 'The magic of the mall: form and function in the retail built environment', *Annals of the Association of American Geographers*, vol. 83, pp. 18-47.

Goss, J. (1999), 'Consumption', in P. Cloke, P. Crang, and M. Goodwin (eds), *Introducing Human Geographies*, Arnold, London.

Halfacree, K. (2003), 'Landscapes of rurality: rural others/other rurals', in I. Robertson and P. Richards (eds), *Studying Cultural Landscapes*, Arnold, London.

Hall, T. (2001), *Urban Geography*, Routledge, London, 2nd edition.

Hamnett, C. (1999), 'The city', in P. Cloke, P. Crang and M. Goodwin (eds) *Introducing Human Geographies*, Arnold, London.

Hamnett, C. (2000), 'Gentrification, postindustrialism, and industrial and occupational restructuring in global cities', in G. Bridge and S. Watson (eds), *A Companion to the City*, Blackwell, Oxford.

Harvey, D. (1989), *The Condition of Postmodernity*, Blackwell, Oxford.

Holcomb, B. (1994), 'City make-overs: marketing the post-industrial city', in J.R. Gold and S.V. Ward (eds), *Place Promotion: The Use of Publicity and Marketing to Sell Towns and Regions*, Wiley, Chichester.

Holcomb, B. (1999), 'Marketing cities for tourism', in D.R. Judd and S.S. Fainstein (eds), *The Tourist City*, Yale University Press, London.

Holloway, L. and Hubbard, P. (2001), *People and Place: The Extraordinary Geographies of Everyday Life*, Pearson Education, Harlow.

Jameson, F. (1991), *Postmodernism, or the Cultural Logic of Late Capitalism*, Duke University Press, Durham, NC.

Judd, D. (1995), 'The rise of the new walled cities', in H. Liggett and D. Perry (eds), *Spatial Practices: Critical Explorations in Social/Spatial Theory*, Sage, Thousand Oaks, Ca.

Lees, L. (2000), 'A reappraisal of gentrification: towards a "geography of gentrification"', *Progress in Human Geography*, vol. 24, pp. 389-408.

Lees, L. (2003), 'Policy (re)turns: gentrification research and urban policy – urban policy and gentrification research', *Environment and Planning A*, vol. 35, pp. 571-74.

Leitner, H. and Sheppard, E. (1989), 'The city as locus of production', in R. Peet and N. Thrift, *New Models in Geography: Volume Two*, Unwin Hyman, London.

Ley, D. (1996), *The New Middle Class and the Remaking of the Central City*, Oxford University Press, Oxford.

MacLeod, G. and Ward, K. (2002), 'Spaces of utopia and dystopia: landscaping the contemporary city', *Geografiska Annaler*, vol. 84, pp. 153-70.

Mingay, G.E. (ed) (1989), *The Rural Idyll*, Routledge, London.

Mitchell, D. (2000), *Cultural Geography: A Critical Introduction*, Blackwell, Oxford.

Page, S. (1995), *Urban Tourism*, Routledge, London.

Ritzer, G. (1999), *Enchanting a Disenchanted World: Revolutionizing the Means of Consumption*, Pine Forge Press, London.

Sassen, S. (1991), *The Global City: New York London Tokyo*, Princeton University Press, Princeton.

Schein, R. (1997), 'The place of landscape: a conceptual framework for interpreting an American scene', *Annals of the Association of American Geographers*, vol. 87, pp. 660-80.

Short, J.R. (1991), *Imagined Country: Society, Culture and Environment*, Routledge, London.

Short, J.R. and Kim, Y-H. (1999), *Globalization and the City*, Longman, Harlow.

Smith, N. (1996), *The New Urban Frontier: Gentrification and the Revanchist City*, Routledge, London.

Smith, N. (2002), 'Gentrification generalised: from local anomaly to urban regeneration as global strategy', paper presented at the Upward Neighbourhood Trajectories: Gentrification in a New Century conference, Glasgow, 26th-27th September.

Smith, N. and Williams, P. (eds) (1986), *Gentrification of the City*, Allen & Unwin, London

Sudjic, D. (1993) *The 100 Mile City*, Flamingo, London.

The Sunday Times (2001), 'Cut-price, courtesy of the council', 12th August.

The Sunday Times (2002), 'Homes of the first water', 6th January.

Urban Task Force (1999a), in association with URBED, MORI and the School for Policy Studies at the University of Bristol, *But Would You Live There? Shaping Attitudes to Urban Living*, Urban Task Force, London.

Urban Task Force (1999b), *Towards an Urban Renaissance*, E & FN Spon, London.

URBED (1994), in association with Comedia, Hillier Parker, Bartlett School of Planning University College London, and Environmental and Transport Planning, DoE, *Vital and Viable Town Centres: Meeting the Challenge*, HMSO, London.

Valentine, G. (2001), *Social Geographies: Space and Society*, Harlow: Pearson Education.

Ward, S.V. (1998), *Selling Places: The Marketing and Promotion of Towns and Cities 1850-2000*, London: E & FN Spon.

Webster, C. (2001), 'Gated communities of tomorrow', *Town Planning Review*, vol. 72, pp. 149-170.

Whitehead, M. (2001), *The Politics of the Environmental City and the Regulation of Environmental Space in the UK*, unpublished Ph.D. thesis, University of Wales, Aberystwyth.

Wyly, E. and Hammel, D. (1999), 'Islands of decay in seas of renewal: housing policy and the resurgence of gentrification', *Housing Policy Debate*, vol. 10, pp. 711-71.

Zukin, S. (1982), *Loft Living*, Johns Hopkins University Press, Baltimore, Md.

Zukin, S. (1991), *Landscapes of Power: From Detroit to Disney World*, University of California Press, Berkeley, Ca.

Chapter 3

Urban Regeneration in a Growing Region: The Renaissance of England's Average Town

Mike Raco

Introduction

The academic and policy discourses of the 'urban renaissance' have been focused on the problems and opportunities of regeneration in Britain's most deprived and largest urban areas. Given the scale of the problems facing Britain's major cities this focus is neither surprising nor unjustified (see Turok and Edge, 1999). However, as the Urban Task Force Report (1999) states, more than 90% of England's population live in urban areas with populations of over 10,000 people. Therefore, understanding the ways in which regeneration programmes have been developed and implemented in a variety of urban contexts is an important element in interpreting the government's broader urban renaissance agendas. It is with this in mind that this chapter examines urban regeneration discourses and practices in Reading, a relatively prosperous town in the South East of England[1]. Whilst its socio-economic characteristics differ somewhat from those facing many of Britain's major cities, the chapter argues that there are significant lessons that can be drawn from the Reading experience for policy agendas elsewhere. Indeed, Reading has been hailed as a model for urban regeneration, with the Office of the Deputy Prime Minister (ODPM), for example, claiming that *'Reading has made impressive progress towards an urban renaissance'* (cited in Reading Borough Council (RBC), 2003, p.3). If this is so, then an examination of what the renaissance has consisted of in the town and what its impacts have been, provides some insight into the possibilities and limitations of projects elsewhere.

The chapter argues that despite the rhetorical shift towards new social democratic brands of urban policy, regeneration agendas in places such as Reading

1 The bulk of this chapter draws on a research project which examined urban regeneration practices in Reading, carried out between October 2000 and May 2001. The research involved the interview of 35 key local actors and organizations that were supplemented by the analysis of policy documents, correspondence, council minutes, accounts, policy briefings and party records to provide a detailed picture of local discourses and practices of regeneration.

are still driven, first and foremost, by economic imperatives, with social and community needs subordinated to those of developers and employers. Moreover, regeneration in buoyant local and regional economies creates particular problems, some of which may impact upon the future sustainability of development and reinforce and reproduce existing socio-economic inequalities. The chapter begins by assessing some of the key influences on urban regeneration in a growing region before investigating the development of regeneration agendas in the town. This is followed by an assessment of the impacts of regeneration and a discussion of the sustainability of growth that has been initiated. The chapter concludes with an outline of the key lessons from the case study concerning the broader agendas of the government's urban renaissance and an assessment of the significance of urban imaginations and development projects.

Fuelling the market: renaissance and regeneration in 'successful places'

Urban and regional inequalities have been on the rise in the UK since the mid 1970s as regional policies have been downgraded and places have been left increasingly to fend for themselves (see Martin, 2001; Johnstone and Whitehead, this volume). Development has increasingly been concentrated in what Allen *et al* (1998) term 'hot spots' of growth where local, regional, national and global factors combine to generate expanding pockets of economic activity. In such places, urban regeneration would appear to be a relatively straightforward matter of tapping into existing development networks and providing new opportunities for developers. Where markets have been successful in supporting local economic development, it might be expected that the regeneration of urban centres could be spearheaded by market-led initiatives, with public agencies playing a guiding and facilitating role.

Yet, in 'successful' places, market-driven prosperity creates its own challenges, as social and environmental objectives cannot always be sustained in a context of rapid economic growth. In the government's latest urban policy initiative, *Sustainable Communities: Building for the Future*, it is argued that the physical regeneration of urban infrastructure will enhance the quality of life and employment prospects of a broad range of social groups, whilst boosting urban economies and property development (ODPM, 2003). Such regeneration is designed to be more holistic and self-sustaining with local people, groups and businesses playing a key role in 'the planning, design, and long term stewardship of their community' (p.2). In line with New Labour, Third Way, thinking, this stewardship role is promoted as a mechanism for local communities to nurture and guide the development process in ways that are mutually beneficial both for them and for investors (see Lunts, 2003). Development, therefore, becomes a market-driven exercise in which market mechanisms are not problematized as the cause of urban inequalities but are promoted as the source of urban salvation. All that is required is for communities and local agencies to steward and steer development in ways that meet their own requirements and needs. In this sense, sustainability is characterized primarily in modernist terms, with economic growth feeding unproblematically into the creation of social equity and environmental protection.

Yet, it is in fast-growing places that some of the contradictions and tensions inherent in such agendas become apparent. Calling on more market to tackle the problems of urban inequalities carries a certain irony, as it is market mechanisms that have played a key role in the generation of such inequalities in the first place. More market only seems destined to increase and reproduce inequalities on a variety of scales. For example, if house price inflation is already creating difficulties for local communities in prosperous places, then the promotion of regeneration agendas that seek, as their objective, to push property prices even higher, will reinforce these problems. Similarly, if areas are already suffering from congestion, then promoting further development in urban centres, in a context where there is insufficient investment in public transport, will only make matters worse. The consequence of this will be to reduce the quality of the local environment and impose additional economic costs which in the longer term may threaten the competitiveness of a 'growth' location.

Such threats to the sustainability of urban locations are further undermined by the deterioration of public services that are an inevitable consequence of rapid, market-driven development. As costs of living increase, so the position of public sector workers *vis-à-vis* local housing and consumption markets is gradually undermined. Shortages of staff in many areas of the South East of England and other 'hot spots' across the UK are having a significant impact on the quality and availability of public services (ODPM, 2003). This is a particular problem in urban areas, where the gulf between public sector pay and costs of living have been at their widest. The ramifications of this are wide ranging. For those most dependent on the public sector, such as the elderly, the disabled and poorer communities, such deterioration impacts directly on their quality of life and their socio-economic well-being. However, even middle-class groups are dependent on public services in a variety of forms to underpin their standards of living. Butler and Robson's (2002) research in London, for example, demonstrates that education is a critical factor in influencing middle-class decisions about where to locate (see also Schoon, 2002). Urban locations where education services are under pressure are, therefore, likely to be less attractive to middle-class communities, something that may undermine the broader rationale of urban regeneration that seeks to encourage a movement of people (particularly those with higher incomes) back in to inner urban areas.

In this context, it is difficult to understand exactly what is meant by 'community stewardship' of the development process. Promoting market-driven development, by definition, empowers those with the market resources to maximize their residential and lifestyle choices at the expense of those who do not. Previous rounds of urban policy, such as the programmes of Urban Development Corporations in the 1980s and 1990s were also market-driven, with the aim of promoting new forms of property-led regeneration (see Cochrane, 1999). However, the new urban renaissance is about more than this. It is about the selective gentrification of inner urban environments through a housing-led strategy which encourages the migration into the city of young, middle-class professionals who tend to have limited family responsibilities and possess high disposable incomes. As such, it is concerned with changing both the form and character of urban places.

David Lunts (2003), Director of ODPM's Urban Policy Unit, for instance cites Brindley Place in Birmingham as one of the best examples of contemporary urban regeneration in British cities. This is the conversion of a former post office sorting depot in the city centre into 200,000 square feet of office space, 200 apartments, 2 new hotels, 40 designer shops and 15 waterside cafes, restaurants and bars. Such a project is typical of what renaissance-style development is seeking to achieve. For critics such as Lees (2003) these can be characterized as a form of state-led gentrification which is 'based on an economy of conspicuous consumption...[and] enclaves designed to attract the middle classes – that is, the consuming and spending classes' (p.71). Alternative conceptions of urban living and the roles and responsibilities of other community groups are pushed aside as regeneration becomes re-interpreted as a form of selective market-building and place reconstruction. In addition, in encouraging 'successful' places to become even more successful in market terms, the urban renaissance may play a significant part in increasing inequalities between cities and regions. In many ways this is institutionalized in the government's *Sustainable Communities* agendas with the establishment of (euphemistically-named) Market Renewal Areas, in towns and cities of northern England, in which swathes of derelict and empty low-value housing will be demolished at the same time as massive increases in housing are planned in southern England (see ODPM, 2003).

Regeneration also focuses attention on some on the visions and imaginations of towns and cities that developers and policy-makers possess. The urban renaissance promotes a particular type of vision for urban centres which are important in shaping concrete forms of development (Lees, 2003). As Harvey (2000, p.159) eloquently argues, 'as we collectively produce our cities, so we collectively produce ourselves. Projects concerning what we want our cities to be are projects concerning human possibilities, who we want...or who do not want to become'. If places such as Reading are leading examples of the type of urban regeneration that the government envisages for Britain's urban centres, then what do its experiences tell us about future trends, visions and practices? What imaginations have characterized the regeneration of Reading and what sort of place have local developers and politicians sought to create? Given this broader context, the next section now examines development agendas and policies in Reading before assessing its impacts on local communities and local environments.

Development agendas and local politics: the renaissance of an 'average' town

Reading's socio-economic history has much in common with towns and cities in other parts of Britain. During the nineteenth century it experienced rapid development as an industrial location built around three significant industries – breweries, biscuit-making, and seed bulbs – which were driven by new transport connections (see Phillips, 1999). In the post-war period its manufacturing trades went into steady decline and by the early 1980s many of the biggest employers had moved away, leaving large areas of derelict and polluted land. However, since then the town has experienced rapid economic growth, primarily in the service industries of IT, insurance and finance, which have increased by almost 50% since 1991 (RBC, 2003a). It is European Headquarters for a number of major firms including Prudential Assurance, Compaq and the Oracle Corporation (RBC, 2000a and 2000b). Between 1991 and 1998 Reading experienced an increase in employment growth of around 10,000 jobs, with most of the growth occurring after 1995. A high proportion of the population (147,700) is well qualified, with 35% of economically active people engaged in managerial and professional employment (RBC, 2003a). Reading also has an extremely low unemployment rate of 1.6% (January 2002) and only around 7% of those have been without work for more than 12 months. The average gross weekly salary in the town is also £531.80 as compared to the British average of £444.30 (*ibid.*).

Much of this growth has been fuelled by the investment decisions of companies that are keen to locate along the M4 corridor, close to London and Heathrow, and the broader spill-over effects of decentralization from London that has been on-going over the last 30 to 40 years. However, more recently, the emergence of Reading as a hot spot of development has also been a reflection of wider discourses of place-building that have been constructed. Given Reading's position in relation to London, its politics has long suffered from a perception that it is an 'edge city' location (see Figure 3.1; Garreau, 1991). For instance, during the 1960s and 1970s Reading acquired a UK-wide reputation for its lack of a dynamic local political culture. It was derided in national newspapers as the 'town without a heart and soul' (*The Times*, 1972), a 'placeless place' in which political relations had become characterized by opaque decision-making processes, structures, and systems (Alexander, 1985; Pinch, 1989). It was in this local political context that Reading's urban centre underwent significant, incremental modernist redevelopment through the 1960s, 1970s, and 1980s. These new urban spaces failed to generate additional large-scale investments or widespread popularity. Retailers and commercial investors saw little opportunity to invest in the area and for existing actors new, higher quality premises, were difficult to find. These commercial weaknesses were reinforced by negative perceptions. For example, national surveys of retail areas, which rank centres by their commercial success and a range of quality indicators, consistently placed Reading in the lower bracket of locations. One survey in 1992 even put the town at the bottom of recommended places to shop in the UK (see *Reading Evening Post*, 1992). The closure of major industrial sites around the town centre in the early 1980s, had also left a scarred, derelict landscape (see Illustration 3.1).

In 1991 RBC came under the control of the local Labour Party and a new generation of younger, more active, and ambitious politicians. Driven by a strong and charismatic Leader, and a political structure which concentrated decision-making power into the hands of a small number of elite councillors, RBC began to establish a new set of development agendas, working in close partnership with private sector developers. The transformation of the town's broader image and the promotion of a new set of commercial and retail investments, became its number one priority. During the 1970s Reading had sold itself as 'England's average town' – a place of normality in which investors and visitors could feel comfortable but clearly a place of relatively low ambition or sense of worth.

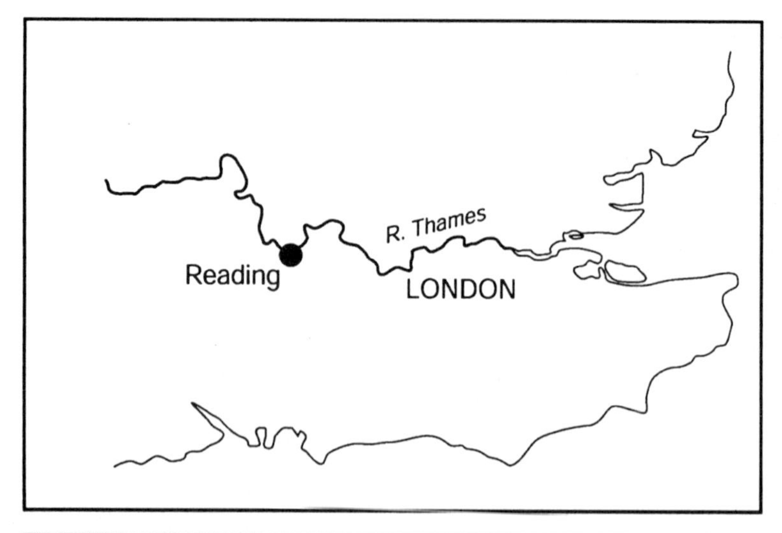

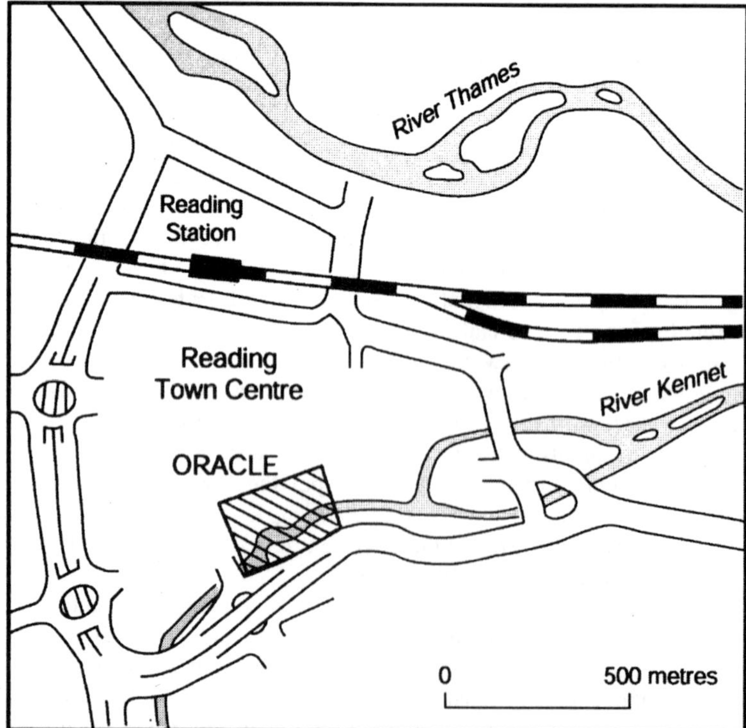

Figure 3.1 Location of Reading and The Oracle shopping centre

Source: Mike Raco

Illustration 3.1 Derelict site adjacent to Reading town centre

In order to change this, RBC initiated a series of measures designed to take advantage of Reading's vacant land (development) opportunities and its wider geographical location. New marketing agendas were supported by new forms of property-led regeneration in an attempt to re-capitalize the area and at the same time tap into wider networks and markets. Reading's position and its extensive road and rail links presented a clear opportunity to develop the town as a central, attractive location for inward investors and visitors. It also possesses a catchment area for retailing (*i.e.* those within a 25 mile radius) of approximately 1.7 million people. The purchasing power of these residents is considerable as it is the fourth most prosperous catchment area of any retailing district in the UK (see Quin, 2000). It is this focus on the investment potential of Reading as a place which has been central to the formation of local RBC-dominated growth partnerships (see Raco, 2003a for a fuller discussion).

The regeneration of Reading's urban spaces, therefore, became a priority for politicians and local planners during the 1980s and 1990s. From 1995 to 1999 a major new development project, named *The Oracle* was established on a large, abandoned town centre site that had formerly been owned by the brewers Courage Plc. It rapidly came to play a key role in RBC's strategy of re-branding the town and creating significant new retail, leisure, and shopping facilities. Built by the developer Hammersons Plc at a cost of £250 million, the centre comprises of 700,000 square feet of retail space (primarily located in a major shopping mall), a waterside public space, a cinema complex and other outlets for retailing and leisure activities (see Illustrations 3.2 and 3.3). Particular imaginations of the town's history have been drawn upon to link the development to particular meanings and understandings of place.

Source: Mike Raco

Illustration 3.2 The Oracle development, Reading

Source: Mike Raco

Illustration 3.3 Waterside public space at The Oracle, Reading

In many ways what has taken place in Reading reflects all that is possible and desirable about the urban renaissance. Reading Borough Council was one of six selected by the government to be Beacon Councils for Town Centre Regeneration in 2001/2002. It was also selected as one of the 24 *Partners in Urban Renaissance* that provided case studies in a government study launched at the Urban Summit in 2002 (see ODPM, 2002 for a thorough discussion). Reading's urban form has been transformed, making it increasingly popular as a visitor destination. Where derelict sites once dominated the landscape, new buildings and public meeting places now stand. New areas of public access have been opened up, with riverside walkways upgraded and made accessible. Moreover, Reading's regional (and national) standing within league-tables and imagined hierarchies has risen as the town has tried to shake off its 'average' image and replace it with one more appropriate to its economic success. During the summer it is possible to compare the town centre and the Oracle development with some of the pictures of urban utopias drawn up in the Urban Task Force Report and other works by Richard Rogers (Urban Task Force, 1999; Rogers and Power, 2000). It is little surprise therefore, that such a transformation appeals to local policy makers intent on fostering local political support and raising the town's profile beyond the locality.

Critically evaluating the impacts of such developments is fraught with difficulties. As Lees (2003) notes, discourses of 'renaissance', with their rhetorical emphasis on inclusion, liveability and sustainability, are particularly difficult to contest and challenge. As with the emergence of partnership discourses in the 1990s, which were portrayed as an inherently 'good thing' (see Peck and Tickell, 1994), the redesigning of urban spaces, to make them more inclusive, people-friendly and welcoming, seems to represent an unchallengeable public 'good'. However, the impacts of renaissance-style developments are by no means straightforward, even in 'successful' towns such as Reading. The regeneration has had a number of impacts which reflect some of the contradictions that are inherent in a market-driven development agenda. The remainder of the chapter assesses these changes and identifies the impacts of regeneration in terms of sustainability and social inclusion, before concluding with a discussion of what such developments tell us about new urban imaginations in contemporary British urban policy. It explores some of the challenges and problems that have arisen and outlines some of the lessons that can be drawn for regeneration schemes elsewhere.

The Reading renaissance – fuelling the flames of market growth

In analysing urban regeneration projects it is incumbent to ask who it is that the developments are aimed at and who benefits from the projects that are developed. It is clear from the above discussion that it is urban-users, rather than urban-dwellers, who represent the focus of policy as attracting people *to* Reading has been the overriding objective of change. In reflecting on the need to expand the range of services on offer for visitors, the Town Centre Manager, for instance, commented in interview that:

> People talk about social exclusion and they always think of poor people. But you could say that the ladies of Henley [sic.] were socially excluded from the town before it was regenerated – they had to travel to Windsor or all the way to London to do their shopping.

Such statements typify much of the thinking that has underpinned the regeneration of the town.

The experiences of Reading also demonstrate that sustaining regeneration in a growing region presents significant difficulties, not least of which has been accessing local labour to service the new developments. There is a dependent relationship between labour markets and renaissance-style regeneration, something that has been conspicuously absent in the government's policy discourses. The urban renaissance *requires* the existence of low-paid, low-skilled workers at the bottom of the labour market – those who are expected to make the cappuccinos, service the bars and restaurants, and clean the streets (see also Amin *et al*, 2000). Development-driven polarization within urban labour markets is not an unfortunate consequence of urban regeneration but a necessary prerequisite for its profitability and 'success'.

In a relatively affluent locality such as Reading accessing such workers on a large scale has represented a significant problem. Employment in Reading is predicted to rise from 91,700 in 1996, to 106,700 in 2006, and 120,400 by 2016, an increase of 31% (RBC, 2003b). The situation in surrounding Berkshire is also one of buoyant growth with employment numbers expected to rise from 426,770 to 561,520 over the same 20-year period. With an unemployment rate of 1.6%, filling new vacancies in Reading has been an on-going challenge. The Oracle development alone has created approximately 3,000 jobs, many of which are in relatively low paid and part time service sectors such as retailing, cleaning and security, something that has been critical to the success of the development and the regeneration more generally. During the late 1990s and early 2000s, strong local partnerships were, therefore, established between local developers, employment agencies, voluntary groups and local communities in a desperate effort to supply cheap and available labour (see Raco, 2003a for a fuller discussion). Women's groups, in particular those from Reading's ethnic communities who had traditionally been marginalized from local labour markets, were targeted and strenuous efforts made to recruit and retain them as low paid employees. In this sense, local partnership formation and development between public, private and community sectors has been a feature of regeneration in Reading but it has been driven by an instrumental need – that of servicing the developments that have taken place.

Turning Reading into a major employment centre has had the additional consequence that its traditional role as a commuter town for London has been turned on its head so that more people now commute into the town daily than leave it (Quin, 2000). Thanks to the Oracle development, Reading has also become a regional centre for shopping, leisure and commerce, with urban-users attracted by the town's specially-built car parking facilities. This deliberate strategy of turning the town centre into a 'honeypot' has come at a price for local residents through significant increases in congestion both on public transport networks and on the roads. A recent report showed that Reading had some of the worst air quality of any urban area in Britain (*Reading Chronicle*, 2001). Traffic volumes in the town have risen by 33% over the period 1991-2001 and at peak times accessibility to the urban centre is seriously restricted (*Reading Evening Post*, 2003). This has been compounded by swingeing cuts to local bus services as the local bus company has found it increasingly difficult to attract drivers on the wages that it is offering – another form of market failure. The regeneration has also meant that traffic in traditionally 'off-peak' periods, such as Sunday afternoons and weekday evenings has become a major problem, again impacting on local residents. Congestion and pollution tends to have a disproportionate effect on poorer urban communities that reside in the most polluted districts, as urban-users drive into urban centres and leave their pollution behind them (see Friends of the Earth, 2000). However, given Reading's relatively small physical size, the negative externalities of worsening air quality have been felt by a wide range of different communities.

It is a similar situation with the growth of leisure facilities in the town and the explicit drive of RBC and local developers to pursue the notion of Reading as a 24-hour city. The driving force behind such ideas is the *City 2020 Vision* that was published in 1999 (RBC, 1999). Reading has campaigned vigorously to be awarded 'city status', even though it is only a symbolic award[2]. A key element of this has been a planning agenda which promotes the concept of a multi-centred city, so that Reading, in the words of its planning briefs, can become the 'Barcelona of Britain' (*The Times*, 2002). One such 'centre' is the establishment of a 'pub quarter' in a commercial zone that had initially suffered from the opening of the Oracle centre. As shops moved out of adjoining streets in the old town centre, to the north of the Oracle, so new properties have become available for national and global entertainment chains to create profitable investment sites. For RBC the development of a 'pub quarter' became a useful development tool in promoting complementary development to the Oracle centre, at the same time as it re-capitalized parts of the town centre which had undergone a short-term loss of trade.

Yet, the promotion of such a quarter, with its explicit focus on alcohol consumption by young people, has generated its own problems. Crime and disorder rates for violent assaults have increased rapidly. There has been a significant increase in petty vandalism on city centre residences and new forms of noise disturbance have been created for urban residents, particularly for the elderly and families living in and around the 'pub quarter'. In the evenings and particularly at weekends, public spaces in the town take on a threatening and exclusionary character and local security measures, such as the cancelling of late running train services and high levels of policing, have had to be adopted, again at the expense of local residents' quality of life. The notion of a vibrant evening economy and the '24-hour city', so popular in the government's renaissance agendas, is highly selective in terms of who it is targeted at. For those who access the services and facilities on offer such a renaissance provides a new experience of a particular place. However, for those who are employed to service the evening economy (often on low-pay and forced to work unsociable hours) and for those who live in urban centres, such services come at a price and can make an urban area less attractive to would-be residents, thereby undermining the broader objective of encouraging greater levels of city centre living.

The regeneration has also created significant security concerns for the local police service, Thames Valley Police, who have the lowest coverage of officers per capita of population of any police force in the UK – another direct consequence of escalating costs of living (Payne, 2002). The 'pub quarter' has generated specific policing problems but it is only a part of a much broader shift in emphasis. Security issues have taken on a new prominence as Reading has moved from being a place with relatively few visitors to become one of the most visited urban spaces in the south of England. Policing resources have not been able to match the new demands which have been generated by increases in activity and it is local residents who have been forced to pay the costs of local policing through major increases in local taxation at the same time as they receive a declining and increasingly limited service. Such pressures on public services do not feature highly in the Urban White Paper or the Task Force Report but in places such as Reading they are a direct and significant consequence of new forms of regeneration.

---

2 It was short-listed but ultimately failed to gain city status in the Queen's Jubilee Cities competition of 2002.

One element of urban renaissance that is also downplayed, yet is enshrined in a range of wider government policies on law and order, is that of making urban spaces more secure. The construction and re-designing of urban spaces has created new opportunities for building exclusion into the fabric of the urban environment. It is ironic that whilst small-scale efforts are being made in many development projects to open up public spaces to those, such as the disabled and elderly, who were previously excluded by the practical difficulties of access, so new forms of exclusion are deliberately being designed-in to the urban fabric to prevent identified problem groups from feeling secure. In Reading, the renaissance has been accompanied by the installation of one of the most vigorous and intensive CCTV schemes in the country[3]; a range of design measures that ensure that there are no potential meeting areas for young people that are not open to CCTV and natural surveillance; and elaborate design measures – from reducing the temperature of pavements (to prevent homeless people seeking shelter in the town centre) to ensuring that no drainpipes are used on buildings to enable people to climb onto roofs (see Raco, 2003b, for a thorough discussion). Such measures are designed to reduce what Urry (1997) terms 'social pollution', or those that could damage the image and reputation of new urban environments.

Alongside this, local housing development has come to represent something of a 'gentrifiers' charter' (see Butler and Robson, 2002). As with development projects elsewhere the construction of houses has been one of the last pieces of the regeneration jigsaw to be put into place. Profitable commercial and retail developments have been prioritized in order to make speedy returns and to generate increases in local housing values by creating 'desirable locations' (see Smith, 2001). Some social housing developments have slowly been established around the town centre but the focus of developers has been on the establishment of high exchange value (although not necessarily high use value) flats in former industrial buildings for high-income professionals, from which maximum profits can be gained. Interviews with local councillors conducted for this research, indicated a frustration that developers had often failed to meet voluntary undertakings to provide more social housing. Frequently, it was suggested, developers used planning regulations to avoid commitments by, for example, building below the agreed number of homes to avoid planning gain. Such findings are not surprising given the Urban White Paper and Urban Task Force Report's silence on the responsibilities of the development industry or corporations more generally, whose right to capitalize on their market investments is uncritically accepted. Again, regeneration agencies should accept this and seek to facilitate market-driven investments, while establishing partnership agreements in and through which social benefits can be accrued.

In Reading such housing developments have had significant consequences for local communities. As house prices have risen, so have the divisions between those with high income streams and those without. This is being translated into a generational divide that is rapidly developing between young, low and middle-

---

3 By mid-2002 Reading had a total number of 327 CCTV cameras to cover its urban centre.

income individuals who are unable to access the property ladder, and middle-aged and elderly house owners who have seen their relative and absolute incomes rise significantly. Inequalities in Reading, as elsewhere in the UK, have risen sharply over the last 20 years. Although Reading is an affluent, fast-growing location there are significant pockets of deprivation that remain, albeit on a much smaller scale than in the bigger metropolitan conurbations. Two of Reading's working class wards, named Witley and Church, have deprivation scores that put them in the top 10% of the most deprived wards in England (RBC, 2003b). Whilst, such trends have not *only* been a consequence of the town centre growth of the last 5-10 years, it has been exacerbated by it as Reading has actively promoted itself as, what Allen *et al.* (1998), term a 'hot spot' of development within the wider Southeast.

Local governance arrangements have proved to be highly adept at promoting economic growth. However, the institutional capacities to tackle the emerging problems of congestion and over-heating have proved to be far more limited. Effective action to tackle housing shortages and transport limitations will require new partnerships to be forged between development agencies, local authorities, and central and regional government. But, thus far, jurisdictional boundaries in the region have been drawn to mollify place-space tensions and political differences, rather than to provide a strategic direction for planning and development policies (Breheny and Hall, 1996). For instance, local politics has long been characterized by tensions over the appropriate role of Reading and the extent to which development takes place in surrounding regions (see Alexander, 1985; Pinch, 1989). Reading is a tightly bounded, Labour-controlled unitary authority, surrounded by affluent, mainly rural borough and authorities, almost all of whom are Conservative controlled and are, at best, cautious about the expansion of their urban neighbour. Since the 1960s fears of urban sprawl and the establishment of a new growth corridor between the M4 and M40 Motorways have paralysed regional planning policy (Pinch, 1989). Yet the only way of tackling Reading's current problems is for RBC to negotiate co-ordinated development strategies with its surrounding neighbours.

The mechanisms to facilitate institutional interaction and co-operation are, however, weak or absent and as a consequence of its growing desperation, RBC has started to lobby central government to give it expanded administrative boundaries and resources. The Leader of RBC, for example, recently argued that such an expansion would give RBC 'control of our regeneration areas and new build areas…this is about the needs of the urban area and the obligations of Reading as an economic driver' (quoted in *Reading Central*, 2003, p.1). Such calls have been met by fierce local resistance from neighbouring boroughs who are opposed to the practical and cultural implications of being subsumed within a larger urban area. The coming of the South East of England Regional Development Agency has provided some strategic direction to development aspirations but it does not have the planning powers to compel co-operation. Consequently, RBC has sought to forge its own partnerships with neighbouring authorities, something that has brought about minor concessions but little in the way of strategic planning or working relationships.

Conclusions: new urban visions and the commodification of Britain's towns and cities

This chapter has examined the form and character of renaissance-style regeneration in Reading, a town which has been relatively successful in market terms since the mid 1970s. It has demonstrated that in such places, regeneration can create new urban spaces that attract visitors and give rise to new forms of commerce and confidence in town and city centres. There are many aspects of such regeneration that should be applauded. Clearly, Reading town centre is a very different place to what it was in the early 1990s, in aesthetic, social and economic terms. Large-scale investments have been made in the urban fabric and, far from declining, it has become a commercial success story with developers keen to establish new projects and activities in the area. However, the chapter has also highlighted some of the difficulties that have been experienced in the town, particularly for local communities who have been faced with the negative externalities that strong market-led growth has brought.

Reading's redevelopment was to be a showcase in which new, locally-sensitive architectural styles and forms were to be established which would both promote economic regeneration and generate new attachments to place. As the design architects for the regeneration project argued, 'the design concept...is to create buildings with a strong character which will enable it to be immediately recognized and associated with Reading...like Harrods is with London' (Haskoll & Company, 1990, p.4). In so doing, it would avoid criticisms of modern centres 'which all seem to look similar and have no individuality' (p.5). This restless search for differentiation and novelty has been taken one step further with new development plans announced in 2002 which called for a major expansion of the urban centre and the construction of new commercial and retail spaces (see RBC, 2003a). In particular, a new 20-storey development has been proposed to create one of the tallest office blocks in the UK, outside of London, in order to give the development an identity of its own and a 'different feel' to similar projects elsewhere.

These new developments have sought to create attachments to place built on new forms of *commodification* and *consumerism*. If urban regeneration tells us about who and what we want to become (see Harvey, 2000), then it is clear that in this form of regeneration citizenship has been re-codified so that acting as a good citizen involves playing the role of a good consumer, avidly purchasing the goods and services provided by multi-national and national companies. Local meanings and attachments to place in Reading have been subsumed under the logic of commercial success so that, for example, the construction of The Oracle around the formerly derelict Kennett and Avon canal is characterized as an initiative which reunites the people of the town with a historical waterfront, when in fact the canal has always been used as an industrial transport route which has never acted as a 'public space'. Whilst the architectural design does possess innovative features, its structure is still dictated by commercial logic – including the need to physically construct 'anchor stores' at each end of the development around which smaller retailers would then be attracted. The main investors who have taken advantage of the new development opportunities are major national and international retail and service firms such as Warner Brothers, Pizza Hut, House of Fraser and Debenhams. Consequently, the town centre has become dominated by the symbols of global capitalism, despite promoting itself as a model for locally-sensitive, inclusive regeneration. Every effort has been made to ensure 'the construction of safe, secure, well-ordered, easily accessible, and above all pleasant, soothing and non-conflictual environments for shopping [as] the key to commercial success' (Harvey, 2000, p.168). Maybe this is a glimpse of the future of renaissance-style British urbanism.

More broadly, the relationships and connections between places, their regeneration and growth, and other areas in the UK and beyond have been systematically downplayed as cities and towns seek to promote themselves within methodologically-limited 'league tables' and imagined national and regional hierarchies. If anything, the renaissance promotes a 'go it alone' attitude within localities, which are encouraged to expand, whatever the implications for other competitors. Moreover, despite the rhetorical promotion of the concept of 'sustainability', the belief that commercial, market-led success represents the basis for new urban spaces still dominates agendas. At a variety of levels the cultivation of ever-expanding economic development is perceived to be politically popular. Promoting sustainability by limiting commercial activity is not. Perhaps the most significant challenge facing towns like Reading is for policy-makers and electorates to accept reduced levels of market-led growth as a way of improving the local quality of life, social mobility and the success of existing investments. With a set of national policy frameworks that encourage the opposite, the chances of a more balanced and more equitable urban future look increasingly remote.

Acknowledgements

The research for this chapter was funded by the University of Reading Endowment Trust Fund (Project Number R104203). The author would like to thank Mark Whitehead and Craig Johnstone for their comments and suggestions on an earlier draft, although responsibility for the final product is, of course, the author's alone.

References

Alexander, A. (1985), *Borough Government and Politics in Reading 1835-1985*, George Allen & Unwin, London.

Allen, J., Massey, D. and Cochrane, A. (1998), *Rethinking the Region*, Routledge, London.

Amin, A., Massey, D., and Thrift, N. (2000), *Cities for the Many Not the Few*, The Policy Press, Bristol.

Breheny, M. and Hall, P. (1996), *The People, Where Will They Go? National Report of the TCPA Regional Inquiry into Housing Need and Provision in England*, Town and Country Planning Association, London.

Butler, T. and Robson, G. (2002), 'Social capital, gentrification and neighbourhood change in London: A comparison of three South London neighbourhoods', *Urban Studies*, vol. 38, pp. 2145-62.

Cochrane, A. (1999), 'Just another failed urban experiment? The legacy of Urban Development Corporations', in R. Imrie and H. Thomas (eds) *British Urban Policy: An Evaluation of the Urban Development Corporations*, Sage, London.

Friends of the Earth (2000), *Urban White Paper – drowning in a sea of carrots,* press release accessed online at: www.foe.co.uk/pubsinfo/infoteam/pressrel/2000/20001116170753.html

Garreau, J. (1988), *Edge City: Life on the Frontier*, Doubleday Press, New York.

Harvey, D. (2000) *Spaces of Hope*, Edinburgh University Press, Edinburgh.

Haskoll & Company (1990), *The Reading Oracle - Architectural Statement*, Haskoll & Company Ltd, London.

Lees, L. (2003), 'Visions of 'urban renaissance': the Urban Task Force Report and the Urban White Paper', in R. Imrie and M. Raco (eds) *Urban Renaissance? New Labour, Community and Urban Policy*, The Policy Press, Bristol.

Lunts, D. (2003) *Urban Renaissance – Fact of Fiction*, a transcript of this speech was accessed online at: www.cem.ac.uk/publec/publec03.htm

Martin, R. (2001) 'Editorial: the Geographer as Social Critic – Getting Indignant About Income Inequality', *Transactions of the Institute of British Geographers*, vol. 26, pp. 267-72.

ODPM (2002), *Towns and Cities: Partners in Urban Renaissance*, HMSO, London.

ODPM (2003), *Sustainable Communities*, HMSO, London.

Payne, S. (2002), 'Police facing cost of living haemorrhage', Daily Telegraph, 17th August, accessed online at: www.telegraph.co.uk/news/main.jhtml?xml=/news/2002/08/17/npc117.xml

Peck, J. and Tickell, A. (1994), 'Too many partners…the future for regeneration partnerships', *Local Economy*, vol. 9, pp. 251-65.

Phillips, N. (1999), *The Story of Reading*, Countryside Books, Newbury.

Pinch, P. (1989), *Locality, Local Government and Central Government: Restructuring Financial Control and the Local State in Reading and Swindon*, unpublished Ph.D. Thesis, Department of Geography, University of Reading.

Quin, S. (2000), *Reading Town Centre Monitor 2000*, Reading Borough Council, Reading.

Raco, M. (2003a), 'Assessing the discourses and practices of regeneration in a growing region', *Geoforum*, vol. 34, pp. 37-55.

Raco, M. (2003b), 'Remaking place and securitising space: urban regeneration and the strategies, tactics and practices of policing in the UK', *Urban Studies*, vol. 40(9), 1869-87.

Reading Borough Council (1999), *City 2020*, Reading Borough Council, Reading.

Reading Borough Council (2000a), *Economic Development Strategy, 2000/2001*, Reading Borough Council, Reading.

Reading Borough Council (2000b), *Reading City 2020 - A Vision of the Future*, Reading Borough Council, Reading.

Reading Borough Council (2003a), *Reading City 2020 Update*, Reading Borough Council, Reading.

Reading Borough Council (2003b), *Reading Housing Strategy Update*, accessed online at: www.reading.gov.uk/athome/hsgstrategy-update2002/

Reading Central (2003), 'Reading Plans to Double in Size', 24th April.

Reading Chronicle (2001), 'Reading's Air Quality Worse Than London', March 5th.

Reading Evening Post (1992), 'Reading the Worst Place to Shop', 13th November.

Reading Evening Post (2003), 'Reality Bites for Boomtown Firms', 16th January

Rogers, R and Power, A. (2000), *Cities for a Small Country*, Faber, London.
Schoon, N. (2002), *The Chosen City*, Spon, London.
Smith, N. (2001), 'Re-scaling politics: Geography, globalism and the New Urbanism', in C. Minca (ed), *Postmodern Geography: Theory and Praxis*, Blackwell, Oxford
The Times (1972), 'The Town Without a Heart and Soul', 18th October.
The Times (2002), 'Reading becomes the Barcelona of Britain', 24th February.
Turok, I. (1999), 'Localization or mainstream bending in urban regeneration? European experience', *Local Economy*, vol. 14, pp. 72-87.
Turok, I. and Edge, N. (1999) *The Jobs Gap in Britain's Cities*, The Policy Press, Bristol.
Urban Task Force (1999) *Towards an Urban Renaissance, Final Report of the Urban Task Force Chaired by Lord Rogers of Riverside*, Spon, London.
Urry, J. (1997) *The Tourist Gaze: Leisure and travel in contemporary societies*, Sage, London.

Chapter 4

The Urban Neighbourhood and the Moral Geographies of British Urban Policy

Mark Whitehead

Introduction

With the possible exception of the region, neighbourhoods have become the dominant spatial motif of Britain's New Labour government. Nowhere is the centrality of the neighbourhood to the New Labour movement expressed more clearly than in the field of urban policy. Although the neighbourhood has regularly been invoked as a framework for area-based urban regeneration initiatives in the UK, this chapter argues that the contemporary incarnation of the neighbourhood is different in two important ways. Firstly, this is because the neighbourhood has now moved from being simply a specific component of urban policy, to become a foundational principle of urban regeneration. Secondly, because the use of the neighbourhood within urban and other policy areas now appears to under-gird a broader set of moral assumptions and practices which are central to the ideologies of central government as a whole. In this context, the neighbourhood provides an important part of New Labour's philosophies and its vision of urban renaissance.

In order to understand the contemporary political utilization of the neighbourhood within British urban policy, this chapter analyses the neighbourhood as a type of moral space. By conceiving of the neighbourhood in this way, analysis draws upon work on moral geography (cf. Driver, 1988; Matless, 1994; Ogborn and Philo, 1994; Smith, 1994a, 1994b, 1998a and 1998b). The study of moral geography is essentially concerned within the inter-relationship between morality and space. In this context work within moral geography has focused on two main issues: first, the ways in which the actions, practices and behaviours of people are judged to be suitable or unsuitable according to the particular places in which they occur (Matless, 1994); and, second, the production of moral judgements which are based on assumptions made about the relationship between patterns of behaviour and particular environments (Driver, 1988; Matless, 2000). This chapter reveals how the neighbourhood is now being utilized as a moral framework through which urban problems in Britain are being identified, codified and addressed. In particular analysis explores the different ways in which the community ethos and support networks associated with the neighbourhood are being tied in to the broader moral discourses of Labour's urban renaissance programme.

This chapter begins by briefly describing the key policy initiatives and institutional changes which have served to resurrect the neighbourhood as a key political category within British urban policy since 1997. Analysis then moves on to reveal a particular set of moral discourses and practices which are embedded within contemporary descriptions of the urban neighbourhood. In the context of these moral geographies of the neighbourhood, this chapter concludes by considering the social struggles which have surrounded the use of neighbourhood space within the town of Walsall, and by questioning the inclusiveness of contemporary urban neighbourhood policy.

The resurrection of the British urban neighbourhood

The nature and number of neighbourhood initiatives developed by the New Labour government is as confusing as it appears to be significant. The Neighbourhood Renewal Unit (NRU), *A New Commitment to Neighbourhood Renewal A National Strategy* (SEU, 2001a), Neighbourhood Management Pathfinders, the Neighbourhood Renewal Community Chest, Neighbourhood and Street Wardens, and the Neighbourhood Renewal Fund, are just some of the initiatives and institutions which now target urban neighbourhoods as their primary concern and site of intervention. In this context, it is important to begin our discussions by clearly establishing what has been happening in the world of neighbourhood-based urban regeneration since 1997.

Early neighbourhood initiatives and the Social Exclusion Unit

The earliest vestiges of the neighbourhood in New Labour's political programme emerged from the Social Exclusion Unit (SEU). The SEU was created to tackle persistent manifestations of social, political and economic exclusion throughout Britain. It rapidly established the neighbourhood as a crucial framework through which to observe various forms of social marginalization. According to the SEU, many forms of social, political and economic exclusion were concentrated in small-scale neighbourhood spaces (SEU, 1998). In this context, it was argued that the most effective way of tackling social exclusion was to concentrate resources in key enclaves of neighbourhood deprivation and dereliction. In 1998 the SEU produced the first national strategy for neighbourhood renewal in the UK entitled *Bringing Britain Together: a National Strategy for Neighbourhood Renewal* (SEU, 1998a). Following on from this strategy the SEU launched a series of policy statements designed to address different forms of social problems – including educational exclusion (SEU 1998b and 1999), anti-social behaviour (SEU, 2000a) and ethnic minority marginalization (SEU, 2000b) through neighbourhood-based projects. These statements led to a range of special purpose, neighbourhood action schemes developed by a range of government departments (including the

Department of Health, the Home Office and the Department for Education and Employment) (cf. Cameron and Gunn, 2002, p.6).

Following the SEU deliberations on the links between neighbourhoods and social exclusion, the neighbourhood began to re-emerge within British urban policy. The earliest manifestations of neighbourhood-based urban policy emanated within the government's restructured Single Regeneration Budget (SRB) programme (DETR, 1998a) and the New Deal for Communities scheme (DETR, 1998b). This early utilization of the neighbourhood by the New Labour government was designed to enable the rescaling of urban funding allocations into smaller units. In the case of the SRB – a programme which New Labour inherited from the previous Tory administration – 20% of its budget was targeted at localized (neighbourhood) pockets of deprivation which were not addressed within more comprehensive projects (DETR, 1998a, p.5). Running alongside the Single Regeneration Budget was the Labour government's freshly devised New Deal for Communities. This *small area programme* ring-fenced parts of the government's regeneration budget for the most severely deprived urban areas – areas which had no specified funding under the SRB (DETR 1998a, p.21). Unlike the majority of funding under the SRB – which continues to be focused upon large urban districts – New Deal for Communities resources are targeted at the smaller neighbourhood scale, and are explicitly devoted to developing better neighbourhood management capacities for the delivery of local services (DETR, 1998b, p.1).

In addition to being incorporated into specific urban programme initiatives, the neighbourhood gradually became a core principle of government thinking on and strategies towards cities. In the comprehensive review of urban problems carried out by the Urban Task Force for example, the neighbourhood was seen as key site around which a range of urban issues could be addressed (see Urban Task Force, 1999, ch.7). In particular, the Urban Task Force emphasized the need to design better physical neighbourhoods, which through their material architectures and spatial structures could help inner cities become more desirable places to live. In order to ensure that the environmental quality and the basic infrastructure of neighbourhoods was maintained, the Urban Task Force Report also recommended that *Neighbourhood Managers* be used to co-ordinate services at a local level (cf. Cameron and Gunn, 2002 for review). The primary difference between the SEU and the Urban Task Force's understanding of the neighbourhood is that while the SEU focused on the social fabric of neighbourhoods, the Urban Task Force was primarily concerned with physical characteristics of neighbourhood space (ibid., p.6).

Rethinking the neighbourhood and 'bending the mainstream'

The centrality of the neighbourhood to New Labour's urban renaissance was further emphasized in 2000. The publication of the new Urban White Paper in 2000 saw the neighbourhood again promoted as a key component of and target for urban policy (DETR, 2000). Within the Urban White Paper, there is a clear attempt to try and combine the social and physical understandings of neighbourhood space developed by the SEU and Urban Task Force, within an integrated urban neighbourhood renewal programme. The White Paper consistently stresses that effectively designed and socially vibrant neighbourhood spaces are vital components within a wider renaissance in urban living throughout Britain. Without physically attractive and socially inclusive neighbourhood spaces, the Urban White Paper claims that it will be difficult to reverse the decline in city living in Britain and generate the investment which is needed to revitalize urban areas (DETR, 2000, ch.4). In order to create neighbourhoods which are *places for people* the Urban White Paper supported the continuation of existing neighbourhood programmes like New Deal for Communities, but also called for new practices within the planning and design of neighbourhoods and the creation of *Neighbourhood Wardens* to oversee the improvement of neighbourhood spaces (ibid., pp.112-3).

In addition to the Urban White Paper, neighbourhood renewal in Britain has also been actively re-thought through a sequence of eighteen Policy Action Teams (PATs) which have reported to the SEU (cf. SEU, 2001a). The PATs were created in 1998 following the publication of the first national strategy for neighbourhood renewal. The purpose of the PATs was to fast-track policy development on neighbourhood renewal and to provide policy guidance on the future direction of neighbourhood policy in Britain. Following the final report of the PATs (SEU, 2001a) the SEU produced a new national strategy for neighbourhood renewal – *A New Commitment to Neighbourhood Renewal: National Strategy Action Plan* (SEU, 2001b). Crucially this document transformed the neighbourhood from being a target for special purpose, area based initiative funding, to a site around which mainstream public spending and services should be focused. The new *National Strategy for Neighbourhood Renewal* called for a *bending* of mainstream resources into deprived neighbourhoods as a prerequisite for effective regeneration. In order to encourage this process, the Neighbourhood Renewal Fund was specifically established to *top-up* local government spending in deprived neighbourhoods and to provide a financial incentive to local authorities to improve the delivery of core public services to such districts (SEU, 2001b, p.48).

In order to bolster and support the government's broad ranging neighbourhood programme, a series of institutions have now also been created to support neighbourhood policies. Prime among these institutions is the *Neighbourhood Renewal Unit* (NRU), which is part of the Office of the Deputy Prime Minister. It is responsible for co-ordinating neighbourhood regeneration at a national level and for implementation of the *National Strategy for Neighbourhood Renewal*. In addition to the NRU a series of Neighbourhood Action Teams have also been set up in the different Government Offices in the English regions. As with the NRU, these teams are responsible for co-ordinating and implementing neighbourhood policy, but this time at a specifically regional level. At a local level, Neighbourhood Management Partnerships have been created between residents, local authorities, the police, health care services and housing associations. These partnerships have been designed to give local residents more influence over the policy decisions which key agencies make concerning their local area (at a national level these partnerships are supported by a Neighbourhood Management Network). Because of the wide range of initiatives, funding streams and programmes which are now converging on neighbourhoods spaces throughout Britain, these institutions appear to have a difficult but vital role in trying to produce integrated patterns of renaissance within urban neighbourhoods.

The moral geography of the urban neighbourhood

This chapter argues that the utilization of the neighbourhood within Labour's urban renaissance programme, under-girds a moral geography of urban community space. According to Driver (1988), moral geography is concerned with the relationship between social conduct and particular environments, or spatial arena. Developing on the work of Driver, Matless (1994) argues that the construction of a moral geography involves the contested production of normative codes of socio-spatial conduct. In this context Matless (1994) emphasizes the ways in which individual morality is always constructed relative to particular spatial contexts – what is historically defined as good and bad always *happens somewhere* and is designated and enforced in relation to some place (p.130). In addition to sensitising us to the spatial character of moral codes, the study of moral geography also involves exploring the historical dialectic that exists between the social and physical ethos of a place. In this context, work on moral geography not only draws attention to the spatial positioning of morality, but also to the different historical ways in which the moral reform of the individual has been related to the production of better physical places, and the material transformation of the environment to changes in individual conduct (Ogborn and Philo, 1994). Understood in this way, I want to argue that the principles of moral geography are useful to contemporary analyses of British urban policy in two main ways: first, because they illustrate how certain codes of conduct and social responsibilities are now being constructed around neighbourhood spaces; and, second, because they reveal how the social and physical reform of neighbourhoods in Britain is being constructed as a single project or act of renaissance.

It is relatively easy to discern the moral geographical currents which run through the history of British urban policy. From the attempts which were made at moral improvement through environmental reforms in the Victorian era, to the ideals of freedom and neo-liberal ideology which informed urban policy during the 1980s and 1990s, British urban policy has continually constructed and addressed urban problems through particular geo-ethical frameworks. The contemporary urban renaissance programme of the New Labour government is no different in this respect. However, the moral geography of the urban renaissance programme does represent at least a partial reaction against many of the moral arguments and ideals of previous Conservative policy initiatives. Drawing on the broad principles and philosophies of the *Third Way* (Giddens, 1998), the New Labour government has used urban policy to support its broader renewal of social democratic ideals (The Commission on Social Justice, 1994). In this context, New Labour has developed a brand of urban policy which attempts to balance the need for economic change and restructuring with important social goals – particularly the renewal of civil society and the creation of more *inclusive* urban communities (DETR, 2000). As described above, the neighbourhood has provided a crucial moral space through which the twin objectives of economic regeneration and social rehabilitation have been pursued.

Initially, the incoming Labour government used the neighbourhood as a spatial target for urban policy. They argued that the competitive allocation of urban funding by the Major administration was unfair for two reasons: first, because many of the most deprived urban areas were not guaranteed the vital funding which they required; and, second, the scale of competitive urban funding allocation meant that unless they were located in larger urban regeneration areas, many smaller neighbourhood pockets of deprivation were being starved of public resources. Through the revised *Index of Multiple Deprivation* (2000), the restructured SRB, the New Deal for Communities programme and, in particular, the Neighbourhood Renewal Fund, the Labour government are using the neighbourhood as a new basis for identifying and addressing urban deprivation and disadvantage. In order to support this use of neighbourhood space, the government have instigated a Neighbourhood Statistics Project to provide a database of social and economic statistics at a neighbourhood scale (NRU, 2002b). Such initiatives are using the neighbourhood as a basis for seeing urban problems in new ways. As the slum and the ghetto have been invoked historically, the neighbourhood is now being used as a moral space through which urban deprivation can be recognized, understood and addressed differently. The difficulties of urban communities are consequently now being interpreted as local bundles of educational, health, employment, crime, transport and housing problems. In this way urban problems are fast being understood first and foremost as problems of neighbourhood space. This chapter argues that this depiction of urban social and economic problems represents a reconstituted moral geography of urban deprivation.

In addition to providing a basis for the fairer allocation of urban funding and for seeing urban problems differently, the ideal of neighbourhood is also being used to define a new type or brand of metropolitan citizenship. Matless (1994) claims that an important aspect of the moral geographies which surround us are the ways in which human behaviour and conduct is derived from and defined in the context of particular spatial expectations. Consequently, the renewal of neighbourhood space appears to depend upon the formation of good neighbours, who will occupy and nourish these community spaces. The clearest paradigm of neighbourhood conduct is articulated in the government's Neighbourhood Warden scheme. Neighbourhood and Street Wardens are meant to provide a 'semi-official presence in a residential area with the aim of improving the environment, quality of life and safety' (NRU, 2002b, p13). Neighbourhood and Street Wardens are meant to keep a *watchful eye* on the neighbourhood in order to prevent *anti-social* behaviour, street crime and vandalism. Neighbourhood Wardens also have a responsibility for ensuring that the different ethnic, age and gender groups within a neighbourhood community are *included* within local projects (SEU, 2001b). Within the Neighbourhood and Street Wardens scheme we see a moral blueprint of the 21st century urban neighbour – vigilant, empowered, concerned for their proximate community and sensitive to the diverse needs of different groups who collectively constitute their neighbours. These community wardens represent key role models and examples of how to behave within neighbourhood space and emphasize the importance of taking personal responsibility for the physical and social fabric of your own local area. This new breed of community activists and social entrepreneurs reflects New Labour's desire to reinvigorate civil society through the creation of more socially responsible citizenship. What is important to recognize here, is that the neighbourhood does not simply represent a passive surface over which new moral geographies are being forged. The prioritization of the neighbourhood as a key space of moral responsibility and citizenship has a direct impact upon the types and scales of conduct, which are being promoted within British cities today.

Encapsulated in the Neighbourhood Renewal Fund, Community Chest and Neighbourhood Management programmes are others codes of conduct which are being promoted in neighbourhood space. These codes of conduct tend to prioritize the importance of local community involvement in regeneration schemes and projects. In its *National Strategy for Neighbourhood Renewal* the SEU (2001b, p.51) states:

> The government is committed to ensure that communities' needs and priorities are to the fore in neighbourhood renewal and that residents of poor neighbourhoods have the tools to get involved in whatever way they want.

It appears that being a *good neighbour* involves getting involved, participating, and making things happen, not simply letting urban policies happen to your community. The idea of the active citizen is central to the New Labour project and is deeply tied to a belief in the role of the neighbourhood in nurturing such a dynamic brand of citizenry:

> Community involvement...can best be approached at a small geographical scale – the neighbourhood itself rather than the wider area covered by the Local Strategic Partnership. Special efforts need to be made to engage communities of interest who may not be concentrated in one place, and those who may be harder to reach because of language and access difficulties (SEU, 2001b, p.52).

Such sentiments reveal how the neighbourhood is being promoted as the grassroots cornerstone of local democracy within Labour's urban renaissance. The scale of the neighbourhood, it would appear, provides the ideal context within which to learn how to participate more effectively within society and to encourage previously excluded groups to become involved in the political process.

There is a final aspect to New Labour's use of the neighbourhood as a strategy for urban renewal which has a bearing on how we understand the new moral geography of urban policy. In addition to recasting visions of citizenship to fit with the ideals of neighbourhoods, the Labour government clearly believes that the physical design and shape of neighbourhoods has a significant bearing on the types of behaviour and conduct which occur in community space. In the Urban White Paper of 2000 and its precursor, the Urban Task Force Report (1999), there is consequently a strong emphasis on the need to re-design cities so that they can provide more open and integrated spaces within which urban residents can mix, share ideas and develop a collective neighbourhood consciousness:

> New urban developments, on brownfield or greenfield land, must be designed to much higher standards if they are to attract people back into our towns and cities. Urban developments should be integrated with their surroundings, optimise access to public transport and maximize their potential by increasing density in appropriate conditions. They should seek diversity; encouraging a mix of activities, services, incomes and tenures within neighbourhoods. Land must be used efficiently, local traditions respected and negative environmental impacts kept to a minimum. Priority should be given to high architectural standards and to the design of public spaces between buildings where people meet and move about (Urban Task Force, 1999).

There is a clear sense here that not only is there a right way to act within neighbourhoods, but that such behaviour has previously been inhibited, or structured out by badly designed neighbourhood spaces. With unsafe or vandalized public spaces, a lack of local facilities and a dearth of meeting places, the Labour government argue that the moral problems of urban neighbourhoods are at least partially a product of their physical condition. The solutions to these problems are presented in the glossy colour pages of the Urban White Paper (DETR, 2000). In *Our Towns and Cities: The Future – Delivering and Urban Renaissance* there is a strong emphasis on the role of squares, recreational parks, boulevards and street environments in the creation of a more inclusive and interactive neighbourhood community (see DETR, 2000, ch.4). The Urban White Paper teems with images of clean and safe public open spaces, because these are the types of environment the government believes are necessary if a new urban citizenry is going to be formed. The vision of a more open, public metropolis supports the strong discursive links which connect the idea of renaissance and a nostalgia for the pre-industrial city (cf. Amin and Thrift, 2002, ch.2). The physical restructuring of neighbourhood space envisioned within the urban renaissance programme appears to belie a desire to create the idyllic public spaces of a cosmopolitan city (cf. Sennett, 1974, pp.294-5; Jacobs, 1994) and engender a new moral geography of tolerance and understanding within British urban life.

Tales from the urban neighbourhood – the case of Walsall

New Labour's urban renaissance appears to be based upon a dual moral geography of neighbourhood space. At one level, the neighbourhood is depicted as a space of social responsibility and participation in the political process. At a second level, the neighbourhood is about the celebration of public space as an arena of interaction and cosmopolitanism. The town of Walsall in the English West Midlands has experienced a long historical struggle over is neighbourhood spaces (cf. Seabrook, 1984; Whitehead, 2003). This historical struggle recently culminated in the implementation of series of government-sponsored neighbourhood renewal programmes in the town. Using the example of the Walsall, the remainder of this chapter analyses the extent to which the moral geographical visions of a neighbourhood renaissance are being realized in British cities.

The historical struggle over neighbourhood space in Walsall

The town of Walsall is in many ways synonymous with the neighbourhood debate. From the early 1970s onwards, a series of attempts have been made by the radical arm of Walsall's local Labour Group to devolve council services and democracy into neighbourhood networks. The 1980s saw the establishment of Neighbourhood Offices in the town. These offices provided practical advice on council house waiting lists, how to access repair services and convenient sites where local people could pay their taxes. In 1995, it was proposed that the neighbourhood should be used more widely as a basis for the delivery of local government services. The incoming local Labour government, led by Dave Church, controversially proposed the formation of Neighbourhood Councils, to which large segments of mainstream council funding and decision-making power would be devolved. The proposals were ridiculed by the Conservative government of the time, and the Labour party suspended the local Labour Group and effectively put an end to its new vision of local neighbourhood democracy.

Significantly, the principle of neighbourhood democracy was re-invented in Walsall in 1996. In that year, the local council won government funding for an SRB scheme entitled *Empowering Local Communities*. The scheme proposed the creation of neighbourhood committees in the seven most deprived areas of the town. These neighbourhood committees are made up of 15-30 elected representatives each from a given local neighbourhood *patch*. The chosen representatives are responsible for deciding how and where neighbourhood regeneration funding should be used in their local communities. Subsequent to the SRB scheme more neighbourhood committees have been created throughout Walsall and now provide the vehicles through which New Deal for Communities and new SRB monies are being spent and service level agreements negotiated with local authority providers. While having far less power and geographical coverage than the Neighbourhood Councils proposed by the local Labour Group, these Local Neighbourhood Committees were seen by the local authority and central government to provide a viable framework within which to develop neighbourhood democracy. The experience of neighbourhood government and policy in Walsall provides a useful framework within which it is possible to begin to analysis the potential of neighbourhood spaces to deliver a wider urban renaissance within the UK.

The problematics of identifying and creating neighbourhood spaces

When initial attempts were made to implement a structure of local neighbourhood committees, Walsall's local authority encountered a series of problems. These problems revolved around the identification of where particular neighbourhood spaces existed and the appropriate scale at which neighbourhoods should be constituted. Initially a team of local facilitators worked with communities to try and identify and delimit neighbourhood districts within the town. This process of consultation was described to me by one community facilitator in the following way:

> The people who wish to become involved in the design team leading up to the elections – typically groups between eight and twenty people – sit down and we draw the map, we agree the map, we think yes well this is the outer boundary (of the neighbourhood)...these proposals are then advertized and promoted at community events and general local meetings, and local opinions on the patches and boundaries are taken on board (Associated Policy Officer, Walsall Metropolitan Borough Council, 1999).

The problem with this process of identifying and delimiting neighbourhood space is of course that one person's perception of neighbourhood space on a design team was obviously very different from another's. Consequently, strong and often divisive debates were often had over where a neighbourhood boundary should be draw and on which side of that line a particular household would fall. These divisions resulted in some people identifying much more with the agreed neighbourhood spaces than others. According to local community facilitators these were normally the people who became much more engaged and involved in the Local Neighbourhood Committees themselves.

The local authority and community facilitators experienced further difficulties when discussions were held on the appropriate scale of a neighbourhood. In order to enable Local Committees to act in a reasonably strategic way, the local authority felt that neighbourhoods should be made up of between 1500 and 3000 households (or between 3000 and 8000 people). However, it was felt that this scale of neighbourhood was really anathema to the types of social attachment and political participation which these neighbourhood spaces were trying to engender. Consequently it was decided that each neighbourhood should be divided into patches of approximately 100 households. These *neighbourhood patches* would then have one representative each on the Local Neighbourhood Committee. While providing a more *humanly scaled* basis for neighbourhood life, neighbourhood patches have also served to divide neighbourhoods into competing turfs.

The difficulties of identifying the spaces and scales of neighbourhoods in Walsall reveals a broader weakness in New Labour's invocation of neighbourhood policy. Throughout the burgeoning literatures on neighbourhood policy produced by the Labour government there is an implicit assumption that neighbourhoods exist and present themselves as natural, organic entities within the urban landscape. Of course, this belief in the pre-existence of established neighbourhood spaces reinforces the moral discourses of community support, solidarity and care which are associated with neighbourhoods. But neighbourhoods do not exist as neatly segregated physical (Smailes, 1955; Carter, 1972) or social spaces (Ley, 1983, p.87) within the city. Neighbourhoods are contested fragments of city space, the formation of which can be as divisive as it is harmonising and as exclusionary as it is inclusive (cf. Whitehead, 2003).

Neighbourhoods and the fragmentation of the city

The problems of identifying neighbourhood spaces in Walsall have been compounded by the tensions which have subsequently been experienced between different neighbourhoods. While the ideal of neighbourhood democracy in Walsall and Labour's broader urban renaissance programme is premised upon the creation of a more open and cosmopolitan urban lifestyle, the experience of Walsall reveals a very different set of processes. Talking to policymakers in Walsall, it is apparent that while neighbourhoods may be good at bringing proximate urban inhabitants together, they can be equally divisive for groups who do not share such propinquity.

The geographically divisive aspects of contemporary neighbourhood policy is evident in Walsall is two main ways. Firstly, because neighbourhood building tends to be concentrated in the most deprived urban communities, great jealousies have been evident in communities adjoining the fortunate neighbourhoods but not receiving funding. Unlike the original plans proposed by the local Labour Group, Local Neighbourhood Committees only exist in a relatively small number of districts in the town. Consequently many local residents express concerns over a two-tier system of democracy emerging in the town between those with neighbourhood representatives and those without.

The second divisive characteristic associated with neighbourhood democracy in Walsall is evident between areas with Local Neighbourhood Committees. Although Local Committee areas all receive funding, the amount and nature of that funding varies from one neighbourhood to another. As a consequence of the differential funding received by Local Neighbourhood Committees, a series of 'neighbourhood feuds' have emerged in Walsall. These feuds tend to focus upon intense inter-neighbourhood comparisons of funding levels and conflicts over who receives funding for issues which cross neighbourhood boundaries. The problems of funding conflict is recognized by policymakers in Walsall's Metropolitan Borough Council (WMBC), but is accepted as an inevitable part of public spending allocations:

> There are always winners and losers and we do recognize this. There is a degree of bleed across the areas, and with schools for example we recognize when feeder schools are outside of an [Local Neighbourhood Committee] area and include them in the funding. I mean we get concerns expressed...but at the end of the day you work within the resources that you are given (Urban Policy Officer, WMBC, 1999).

While there may be a sense of inevitability over funding conflicts between different areas of a city, the case of Walsall does bring in to question the idyllic depiction of neighbourhoods within Labour's urban renaissance programme. The creation of stronger neighbourhood identities may bring local urban communities together, but neighbourhoods can also serve to fragment and dislocate the wider urban community. In the case of Walsall it is apparent that the creation of neighbourhoods has opened up new frontiers of urban social conflict and formalized urban political division in new ways. Consequently, with funding feuds

raging between neighbourhoods, there is a clear danger that neighbourhood policy has the potential to create what Sennett (1974, pp.294-5) describes as *barricaded communities* just as much as they can produce *territorial communities of intimacy*. Indeed, in Goscote, Walsall New Deal for Communities funding has paid for the erection of fencing around neighbourhood communities (see Illustration 4.1). Crucially this type of divided cityscape seems to fundamentally oppose the types of moral geographies and codes of neighbourly conduct which the Labour government are trying to promote.

Source: Mark Whitehead

Illustration 4.1 Cosmopolitan neighbourhoods or barricaded communities?

Neighbourhoods and the issue of political power

A final issue which the experience of neighbourhood democracy in Walsall reveals regarding the principle of neighbourhood renewal, concerns the issue of political power and participation. As described above, one of the key justifications given for neighbourhood-based urban policy was that neighbourhoods would provide a more accessible basis for local political participation and decision-making. In Walsall, however, the political value of neighbourhood democracy is being questioned both by local residents and the policymakers responsible for delivering neighbourhood renewal.

One of the main limitations of neighbourhood democracy in Walsall has been the inability of Local Neighbourhood Committee to actually set the policy agenda within their own communities. As one community facilitator pointed out:

> It's a funny thing really because in a sense one of the prerequisites of the [Local Neighbourhood Committee] programme is that there is consultation at the local level, on the other hand funding bids are approved before people really have a proper chance to participate in the bidding process (Community Facilitator, WMBC, 1999).

Local authorities when bidding for SRB and New Deal for Communities monies were required to establish key priorities and policy objectives. With strict auditing and monitoring systems in place, once such objectives were established at the bidding stage it proved difficult for local neighbourhood committees like those found in Walsall to really influence the ways in which urban regeneration funding was actually spent.

Beyond special purpose urban funding (like the SRB), the Local Neighbourhood Committees in Walsall have also experienced severe limitations in trying to *bend the mainstream* spending of the local authority. For different legislative reasons and because of their perceived lack of technical expertise, the Local Neighbourhood Committees have been denied meaningful access to wider council budgets. The seemingly limited influence of the Local Neighbourhood Committees in Walsall over special purpose funding, combined with their inability to shape local authority spending, has had a serious impact on the levels of political participation on these committees. Only 111 of the 151 seats available on Local Committees have been filled. Even more concerning is that only 27 of the 111 occupied seats were contested in local neighbourhood elections. Without the delegation of power and resources to neighbourhoods, it appears that their ability to act as spaces of metropolitan participation and crucibles of urban social and economic renaissance will be compromised and undermined.

Reflections on the neighbourhood ideal

This chapter has charted the emergence of neighbourhood policy as a key component of New Labour's urban renaissance programme. It has also illustrated how the re-emergence of the neighbourhood has provided a spatial context for a new moral geography of British urban policy. This moral geography has used the neighbourhood as a strategy for identifying, understanding and addressing urban social problems. Despite the sanguine moral discourses of neighbourhood space, analysis has questioned the use of the neighbourhood as a strategy for urban renewal in Britain.

Using the example of Walsall, this chapter has criticized New Labour's use of the neighbourhood at two levels. Firstly, it has questioned the validity of the moral associations which are being made between neighbourhood spaces, community care and cosmopolitan tolerance. As the work of planners (Jacobs, 1994) and urban sociologists (Sennett, 1974) in the 1960s and 1970s first revealed, this chapter has shown that neighbourhoods can be as divisive as they can be unifying, as much about the *barricading-off* of urban space as the creation of vibrant spaces for social interaction. Questions undoubtedly remain concerning whether neighbourhoods can generate the broader spatial scope of moral responsibility towards the whole urban community envisaged within New Labour's urban renaissance (Smith, 1998b). At a second level, analysis has also revealed that the ways in which urban policy is currently constructing neighbourhoods is acting as anathema to their purported moral function. Consequently, while neighbourhood areas continue to have insufficient power to influence the ways in which urban funding is being spent, and remain unable to access mainstream public funding, it is difficult to imagine neighbourhoods providing a new democratic foundation for metropolitan life in the UK.

References

Amin, A. and Thrift, N. (2002), *Cities – Reimagining the Urban*, Polity Press, Cambridge.

Cameron, S. and Gunn, Z. (2002), 'Increasing Urban Capacity – From Land Constraints to Neighbourhood Renewal', paper presented at the 3rd Regeneration Management Research Workshop – Urban Renaissance in Question, University of Durham 14th November.

Carter, H. (1972), *The Study of Urban Geography*, Edward Arnold, London.

Commission on Social Justice (1994), *Social Justice – Strategies for National Renewal*, Vintage, London.

DETR (1998a), *The Single Regeneration Budget: A guide for Partnerships*, DETR, London.

DETR (1998b), *A New Deal for Communities*, DETR, London.

DETR (2000), *Our Towns and Cities: the Future – Delivering an Urban Renaissance*, HMSO, London.

Driver, F. (1988), 'Moral geographies: social science and the urban environment in mid-nineteenth century England', *Transactions of the Institute of British Geographers*, vol. 13(3), pp. 275-87.

Giddens, A. (1998), *The Third Way: The Renewal of Social Democracy*, Polity Press, Cambridge.

Jacobs, J. (1994), *The Death and Life of Great American Cities*, Penguin Books, London.

Ley, D. (1983), *A Social Geography of the City*, Harper Row, New York.

Matless, D. (1994), 'Moral geography in Broadland', *Ecumene*, vol. 1, pp. 127-55.

Matless, D. (2000), 'Moral geographies', in R.J. Johnston, D. Gregory, G. Pratt and M. Watts (eds), *The Dictionary of Human Geography*, Blackwell, Oxford.

NRU (2002a), *Fact Sheet 1 – What is Neighbourhood Renewal.* (ODPM, London).

NRU (2002b), *Changing Neighbourhoods, Changing Lives: The Vision for Neighbourhood Renewal* (ODPM, London).

Ogborn, M. and Philo, C. (1994), 'Soldiers, sailors and moral locations in nineteenth century Portsmouth', *Area*, vol. 26, pp. 221-31.

Seabrook, J. (1984), *The Idea of Neighbourhood: What Local Politics Should be About*, Pluto Press, London.

Sennett, R. (1974), *The Fall of Public Man*, Cambridge University Press, Cambridge.

Smailes, A. (1955), 'Some reflections on the geographical description and analysis of townscapes', *Transactions of the Institute of British Geographers*, vol. 21, pp. 99-115.

Smith, D.M. (1994a), 'On professional responsibility to distant others', *Area*, vol. 26, pp. 359-67.

Smith, D.M. (1994b), *The Moral Problem*, Blackwell, Oxford.

Smith, D.M. (1998a), 'Geography and moral philosophy', *Ethics, Place and Environment*, vol. 1, pp. 7-34.

Smith, D.M. (1998b), 'How far should we care? On the spatial scope of beneficence', *Progress in Human Geography*, vol. 22, pp. 15-38.

SEU (1998a), *Bringing Britain Together; a National Strategy for Neighbourhood Renewal*, Cabinet Office, London.

SEU (1998b), *Truancy and School Exclusion*, Cabinet Office, London.

SEU (1999), *Bridging the Gap: New opportunities for 16-18 year olds not in education, employment or training*, Cabinet Office, London.

SEU (2000a), *Anti-Social Behaviour Report: Report of the Policy Action Team 8*, Cabinet Office, London.

SEU (2000b), *Minority Ethnic Issues in Social Exclusion and Neighbourhood Renewal*, Cabinet Office, London.

SEU (2001a), *National Strategy for Neighbourhood Renewal* – Policy Action Team Audit, Cabinet Office, London.

SEU (2001b), *A New Commitment to Neighbourhood Renewal: National Strategy Action Plan*, Cabinet Office, London.

Urban Task Force (1999), *Towards an Urban Renaissance – Final Report of the Urban Task Force*, E & FN Spon, London.

Whitehead, M (2003), 'Love thy neighbourhood – rethinking the politics of scale and Walsall's struggle for neighbourhood democracy', *Environment and Planning A*, vol. 35, pp. 277-300.

Chapter 5

Crime, Disorder and the Urban Renaissance

Craig Johnstone

Introduction

Crime and disorder are persistent and pervasive social problems in Britain's towns and cities. They are probably not, however, two ills many readers would typically expect urban policy to address. Anyone with a little knowledge about how the British government divides responsibilities between its departments knows that crime and disorder problems, in England and Wales at least, traditionally fall within the remit of the Home Office, which runs the criminal justice system, while urban policy is now formulated by the Office of the Deputy Prime Minister (ODPM). Recent history would seem to suggest, moreover, that the urban policy agenda is dominated by the physical regeneration of city centre real estate and the revitalization of urban economies. Social issues such as crime, in contrast, have received scant attention. It is significant though that until the Department of the Environment assumed responsibility for it in 1975 such social problems were amongst the principal concerns of urban policy. Indeed, it was partly fears that deprivation and associated racial tensions might fuel a breakdown in social order that led the Home Office to deploy the first urban policies in 1968 (CDP, 1977; Deakin and Edwards, 1993). By the time the New Labour government was elected 29 years later, fears of Watts-style race riots and the spectre of Enoch Powell's 'rivers of blood'[1] had receded. But other social problems, including crime, identified in the 1960s and detailed in the 1977 Urban White Paper (DoE, 1977) did not fade away during the intervening years. If anything, their neglect by central government made them more acute. The situation was such by 1997 that, in his

---

1 The mid-1960s witnessed race riots in the Black inner city ghettos of a number of cities across the USA. One of the most notorious occurred in Watts, Los Angeles, where six days of violence in August 1965 left 36 people dead. It was highly unlikely at the time that such riots would occur in the UK, but in a speech delivered in Birmingham on April 20th 1968, the Conservative MP Enoch Powell argued that Britain needed to turn back the immigrant tide if the US experience was to be avoided. He also painted a picture of growing disaffection amongst the white working classes who felt they were being displaced by immigrants from the jobs, neighbourhoods and public services they believed were rightfully theirs.

first major speech as Prime Minister, delivered at the Aylesbury Estate in Southwark, Tony Blair (1997) spoke of 'an underclass of people cut off from society's mainstream, without any sense of shared purpose'. He deemed such severe social marginalization and exclusion unacceptable in 21st century Britain and to this end New Labour has returned social problems including crime and disorder to the urban policy agenda. Alongside the design-led renewal of town and city centres and the realization of greater economic competitiveness, the resolution of key social problems is now central to the delivery of an 'urban renaissance' (Department of Environment, Transport and the Regions (DETR), 2000).

My intention in this chapter is threefold. First, to introduce British crime and disorder problems, and the responses of the New Labour government to them, to a readership that may not be familiar with this area of public policy. Second, to examine the role of contemporary urban policy in the delivery of a reduction in crime, anti-social behaviour and the fear of crime, and the significance of this reduction for the realization of New Labour's urban renaissance. Third and finally, the chapter critically assesses the threats to the Blair government's vision of a socially inclusive renaissance posed not by crime and disorder but by policy responses to them and also by changing social attitudes. I argue that New Labour's urban renaissance vision is contradictory, promoting inclusion while simultaneously reinforcing the exclusion of the socially disadvantaged through the intense risk-management of gentrified urban space and attempts to recreate place-based communities that are inherently insular and solipsistic.

The extent and impact of crime and disorder

Crime and disorder were the first urban problems against which the 19th century *laissez-faire* state felt it necessary to take action – the Home Office creating the Metropolitan Police in 1829[2]. The high crime rates experienced today are, however, relatively recent phenomena, only emerging in the last decades of the 20th century. The number of police-recorded offences in England and Wales passed 1 million in a year for the first time in 1964. Thereafter the rate rose rapidly, reaching 2.7 million in 1979 and a 20th century peak of 5.6 million in 1992[3]. Although the rate then fell slightly before levelling off, new recording procedures introduced in 2002 caused it to climb to a new high of 5.8 million[4] (Povey, Nicholas and Salisbury, 2003). The problem of disorder is much more difficult to quantify because until recently incidents of it were only recorded when a criminal act was involved. The situation was compounded by the under-reporting of

---

2 Central government intervention in public health and housing problems did not follow until 1848 and 1883 respectively.

3 Police-recorded crime reflects both recording and reporting practices. A more accurate indicator of crime levels, although it does not include offences against minors, is thought to be the now-annual British Crime Survey. This was first conducted in 1982 and has consistently estimated crime to be three or more times the official figure.

4 427,000 crimes were recorded in Scotland in 2002 (Scottish Executive, 2003).

incidents, inadequate definition of the term 'anti-social behaviour'[5], and because, as Policy Action Team (PAT) 8 found in 2000, 'no agency has a specific requirement to reduce it [and] there are no national objectives or targets for anti-social behaviour. It is no agency's priority so risks their collective neglect' (PAT 8, 2000, p.49). The only national guide to the severity of disorder is the British Crime Survey which, in 2002, found that over 30% of people believed teenagers hanging around on the streets; vandalism, graffiti and other deliberate damage to property; and people using or dealing drugs were very or fairly big problems in their local area.

The highest levels and most serious incidents of crime and disorder tend to be found in the decaying inner suburbs and 'sink' peripheral housing estates of Britain's towns and cities (see *The Guardian*, 2003a). It is here that the most socially and economically disadvantaged members of society have been physically concentrated over the last 20 years as a result of the interaction between housing and labour markets. Tony Blair (1997) painted a bleak picture of such places in his Southwark speech, evoking images of neighbourhoods where the working class had been replaced by a workless class, welfare dependence was almost total, crime endemic and hope in short supply. Indeed, high levels of criminality and anti-social behaviour typically co-exist with mass unemployment, low household incomes, widespread ill health, limited educational attainment and housing market failure in the most deprived neighbourhoods. These different forms of disadvantage are interlinked and prone to fuel one another in a destructive cycle.

In many cases the origin of the social breakdown evident today in deprived neighbourhoods can be traced back over 20 years to the far-reaching restructuring of labour markets instituted by Thatcher's Conservative government during the early 1980s. By the mid 1990s Will Hutton (1995) could argue that restructuring had given rise to a '40:30:30 society' wherein just 40% of the workforce remained in secure employment. Of those outside this elite group, 30% were in employment that was insecure and the other 30% on the margins of society, drifting in and out of the most poorly paid work or idle and in some cases unemployable. Jock Young (1999) likens this last segment to the spectators at a race. Many of them would like the opportunity to compete but most are held back from the racetrack by barriers and a cordon of police: 'they are denied real access to the race but are perpetual viewers of the glittering prizes on offer' (ibid, p.8). The tantalizingly excluded are just as eager to participate in consumer culture as those with 'credit card' citizenship. Unable to gain membership of the consumer society, or at least not meaningful membership, some try to enter illegally: they choose crime. Critics on the Left argue that, as they are functions of social exclusion, the only way to reduce crime and disorder is to deliver social inclusion. Thus, policies that target crime and disorder in isolation are doomed to fail because they ignore the roles played by other forms of deprivation. Launching a crackdown on crime may

---

5 The Anti-Social Behaviour Act 2003 defines such behaviour as that 'by a person which causes or is likely to cause harassment, alarm or distress to one or more persons not of the same household as that person'.

produce short-term benefits but the problem will surely reappear if its underlying causes remain untouched.

Crime and disorder may seldom be the initial catalyst of urban decline but they can still contribute greatly to it and even cause its acceleration (SEU, 1998; PAT 8, 2000). The downward spiral they fuel is thought to begin with fairly minor criminal acts, like vandalism, which, combined with anti-social behaviour, serve to increase the fear of crime and reduce the quality of life for residents of affected areas. Indeed, speaking at the Home Office Anti-Social Behaviour Conference in October 2003, the Regeneration Minister Yvette Cooper stated that 'Tackling anti-social behaviour is a fundamental part of the drive to improve the quality of life for people in our towns and cities and is key to creating sustainable communities' (Home Office Press Release 278/2003). There can be little doubt that neighbourhoods where children congregate in large groups and verbally harass passers by, empty properties are vandalised and, in some case, set on fire, teenagers joyride stolen cars before burning them out, parents threaten victims of their children's crime with violence to dissuade them from going to the police, and drug dealers set up shop, quickly become very undesirable places to live. The constant fear of crime and daily exposure to disorder discourages residents from using the streets and eventually convinces those with the wherewithal to do so to move elsewhere. In the worst cases, as an exodus of well-established residents and role models gathers momentum, community bonds are broken, a social malaise infects the neighbourhood, and the ability or desire of those that remain to enforce a decent standard of behaviour is greatly diminished (see Wilson, 1987).

Once an area gains a bad reputation, demand for property drains away and their values plummet, meaning those owner-occupiers who remain may slip into negative equity and be unable to afford to buy elsewhere. Properties may be abandoned or sold to private landlords, many with no interest in the neighbourhood or the behaviour of their tenants, who rent them to those who have no other option – asylum seekers or people previously evicted from social housing – and a transient population, including drug addicts and prostitutes, seeking cheap accommodation (PAT 8, 2000). Serious crime, violence and, in some places, racial conflict become common currency. The demise of the neighbourhood is complete.

They may be most prevalent in deprived neighbourhoods but incidents of crime and disorder are much less geographically concentrated than poverty and other forms of extreme socio-economic disadvantage. The probability of victimization even within a town or city depends greatly on age, gender, lifestyle, social class and place of residence, yet concern about crime is widespread. The adaptations we have made to the urban environment reflect our fears. Although the suburb of south Liverpool in which I live seems fairly safe, signs and sounds of security are everywhere. Nearly every house on my street is wired with a burglar alarm and a few months ago the city council fitted gates to the alley that runs behind my back yard to prevent any would-be burglars from gaining access to the rear of properties. Businesses have also taken additional precautions. At the local petrol station signs ask customers to pay for fuel before they pump after a spate of drive-away thefts[6]. Similarly, in the off licence up the road, thick Perspex screens bar consumers from handling the merchandise before they buy – the cashier is the only person with access to the shelves. The concern about crime that drives investment in security measures, while sometimes justifiable often has no real basis in the local crime situation, having been informed by the accounts of friends, family and the media[7]. It is young men who are most at risk of being victimized yet a survey conducted by Age Concern in 2003 found that 72% of older people believed that you are more likely to become a victim of street crime as you get older. Significantly, only 2% of respondents had experienced such crime. A certain level of fear about crime is necessary if the public are to take steps to avert crime. The Prime Minister (Blair, 1997) has also tried to exploit the widespread fear of crime amongst the middle classes in order to generate popular support for his social inclusion agenda, observing rather ominously in his Southwark speech that 'comfortable Britain…knows the price it pays for economic and social breakdown in the poorest parts of [the country]'. However, fear of crime now seems to have taken on a life of its own – seemingly increasing while crime levels, to which it is supposedly a response, have diminished. The impact the fear of victimization can have on lifestyles, especially those of the vulnerable (see Koskela and Pain, 2000; Pain, 2000 and 2002), is such that its reduction is now a policy objective in its own right.

The New Labour approach to crime and disorder

Since the 1970s 'law and order' has been a key party political battleground and one on which the Conservatives, offering populist, authoritarian solutions, have excelled. Although (and perhaps because) social democratic Labour governments of the past often found it difficult to fend off accusations that they were 'soft' on crime, New Labour has chosen to make crime and disorder signature issues on which it is prepared to stake its reputation. Pledging to be, 'Tough on crime, tough on the causes of crime' – a soundbite coined a few years earlier by his predecessor as Labour Home Affairs Spokesman, Tony Blair – Jack Straw spent the campaign for the 1997 General Election trading political blows with Michael Howard, arguably the most right wing of all the post-1979 Conservative Home Secretaries. As the Guardian observed at the time:

> Mr Straw's main ambition – sometimes, it seems, his only intention – is to prove he wields a thicker baseball bat than Michael Howard...Whenever Mr Howard pops up with a "crackdown", Mr Straw's standard response is to say that it was his idea first

6 Although it is standard practice in some countries to pay for fuel in advance, at the time of writing it remains unusual to do so in the UK. Interestingly, it appears only to be those who, due to the car they drive, clothes they wear or general demeanour, 'look' like they might pose a risk that are not served unless they pay first.

7 Two classic accounts of the way the media defines deviance and then stimulates public concern about it are Cohen (1972) and Hall et al (1978).

> and, what's more, his crack downwards would be that much harder (*The Guardian*, 1996).

But while there can be little doubt that in some cases New Labour was prepared to be more punitive than the Tories, it also acknowledged that stiff punishments needed to be supplemented by preventative intervention if real progress towards lower crime rates was to be made (see Straw and Michael, 1996). Following Wilson and Kelling (1982), New Labour also advocated greater attention be paid to anti-social behaviour and disorderly conduct, arguing that there was a direct link between these and criminality (see Straw and Michael, 1996, p.4). In their 'broken windows' thesis, Wilson and Kelling (1982) claim that, 'disorder and street crime are usually inextricably linked, in a kind of developmental sequence' (p.31) and 'serious street crime flourishes in areas in which disorderly behaviour goes unchecked' (p.34). They maintain that unless disorderly behaviour is stamped out quickly those committing it are emboldened by the perception that no one cares and so move on to more serious law breaking. Furthermore:

> The prospect of confrontation with an obstreperous teenager or a drunken panhandler can be as fear-inducing for defenceless persons as the prospect of meeting an actual robber; indeed, to a defenceless person the two kinds of confrontation are often indistinguishable (p.32).

Thus, it is their belief that clamping down on disorder not only prevents more serious crime from occurring at some point in the future it also improves public perceptions of safety. These arguments led to the formation of PAT 8 to investigate the problem of anti-social behaviour and informed the Crime and Disorder Act 1998, the Anti-Social Behaviour Act 2003 and the Anti-Social Behaviour (Scotland) Bill. In addition, the Home Office has created an Anti-Social Behaviour Unit and, in October 2003, launched an Anti-Social Behaviour Action Plan, backed by £75 million of funding, which included amongst its proposals pilot or 'trailblazer' anti-begging schemes (Home Office Press Release 278/2003).

In a manner typical of Third Way politics, the Blair government's approach to law and order mixes solutions drawn from a number of different political traditions. Such blending was a radical departure in most spheres of public policy, but here it has built upon the two-pronged strategy developed during Margaret Thatcher's premiership. This was at the same time neo-conservative – advocating the maintenance of a strong state able to uphold law and order and punish the deviant – and neo-liberal – preferring to managed the crime problem in a cost-effective manner via networks of active citizens and local partnerships (see Brake and Hale, 1991; Gamble, 1994; Garland, 1996). New Labour has intensified managerial efforts – where the focus of attention is the potential target or victim rather than the offender and crime causation – and directed tough crackdowns at disorderly and anti-social behaviour. At the same time, however, it has adopted a traditional social democratic approach – one that aims to reduce crime by fostering social inclusion – and attempted to reactivate community crime control through measures designed to stimulate community cohesion and civic renewal. It is these approaches distinct to New Labour that I now turn.

The New Labour government has realized that tackling the causes of offending should be an essential aspect of its crime and disorder reduction strategy. The 'fortressing' of the urban environment (for review, see MacLeod and Ward, 2002), the securing of personal property with locks, alarms and surveillance cameras, and the abandonment of certain urban streets and public spaces by fearful citizens may have contributed to a stabilization of crime rates during the last decade, but this status quo has been reached without any diminution in violent crime, petty crime, and disorder. Most crucially, state of the art security measures do nothing to block the pathway into a criminal career taken by the 10 year old from the deprived housing estate or to convince him that there is an alternative to crime. The Blair government believes that the reduction of the economic and social disadvantage and high levels of disaffection found in areas with the highest crime rates will impact positively on crime and disorder. As a consequence, a multitude of initiatives have been implemented by government departments and newly created policy units since 1997 to tackle both national and smaller scale manifestations of deprivation and exclusion. Even the New Deal for Young People, which sought to get 18 to 25 year olds into work, was described by Straw and Michael (1996, p.12) as being 'as much an anti-crime policy as it is an economic policy'. The social inclusion New Labour seeks to foster is not, however, just a means to an end. For a government that claims to believe in social justice and other social democratic values it is an end in itself (see Blair, 1997). But the extent to which social inclusion policy will actually have any real impact on either social injustice or crime remains to be seen. Jock Young (1999), for example, although supportive of attempts to increase genuine socio-economic inclusion, warns that if inclusion is only partial and unmeritocratic – for example, the 'dragooning' of the unemployed into poorly paid work with no prospects – then all that is achieved is the redrawing of the lines of social exclusion (p.186).

Nevertheless, New Labour's inclusive urge has filtered into the criminal justice system. Steps have been taken, especially since the introduction of the Youth Justice and Criminal Evidence Act 1999, to reduce the number of young offenders receiving custodial sentences. Community sentencing – a key facilitator of which has been the establishment of multi-agency Youth Offending Teams (YOTs) – and restorative justice, whereby offenders apologize and make reparation to their victims or communities for their misdemeanours, are being piloted as alternatives (see Crawford and Newburn, 2002). Key here is the forgiveness, rehabilitation and reintegration of offenders into society. Considerable resources are also being ploughed into schemes providing diversionary activities for potential young offenders. To this end the Youth Justice Board is co-financing Youth Inclusion Projects or Partnerships (YIPs) in approximately 70 of the most deprived neighbourhoods across England and Wales. YIPs provide educational and diversionary activities for those 13 to 16 year olds deemed most likely to offend by schools, the police, social services and YOTs. More recently the Children's Fund has financed a number of what have often become known as 'Junior YIPs' or 'Yiplets' for children aged 9 to 12. Earlier intervention is viewed as crucial because by the time many 13 year olds are inducted into a YIP they have well-established criminal careers and a long history of exclusion from school.

Stable, cohesive communities are viewed as key building blocks of its inclusive society by the Blair government and it has supported a range of initiatives that have directly and indirectly contributed to this objective. Crucially, crime, disorder and the conditions in which they can flourish are viewed as the products of disorganized communities, while a by-product of well-organized and responsible communities is perceived to be their ability to set and police boundaries to acceptable behaviour (on this perspective see Crawford, 1995). Thus, New Labour's rhetoric envisions strong communities of active and responsible citizens willing and able to stand up against 'the minority that cause misery and distress' (Home Office, 2003, p.12). Its approach to community renewal is informed by the vision of society developed by Communitarian thinkers and shared by the Christian democratic wing of the Labour Party, whose members are known to include Tony Blair and the Home Secretaries since 1997, Jack Straw and David Blunkett. Communitarians, most notable amongst them being Amitai Etzioni, argue that in recent decades individual entitlements have become disconnect from reciprocal social duties as a 'me first' society has emerged, actively encouraged during this period by the New Right's reification of individualism (Etzioni 1995 and 1998; see also Hoggett, 1997; Levitas, 1998; Young 1999; Crawford 2001). They call for this situation to be reversed through the reactivation of the institutions of civil society – communities, families and schools – through public acceptance of civic duties.

New Labour has wholeheartedly adopted the Communitarian notion of a 'something for something society' (Blair, 1997). In 1996, Straw and Michael wrote:

> As citizens we all have responsibilities as well as rights, duties as well as freedoms. Indeed real freedoms and liberties can only be effectively exercised if we have a society in which government and people accept their civic duties and obligations (1996, p.6).

This sentiment has been maintained throughout Blair's premiership:

> Active citizenship is built on [the] principles of mutuality. It is about engagement with the community that you are a part of, for the benefit of yourself, your family and those around you (Blunkett, 2002).

> Our aim is a society where we have an understanding that the rights we all enjoy are based in turn on the respect and responsibilities we have to other people and to our communities (Home Office, 2003, p.6).

The rhetoric employed appears to vary depending on the relative importance placed on public engagement in different policy spheres. So whereas residents of deprived neighbourhoods are encouraged to get involved in local regeneration initiatives, they are *told* that it is their duty to take a stance against disorderly conduct. Crucially, New Labour seems to accept that, in a society characterized by individualism, the 'disciplining' of certain groups may be necessary before everybody accepts their civic responsibilities. According to Eugene McLaughlin (2002, p.55):

> Community is utilised by New Labour not just in a traditional sociological sense to bemoan fragmentation and breakdown, but also in a governmental manner to signal its determination to use the disciplinary powers of the state to tackle not just 'crime' but to restore order and pro-social behaviour. This civilising mission is a defining difference between New Labour and previous New Right administrations.

He maintains that this coercive resocialization is most evident in 'work deprived, welfare dependent, "hard of hearing", multi-problem estates which were deemed to be "outside" conventional society' (p.58). It involves what could best be described as 'enforced inclusion' whereby the State provides opportunities that the socially and, in particular, economically marginalized have no real choice but to accept. The government's message to the 'hard of hearing' – those who, for example, show no interest in working for a living, turning away from crime or becoming better parents – seems to be: accept this chance or we will take steps to mitigate your drain on, and risk to, society.

Where gentle persuasion fails, the Blair government has shown that it is quite prepared to be as tough as any Conservative administration[8]. Its crackdown on anti-social behaviour has been particularly notable in this regard. Measures introduced have especially, although not exclusively, targeted the behaviour of young people. This has been done directly through, for example, the creation of the Anti-Social Behaviour Order (ASBOs)[9] and Child Curfew, and indirectly by forcing parents to take greater responsibility for the actions of their children through Parenting Orders and the proposed imposition of fixed penalty fines on minors that parents are then required to pay (see Home Office, 2003). Although the eviction of 'neighbours from hell' from social housing has also been promoted by the government as a way of averting decline, and the Anti-Social Behaviour Act 2003 permits the tougher regulation of public spaces activities such as begging and congregation, some Labour politicians advocate much more draconian solutions that include tougher, custodial sentences for 'yobs' and the removal of social security benefits from parents who refuse to fulfil their duties (see Field, 2003). There are echoes here of the vision of Charles Murray (1990 and 1994), the right wing commentator famous for his controversial essays on the emerging underclass in the USA and UK. But this authoritarian impulse amongst Labour politicians should not automatically be read as evidence of a rightward drift in British politics.

8 The Conservative government used a tough stance on law and order as a means of generating political legitimacy (Hall, 1980; Norrie and Adelman, 1989; Gamble, 1994; Garland, 1996). While New Labour is much less politically reliant on populist law and order policy than was the Major administration, punitive and well-publicized initiatives are a way of demonstrating to the public that something is being done about crime and disorder.

9 ASBOs are awarded by the civil courts and require their recipients to desist from certain behaviour or refrain from entering designated geographic areas (for example, a neighbourhood). Failure to comply can result in a custodial sentence.

It is important to remember that it is in the traditional 'working class' Labour-voting constituencies of urban Britain that disorder is most prevalent and therefore a key electoral issue that their MPs cannot ignore.

The delivery of much of New Labour's strategy for reducing crime and disorder is reliant on the agencies and institutions of the criminal justice system. Many other targeted initiatives have quite logically been devised and funded by the Home Office. But, as the next section shows, urban policy has still had an important role to play.

Crime and disorder reduction through urban policy[10]

Since 1997 urban policy programmes have aimed to deliver time-limited and often capital-intensive physical, social, economic or environmental regeneration projects and/or to reform the way agencies and government institutions work to deliver change to disadvantaged communities. Their principal scale of operation has been the neighbourhood (see Whitehead, this volume), although the introduction of Local Strategic Partnerships and (in spite of its name) the Neighbourhood Renewal Fund has encouraged local stakeholders to focus on certain policy themes – crime, education, health, housing and worklessness – at the borough or district level. The programmes and initiatives mounted by New Labour have addressed crime and disorder directly and, in tackling some of the other forms of deprivation that have a tendency to fuel neighbourhood decline and create conditions conducive to crime and disorder, also indirectly.

Crime, disorder and the fear of crime have been targeted for direct intervention by area-based programmes such as New Deal for Communities and Neighbourhood Management. Projects developed have focused on reducing opportunities for crime, by installing physical crime prevention measures and deploying new technologies such as closed circuit television (CCTV), and enhancing 'community safety' by curbing anti-social behaviour, reducing the fear of crime and generally trying to improve the quality of life for residents of deprived neighbourhoods. At the simplest level this has involved funding the recruitment of additional police officers to work with specific communities. Neighbourhood Wardens[11] have also been employed to patrol certain residential estates where they act as additional eyes and ears for the police, and act as a bridge between the police and local residents, many of who may be suspicious of authority figures. It is intended that the mere presence of Wardens will provide reassurance for older residents while, simultaneously, discouraging young people from engaging in certain forms of anti-social behaviour. They can also perform a coordinating role, organising, for example, with relevant agencies for signs of disorder such as burnt out cars and graffiti – the 'broken windows' that suggest

10 Many of the observations made here are based on research I have conducted in the last year as a result of my involvement in the evaluation of various New Labour urban policy initiatives.

11 This initiative is part funded by the Home Office.

nobody cares – to be removed and vandalism repaired. A number of regeneration programmes have also opted to co-finance Youth Inclusion Projects and other similar initiatives in an attempt to prevent young people thought to be at risk of drifting into crime from doing so. Many other initiatives funded by the main urban regeneration programmes of the ODPM and its forerunners and also by other government departments can impact positively on crime and disorder even though their primary aims and objectives lie elsewhere. These range from keeping young people out of trouble by getting them into work, organized leisure activities or back into education, to the stabilization of communities through housing market renewal.

In addition to funding projects that contribute in some way to the reduction in crime and disorder, urban policy is also being used to promote the more effective usage of the millions of pounds spent every week in deprived neighbourhoods by public service providers – sums that dwarf the public investment that can be realistically channelled through special regeneration programmes. This approach is not new (CDP, 1977; DoE 1977) but is popular with governments because, critics argue, calling on public service providers to change the way they operate is a low cost regeneration option that also enables the State to avoid blame should the desired change fail to materialize (Deakin and Edwards, 1993). But unlike earlier governments, which did little more than appeal for reform, New Labour has taken concerted action to institutionalize mainstream change. Firstly, Neighbourhood Management and Community Cohesion Pathfinders, funded by the ODPM and the Home Office respectively, are attempting to stimulate 'joined-up' governance and inter-agency collaboration at the neighbourhood level. As many local stakeholders, notably the police, primary care and housing trusts, and social services, receive much of their 'trade' from disadvantaged areas this does not seem unreasonable. Secondly, but again only in England, membership of Local Strategic Partnerships (LSPs) has been imposed on agencies responsible for delivering mainstream public services in an attempt to force them to collaborate with each other more closely at the district- or borough-wide level, to reshape services to meet the needs of the socially disadvantaged and to 'bend' their mainstream budgets accordingly. The 88 most deprived boroughs and districts have also been required to produce Neighbourhood Renewal Strategies outlining the ways in which they intend to reduce the gap between their electoral wards ranked in the 10% most deprived in England and the rest.

The job of coordinating and joining up the work of agencies is complicated in the case of crime and disorder, especially at the neighbourhood level, by the existence of the Crime and Disorder Act 1998. In placing a statutory duty on local authorities to take action to reduce crime and disorder the Act means that they can no longer dismiss this task as the responsibility of the police. Indeed, it may mean local authorities are open to opportunities to demonstrate their crime and disorder credentials. However, the Act already requires local authorities to join with the police and other agencies having an influence over crime – probation service, NHS, educators, etc – to form Community Safety Partnerships whose job it is to devise and implement a district- or borough-wide Community Safety Strategy. While Community Safety Partnerships may integrate quite neatly with LSPs as they operate at the same geographic scale, the problem faced by more localized resource management initiatives is that the crime and disorder reduction priorities they identify may be incompatible with those developed for the wider area. As a consequence it may be impossible for agencies to support them. But even when there is no clash of priorities, the proliferation of local management initiatives means public service providers must cope with multiple demands for the bending of mainstream resources. The government seems to have forgotten that most agencies already target their resources at areas of greatest need. The police, for example, know where the highest crime within each division occurs and deploy officers accordingly.

- Urban policy is contributing to all areas of New Labour's crime and disorder reduction agenda: the management and administration of crime risk through local partnerships and crime prevention projects, the deterrence of petty crime and anti-social behaviour through increased surveillance and diversionary activities, the enhancement of quality of life through initiatives designed to increase real and perceived levels of safety, attempts to build community capacity and cohesion, and the tackling of the broad array of socio-economic problems that fuel crime. This holistic approach that crosses barriers between policy sectors is to be welcomed but progress so far has been slow and with the gap between the richest and poorest members of society apparently widening during Tony Blair's premiership (*The Guardian*, 2003b), the challenge remains considerable. As the next section shows moreover, certain approaches to crime reduction and order maintenance, although crucial to the delivery of the urban renaissance, may be fuelling greater exclusion.

Towards an exclusive renaissance?

Logic would suggest that by improving the quality of life for town and city dwellers and reassuring investors, successful crime and disorder reduction strategies contribute directly to the delivery of New Labour's urban renaissance. While this may be true as far as the principal beneficiaries are concerned, it is not always the case. Indeed, the crime and disorder reduction measures employed in an attempt to ensure the success of certain aspects of the urban renaissance vision appear to actively undermine progress elsewhere. In the ideal situation, less crime and disorder, more widespread social inclusion and greater community cohesion would occur concurrently. But instead it appears that some attempts to curb crime and disorder may actually exacerbate social exclusion and reinforce marginalization. In addition to these contradictions within New Labour's vision for urban Britain, this section explores the more intransigent challenge to the delivery of a socially inclusive renaissance posed by fundamental shifts in social attitudes.

Exclusion from new urban spaces

This chapter has concentrated so far on the social problems of urban Britain. It is important to remember, however, that the 'urban renaissance' that New Labour seeks is much broader. Indeed, the Urban White Paper (DETR, 2000) focuses primarily on the design-led revival of town and city centres. It is here that contradictions within the vision of renaissance begin to emerge for, as Hoskins and Tallon (this volume) point out, the repackaging of city centre neighbourhoods as chic lifestyle choices for young middle-class professionals has done little to advance social inclusion. Instead, those who do not fit the image of the urban idyll, who seem 'out of place' due to their behaviour, apparent status, dress or age, are being gradually purged from the streets of these new solipsistic enclaves (see Hannigan, 1998; Norris and Armstrong, 1999; MacLeod, 2002; MacLeod and Ward, 2002). The removal of visible signs of disorder from the streets is an essential element of any entrepreneurial urban regeneration strategy reliant on businesses and homebuyers relocating to new town and city centre developments, as 'the city has to appear as an innovative, exciting, creative, and safe place to live or to visit, to play and consume in' (Harvey, 1989, p.9). Activities once tolerated such as begging, rough sleeping and public drinking are steadily being reclassified as criminal or anti-social behaviour against which the authorities can take action.

The assessment of risk, the enforcement of local bye-laws and the removal of those perceived to pose a danger to the well being of town and city centres has been greatly assisted in recent years by the proliferation of public space CCTV. Video surveillance may help in the identification of the unusual, for example someone running down a busy shopping street in the middle of the afternoon, but John Fiske (1998) argues that in order to be preventive rather than reactive, risk can only be identified by *what it looks like rather than what it does*. Research in the UK (Norris and Armstrong, 1999) found that targets for surveillance were selected based on who CCTV operatives, sometimes influenced by the police, believed were out of time and place and posed the greatest threat to law and order. Their views were invariably shaped by popular stereotypes, leading to young black men being watched far more than any other group. Fiske (1998, p.71) observes:

> Street behaviours of white men (standing still and talking, using a cellular phone, passing an unseen object from one to another) may be coded as normal and thus granted no attention, whereas the same activity performed by Black men will be coded as lying on the boundary of the normal, and thus subject to disciplinary action.

Here Fiske is writing about the North American city but it is evident that 'categorical suspicion' (Lyon, 2001, para. 1.21) also shapes the use of CCTV in the UK. Norris and Armstrong (1999) found that the street behaviour of teenage girls attracts considerably less attention than that of teenage boys, while the closest surveillance is reserved for Black youths and those who are 'known' to the authorities.

The purging from gentrified and redeveloped parts of towns and cities of those deemed to pose a threat to renaissance compounds and underlines the social exclusion of these people while often exacerbating the problems faced by their already deprived communities. MacLeod (2002) found in Glasgow that the police would remove homeless people and 'winos' from the city centre but were prepared to tolerate their presence in a deprived inner suburb nearby. Likewise, research by Short and Ditton (1998) revealed that the introduction of CCTV to Airdrie town centre had displaced fighting from the streets under surveillance to the 'schemes'[12] where many of those involved lived. The removal of these signs of disorder from high status locations may be good for business and reassuring for consumers and residents alike, but the further ghettoization of urban social problems reinforces the outcast status of the underclass. Urban regeneration programmes have heralded the extension of CCTV into deprived residential areas as a sign of the government's commitment to improving community safety in these neighbourhoods. But it remains to be seen whether the reduction of local crime and disorder or the containment of the risk certain residents of these neighbourhoods pose to renaissance elsewhere is the primary purpose of this expanded surveillance web. The further displacement of disorder from the sink estates under surveillance to more affluent suburbs nearby is clearly politically unacceptable and, consequently, in the context of disadvantaged neighbourhoods, CCTV may well be used to assist in the disciplining of their resident population.

Community mis-conceptualization

New Labour seeks the revitalization and remoralization of civil society through the renewal of its key institutions: the family and the community. It is apparent, however, that it is only deprived communities lacking in organization and discipline that are being targeted for intervention. The government has not felt it necessary to plough millions of pounds to stimulate social cohesion into the newer commuter housing estates found across Britain where residents may not even know their immediate neighbours and there are no shops let alone community and leisure facilities. Significantly, such places are rarely hotbeds of crime and disorder, responsible parents making community social control unnecessary. A recent government White Paper stated that, 'Healthy communities are built on strong families' (Home Office, 2003, p.21). But while this may be the case, there seems to be little evidence that strong families necessarily want to come together to form traditional neighbourhood-based communities, or have any need to do so. Indeed, to update one of Margaret Thatcher's famous phrases, there appears in such places to be no such thing as community, only individuals and their families. It is perhaps ironic that healthy communities capable of disciplining their members are most needed in areas where families are weak and unable or unwilling to fulfil their civic duty.

The rhetoric of New Labour not only over-emphasizes the importance of strong communities to the maintenance of social control, it also contains the assumption that social order automatically stems from community strength, ignoring the evidence that organized communities can 'produce and foster high levels of crime' (Crawford, 2001, p.73). Moreover, the nostalgic, conservative and utopian vision of community that New Labour shares with Communitarians fails to acknowledge that communities can become 'pockets of intolerance and prejudice' (ibid.; see also Hoggett, 1997). Indeed, Adam Crawford (2001, p.74) argues that

12 'Scheme' is a colloquial Scottish term used to describe a council housing estate.

strong communities are 'intrinsically exclusive' in that they are inward-looking entities that define themselves in opposition to other groups or geographic areas perceived to be somehow different. Investigations into the causes of the violent disorder that erupted in Bradford, Burnley and Oldham in 2001 found that an underlying cause was not the weakness of local communities but the existence in each place of strong but geographically and racially distinct communities that each viewed the other as the cause of its problems (Denham Committee, 2002, pp.11-12; see also Burnley Taskforce, 2001; Cantle, 2001). The problem here, as in many other places, is that the norms of behaviour condoned by powerful community leaders are far from those envisaged by the State.

Even where communities are active in crime and disorder reduction, their methods may not be quite what the government intends. Perceiving the police to be ineffective, it is not unknown for strong communities to resort to intimidation and vigilantism. This is particularly evident when poor education and a lack of understanding cause intolerance of certain individuals or groups. The hounding of paedophiles from their homes on the Paulsgrove Estate, Portsmouth in 2001 is one such example. In other places where communities reacted strongly against the presence of paedophiles, their vigilantism was so indiscriminate that men who bore slight physical resemblance to the convicted offenders pictured in the tabloid Sunday newspaper *News of the World* were attacked, along with others who 'looked' like paedophiles, and a female paediatrician who those with a poor grasp of English assumed was the same as other 'paedos'.

The punitive society

While the contradictions in New Labour's urban renaissance vision present a clear threat to the delivery of the fairer, more socially inclusive society that Party rhetoric promotes, a much more fundamental challenge is posed by the shift in social values that has occurred in Britain during recent decades. According to the criminologist David Garland (2000), the punitive and exclusionary political responses to crime and disorder common in contemporary Britain are not simply occurring at the whim of government but reflect growing intolerance of deviance and difference amongst the influential professional classes – the liberal elite. Indeed, Garland argues that government policy could not have become so authoritarian without the acquiescence of the educated middle classes. Until the 1970s this group experienced very little crime and disorder and as a consequence was not fearful of it. This physical and social distance from the crime problem along with the assured position in life that a good education and secure job afforded, allowed the liberal middle class elite to adopt a 'civilized' attitude to towards crime. They blamed it on social circumstances, believed that criminals deserved helped not harsh treatment, and had faith in the policy decisions made by criminal justice experts (ibid., pp.355-7) much as they did with doctors, planners and other experts.

This golden age was short-lived and 'within a generation crime became a prominent fact of life not only for the urban middle classes, but for many middle-class suburbanites as well' (ibid., p.359). Meanwhile, failure to control the spread of incivilities and minor disorder into the public spaces used by the middle classes fuelled fear and confirmed to many that experts no longer had the answers to law and order problems. To compound matters, as media, and especially TV coverage of crime, both as news and drama, increased during the closing decades of the 20th century so it tended to 'distort public perception of the [crime] problem', in particular its severity (ibid., p363). Yet Garland maintains that the more widespread experience of crime and disorder across the social classes is not enough on its own to explain the willingness of the liberal elite to support the exclusionary risk-aversion and criminal justice strategies favoured by recent British governments. Instead he identifies the primary catalyst as 'the deep sense of vulnerability, of insecurity, of precariousness' (ibid., p.361) felt by the middle classes as a consequence of the profound socio-cultural and economic changes that swept Britain in the latter decades of the 20th century. Jock Young (1999) apportions most blame to the restructuring of the labour market (see Hutton, 1995), arguing:

> Like pincers on our society, crime and punishment stem from the same source...The obsessive violence of the macho street gang and the punitive obsession of the respectable citizen are similar not only in their nature but in their origin. Both stem from dislocations in the labour market: the one from a market which excludes participation as a worker but encourages voraciousness as a consumer, the other from a market that includes but only in a precarious fashion. That is, from tantalizing exclusion and precarious inclusion (Young, 1999, pp. 8-9).

The precarious nature of middle class inclusion has been further fuelled by the erosion of traditional family and community structures, the breaking up of the welfare state, increasing crime and disorder, and the liberalization of social values. Such change has produced new risks that citizens must try somehow to manage. Garland (2000) argues that in an increasingly complex and insecure world, the fear, aggravation and expense – both of prevention and making good any loses to it – that crime and disorder have foisted upon the professional classes are an unwelcome additional burden. Their apparent powerlessness over risk generates, 'the feeling that "something must be done" and "someone must be blamed" [that] increasingly finds political representation and fuels political action' (2000, p.368).

We can conclude from this that in a high crime society such as our own, where the fear of difference and deviance has been ratcheted to new heights by media scaremongering about asylum seekers and the post-9/11 terrorist threat, public support, demand even, for uncompromising responses to crime and behaviour that is now viewed as anti-social is unlikely to diminish. Indeed, Garland (ibid.) suggests that:

> Our attitudes to crime – our fears and resentments, but also our common sense narratives and understandings – become settled cultural facts that are sustained and reproduced by cultural scripts and not by criminological research or official data.

So while New Labour may maintain that social inclusion is r
but also a route to safer, more 'liveable' towns and cities,
whether the public is committed to this agenda.

Conclusion

The twin problems of crime and disorder have risen rapidly up
in recent decades as they have become increasingly more severe, especially in urban areas. New Labour is committed to tackling both of them, not only because they impact severely on the quality of life of those who are their victims but also because they act as fuel for urban decline and pose a threat to the urban renaissance that it seeks to deliver. In addition to continuing the crime prevention tradition established in the 1980s, the Blair government is attempting to tackle the causes of crime by reducing social exclusion and to enhance social control through the rebuilding of place-based communities. As crime and disorder are perceived to have a wide range of catalysts, action taken in a number of policy spheres is thought likely to impact upon them. Thus, urban policy is playing a significant role in both the direct reduction of offending and the co-ordination of the work of other agencies whose work is relevant here. Crucially though, this chapter identifies contradictions between the different approaches that have been deployed to reduce crime and disorder and likewise within the Blair government's vision of urban renaissance. While New Labour rhetoric emphasizes social inclusion, I argue that the social control processes associated with physical urban regeneration and community renewal in fact compounds exclusion and reinforces marginalization. Moreover, as a consequence of a cultural shift in attitudes towards crime that has occurred in recent decades as Britain has undergone a transformation into a 'the high crime society' (Garland, 2000), it seems unlikely that this exclusive impulse will be quick to wane.

References

Blair, T. (1997), *Welfare Reform: Giving People the Will to Win*, speech delivered at the Aylesbury Estate, Southwark, 2nd June.

Blair, T. (2001), 'Third Way, phase two', *Prospect Magazine*, March.

Blunkett, D. (2002), *How government can help build social capital*, presentation to the Performance and Innovation Unit Seminar on Social Capital, 26th March, accessed online at www.homeoffice.gov.uk/piuspeech.html

Brake, M. and Hale, C. (1991), *Public Order and Private Lives: the Politics of Law and Order*, Routledge, London.

Burnley Task Force (2002), *Burnley Speaks, Who Listens...? A summary of the Burnley Task Force Report on the disturbances in Burnley in June 2001*, Burnley Task Force, Burnley.

Cantle, E. (2001), *Community Cohesion: A report by the Independent Review Team, chaired by Ted Cantle*, Home Office, London.

Cohen, S. (1972), *Folk Devils and Moral Panics*, Granada, London.

…nity Development Projects (1977), *Gilding the Ghetto: The state and the poverty …xperiments,* CDP Inter-project Editorial Team, London.

…wford, A. (1995), 'Appeals to community and crime prevention', *Crime, Law and Social Change*, vol. 22(2), pp. 97-126.

Crawford, A. and Newburn, T. (2002), 'Recent developments in restorative justice for young people in England and Wales: community participation and representation', *British Journal of Criminology*, vol. 42, pp. 476-95.

Deakin, N. and Edwards, J. (1993), *The Enterprise Culture and the Inner City*, Routledge, London.

Denham Committee (2002), *Building Cohesive Communities: A Report of the Ministerial Group on Public Order and Community Cohesion*, Home Office, London.

DETR (2000), *Our Towns and Cities: The Future – Delivering an Urban Renaissance*, HMSO, London.

DoE (1977), *Policy for the Inner Cities*, HMSO, London.

Etzioni, A. (1995) *Rights and the Common Good: the Communitarian Perspective*, St Martin's Press, New York.

Etzioni, A. (1998) *The New Golden Rule: Community and Morality in a Democratic Society*, Basic Books, New York.

Field, F. (2003), *Neighbours from Hell*, Politicos, London.

Fiske, J. (1998), 'Surveilling the city: whiteness, the Black man and democratic totalitarianism', *Theory, Culture & Society*, vol. 15(2), pp. 67-88.

Gamble, A. (1994), *The Free Economy and the Strong State: the Politics of Thatcherism*, Macmillan, Basingstoke.

Garland, D. (1996), 'The limits of the sovereign state: strategies of crime control in contemporary society', *British Journal of Criminology*, vol. 36(4), pp. 445-71.

Garland, D. (2000), 'The cultures of high crime societies: some preconditions of recent "law and order" policies', *British Journal of Criminology*, vol. 40, pp. 347-75.

Hall, S. (1980), *Drifting into a Law and Order Society*, Cobden Trust, London.

Hall, S., Critcher, C., Jefferson, T., Clarke, J. and Roberts, B. (1978), *Policing the Crisis*, Macmillan, Basingstoke.

Hannigan, J. (1998), *Fantasy City: Pleasure and Profit in the Post-Modern Metropolis*, Routledge, London.

Harvey, D. (1989), 'From managerialism to entrepreneurialism: The transformation in urban governance in late capitalism', *Geografiska Annaler*, vol. 71B(1), pp. 3-17.

Hoggett, P. (1997), 'Contested communities', in P. Hoggett (ed), *Contested Communities*, The Policy Press, Bristol.

Home Office (2003), *Respect and Responsibility – Taking a Stand Against Anti-Social Behaviour*, HMSO, London.

Home Office Press Release 278/2003, *Home Secretary: "Communities must not take no for an answer on anti-social behaviour"*, 14th October 2003.

Hughes, G., McLaughlin, E. and Muncie, J. (eds) (2002), *Crime Prevention and Community Safety: New Directions*, Sage, London in association with The Open University.

Hutton, W. (1995), *The State We're In*, Jonathan Cape, London.

Koskela, H. and Pain, R. (2000), 'Revisiting fear and place: women's fear of attack and the built environment', *Geoforum*, vol. 31(2), pp. 269-80.

Levitas, R. (1998), *The Inclusive Society*, Macmillan, Basingstoke.

Lyon, D. (2001), 'Surveillance after September 11', *Sociological Research Online*, vol. 6(3), available at: www.socresonline.org.uk/6/3/lyon.html

MacLeod, G. (2002), 'From urban entrepreneurialism to a "revanchist city"? On the spatial injustices of Glasgow's renaissance', *Antipode*, vol. 34(3), pp. 602-24.

MacLeod, G. and Ward, K. (2002), 'Spaces of utopia and dystopia: landscaping the contemporary city', *Geografiska Annaler*, vol. 84, pp. 153-70.
McLaughlin, E. (2002), '"Same bed, different dreams": postmodern reflections on crime prevention and community safety', in G. Hughes and A. Edwards (eds), *Crime Control and Community*, Willan, Cullompton.
Murray, C. (1990), *The Emerging British Underclass*, IEA Health and Welfare Unit, London.
Murray, C. (1994), *Underclass: The Crisis Deepens*, IEA Health and Welfare Unit, London.
Norrie, A. and Adelman, S. (1989), '"Consensual authoritarianism" and criminal justice in Thatcher's Britain', in A. Gamble and C. Wells (eds), *Thatcher's Law*, University of Wales Press, Cardiff.
Norris, C. and Armstrong, G. (1999), *The Maximum Surveillance Society*, Berg, Oxford.
Pain, R. (2000), 'Place, social relations and the fear of crime', *Progress in Human Geography*, vol. 24(3), pp. 365-88.
Pain, R. (2002), 'Gender, race, age and fear in the city', *Urban Studies*, vol. 38(5-6), pp. 899-913.
PAT 8 (2000), *Report of Policy Action Team 8: Anti-Social Behaviour*, Cabinet Office, London.
Povey, D., Nicholas, S. and Salisbury, H. (2003), *Crime in England and Wales: Quarterly Update to December 2002*, Home Office, London.
Scottish Executive (2003), *Recorded Crime in Scotland, 2002*, Scottish Executive, Edinburgh.
SEU (1998), *Bringing Britain Together: A National Strategy for Neighbourhood Renewal*, Cabinet Office, London.
SEU (2001), *A New Commitment to Neighbourhood Renewal: National Strategy Action Plan*, Cabinet Office, London.
Short, E. and Ditton, J. (1998), 'Seen and now heard: talking to the targets of open-street CCTV', *British Journal of Criminology*, vol. 38(3), pp. 404-28.
Straw, J. and Michael, A. (1996), *Tackling the Causes of Crime: Labour's Proposals to Prevent Crime an Criminality*, Labour Party, London.
The Guardian (1996), 'Strange case of the vanishing Opposition party', 2nd June.
The Guardian (2003a), 'The war on crime: at the frontline', 10th July.
The Guardian (2003b), 'Tax is out of the bag', 25th June.
Wilson, J. and Kelling, G. (1982), 'Broken Windows', *The Atlantic Monthly*, March, pp. 29-38.
Wilson, W. (1987), *The Truly Disadvantaged*, University of Chicago Press, Chicago.
Young, J. (1999), *The Exclusive Society*, Sage, London.

Chapter 6

Urban Policy Integration in London: The Impact of the Elected Mayor

Andy Thornley and Karen West[1]

Introduction

The establishment of the Greater London Authority (GLA) in May 2000 has significance beyond London. First it is an element of New Labour's broader programme of modernization (Hill, 2000) and, second, the provisions in the GLA Act, particularly those relating to the development and co-ordination of strategic policy for London, reflect New Labour's more general aspirations for an urban renaissance. The problems of integrating economic, social and environmental goals – key goals of the Urban White Paper (Department of Environment, Transport and the Regions (DETR), 2000) – is one with which all cities must grapple. Thus, there are broader lessons here for the Blair government's Local Strategic Partnerships, which, like the GLA, are tasked with integrating a number of strategic policy areas over which they have limited day-to-day control. In fact, the GLA could be viewed as a test-bed for the kind of joined-up governance the Urban White Paper seeks to promote.

The creation of a new strategic body for London responded to the yawning fourteen-year gap in policy that was left by Thatcher's disbanding of the Greater London Council (GLC) (Newman and Thornley, 1997; Travers and Jones, 1997; Dowding et al, 1999), but the GLA is not the GLC reinvented. While the Act places many duties on the Mayor and the GLA, the powers and resources to implement these duties are significantly constrained. The Mayor is statutorily required to produce, and keep under review, strategies in eight spheres of urban policy – spatial development, economic development, transport, waste management, air quality, biodiversity, noise and culture. Yet, in most cases (the notable exceptions being transport and spatial development), the Mayor has little or no authority to ensure action by those who will actually implement the strategies –

1 This chapter is based upon the research project 'Institutional Change, Networks and Agendas – Planning under the GLA' carried out at the LSE and funded by the ESRC (Grant No. R000223095). Yvonne Rydin and Kath Scanlon were our co-researchers on this project and we are deeply indebted to them for their contribution to the research and ideas that are contained in this chapter. The research involved interviewing key actors in the GLA and outside, attending both public and internal meetings, and analyzing documentation.

the boroughs, the private sector, the voluntary sector, and central government bodies. Instead his role is largely confined to one of brokering partnerships and agreements. In this environment of networking and collaboration the issue of how to ensure consistency and co-ordination between different aspects of urban policy becomes particularly pertinent. Rhodes has described how New Labour is adopting a new approach to governance in which policy integration or joined-up thinking plays a key role:

> New Labour rejects the command bureaucracy model of Old Labour with its emphasis on hierarchy, authority and rules...Distinctively, it advocates 'joined-up government', or delivering public services by steering networks of organizations where the currency is not authority (bureaucracy) or price competition (markets) but trust. In the parlance of the chattering classes, it is the 'third way' in action...the arrival of joined up government signals a further switch from management to diplomacy (Rhodes, 2000, p.163).

However this aim of integration is not an easy one. As Johnstone and Whitehead demonstrate in the introductory chapter of this book, national urban policy is notoriously devoid of integration and subject to independent thinking by different government departments. As they observe, since 1997 there has been an apparent lack of co-ordination between the various Units even within the same department. We explore this issue at the level of London government and identify some of the barriers that have to be overcome if its stated aim of strategic policy co-ordination is to be achieved in the capital.

In this chapter, therefore, we are not exploring the way that the Mayor and the GLA interacts with all the other agencies in London involved in policy development and implementation. Rather our focus is on the GLA's first ten months, and on the intensive policy development stage. During this period it was policy development and integration *within* the various institutional entities that were brought together to make up the GLA itself which were the preoccupation, and therefore the subject of our research. What role does the Mayor play in this internal exercise? To what extent does this role display the characteristics of trust and diplomacy that Rhodes suggest are essential to joined-up thinking? We examine the extent to which some of New Labour's new aspirations for urban development – humanised and environmentally sustainable urban growth, integrated and consistent policy, and public consultation – can be delivered by this new kind of institution. Our specific focus is on the formation and integration of policy in the first ten months of the life of the GLA as this was a crucial period during which the priorities of its strategic agenda were determined.

The nature of the GLA and policy formation in the GLA Act

The GLA is a new kind of strategic authority for London whose purpose is to, 'generate strategic action on pan-London issues and solve problems of co-ordination across the capital' (Rydin et al, 2002 and forthcoming). The Act awarded the Authority general powers to promote the economic, social and environmental development of London. However, while the purpose of the new Authority was to lend coherence to the fragmented and ad hoc development that had characterized London in the interregnum between the disbanding of the GLC and the establishment of the GLA, it was not intended to usurp the role of the boroughs, nor many of the other bodies which had played a policy role during that period.

The new Authority is composed of a number of different bodies that make up the GLA 'family'. The 'core' of the Authority, that has the responsibility for developing key strategies for London's development, comprises the Mayor and his Office plus a bureaucracy that includes the Strategy Directorate. This Directorate absorbed many of the previous bodies that were involved in some kind of strategic thinking – the London Planning Advisory Committee (LPAC), the London Ecology Unit (LEU) and the London Research Centre (LRC). While absorbing these bodies was intended to lend consistency and continuity to the development of policy within the new GLA, as we will discuss later, working relations in the early days of the GLA were problematic. Outside this 'core' is the operational arm of the GLA, referred to as the four 'functional bodies' – the London Development Agency (LDA), Transport for London (TfL), the London Fire and Emergency Planning Authority and the Metropolitan Police Authority. This division between strategy formulation and operational activity was however blurred and the LDA and TfL were to become involved in strategy development. A further element of the Authority is the Assembly, which is made up of 25 elected members. Its purpose is to scrutinize or check the policies of the Mayor, but its powers are very limited.

During the first ten months of the GLA, strategy development and co-ordination absorbed much of the core GLA's time and resources. The process of policy formation and integration is presented in the GLA Act (GLA Act, 1999, Part II, sections 30, 33 and 41) as a highly rational process (depicted in Figure 6.1) that involves: the laying down of broad policy objectives – economic development, social development and an improvement in London's environment; the development of key urban policy strategies for delivering these broad objectives; and checking these strategies for consistency with three cross-cutting objectives of health, sustainable development, and equality of opportunity.

However, different power centres within the core GLA held different ideas about how the GLA's strategic policy mission should be interpreted. Much time and energy was, therefore, expended on pursuing different approaches to policy formation and integration. Different interpretations soon emerged around the key power centres within the core GLA with responsibility for policy formation – the Mayor and his Office, the bureaucracy and, to a much lesser extent, the Assembly – each of which had different perceptions of what this new institution of governance could and should achieve for London. We briefly outline these power centres as they provide an important context for our discussion of policy integration.

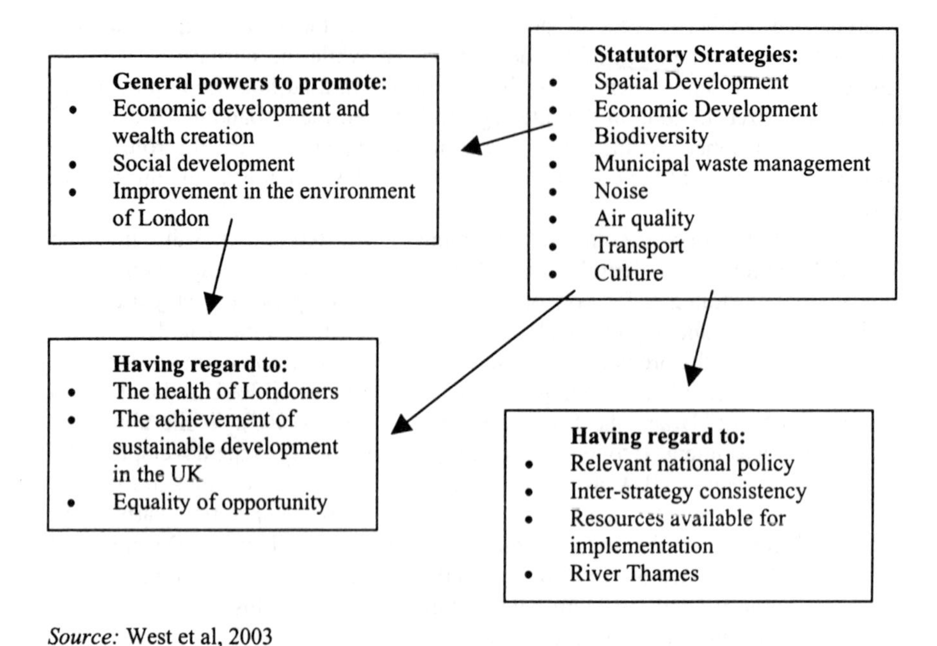

Source: West et al, 2003

Figure 6.1 Policy formation as envisaged in the GLA Act

The power centres of the core GLA

We have analysed the power centres of the core GLA from an institutionalist perspective elsewhere (see Rydin et al, 2002 and forthcoming), using the lenses of cultural theory to understand their respective policy stances. We also discuss the role of the Assembly. For the purposes of this chapter, however, we focus on the two more important centres, the Mayor's Office and the bureaucracy, and explore their differences in relation to the key parameters of decision-making – who are the key actors, what are the drivers of the policy, what are the timescales, focus, and main concerns and what are the perceived constraints? These are set out in Table 6.1.

The Mayor and his Office

The Act gave the Mayor far-reaching executive power, but its architects did not foresee that the first Mayor (one without the support of a party machine) would create a large personal office. Section 67 of the Act provided for a personal office made up of two senior political advisors, who would be personally chosen by the Mayor and did not have to go through a formal selection procedure, and ten other members of staff. However, Ken Livingstone struck a deal with the Assembly to greatly expand this. (In exchange, the Assembly was given the right to hire

Table 6.1 The Mayor's Office and the Bureaucracy

	Mayor	Bureaucracy
Key Actors	Mayor and his Office	Policy officers
Drivers	Personal agenda/manifesto	Statutory and national policy framework and previous policy consensus
Timescale	Short-term/electoral	Medium to long-term
Focus	Project or issue based	Strategy framework
Concerns	Implementation barriers	Co-ordination
Constraints	Access to resources	Conflicting interests/priorities Statutory requirements

Source: Adapted from Rydin et al, 2002

dedicated political staff, for which the Act did not provide.) The Mayor's Office at the time of our research had about 30 staff.

What then were the policy drivers of the Mayor's Office? Their touchstone was the Mayor's election manifesto and his political priorities, and their paramount objective getting him re-elected. During our research period the Mayor leaned heavily towards transport: congestion charging and short- to medium-term public transport improvement, and an attempt to change the view of central government on the management and financing of the London Underground system. This political focus on transport meant that as far as the Mayor was concerned the Transport Strategy was central. He saw transport improvement as the public's top priority and hence essential for re-election. It would clearly be simplistic to suggest that the Mayor was only interested in the short term: he also saw the improvement of London's ailing public transport system as a key step to improving London's environmental impact in the longer term. His strategy, in the immediate term was, however, to focus on achieving a narrow set of objectives. Several officials interviewed during the course of our research observed that the Mayor effectively had two agendas: one covering short-term operational goals, which we call his central agenda, and a peripheral 'Big Tent' agenda, covering much wider ground, through which he attempted to maintain a broad coalition of support. To maintain this support this agenda included goals such as improving the environment, securing affordable housing and delivering an urban renaissance. Underlying both the central and the Big Tent agendas was Livingstone's long-term goal of drawing down more resources and strategic power from central government. London's status as a 'world city' also emerged as an important theme during the course of our research, and came to dominate both the central and Big Tent agendas.

Work that contributed towards the realization of the central agenda was tightly managed by Livingstone's senior personal staff, while the Big Tent agenda was delegated to others in the organization. For example, Darren Johnson, leader of the Green Group in the Assembly and the Mayor's cabinet advisor on the environment, handled liaison with environmental groups. These advisors and the Strategy Directorate were essentially left to manage secondary policy areas, while the Mayor's personal staff were deployed on congestion charging, the operation of TfL, and winning the argument with central government over the financing of London Underground[2].

The Strategy Directorate

In the early days at least, the Mayor seemed happy to allow the Strategy Directorate to do what its name implied: develop strategy. Most of the Directorate's staff at that time came from pre-existing London organizations absorbed into the GLA, each of which had its own history, legitimacy, problem definitions and visions. These did not necessarily coincide with those of the Mayor. As we have already noted, staff from three organizations joined the Strategy Directorate[3]: the London Planning Advisory Committee (LPAC), the London Ecology Unit (LEU) and the London Research Centre (LRC). Staff from LPAC and the LEU made pivotal contributions to the spatial development, transport and environmental strategies. The policy approach of the Directorate was shaped, therefore, by bureaucrats with experience of London government who were oriented towards the legal and statutory framework. Their touchstone was the Act and subsequent regulations. They were always concerned about the legal status of their policies and whether they could be successfully challenged. They were also informed by the policy work with which they had been involved during the period leading up to the formation of the GLA. Crucially, they appeared to operate within a timescale with a ten or twenty year horizon.

LPAC, a committee made up of one elected member from each London borough, was established after the abolition of the GLC to draft strategic planning advice for London. It had its own very clear and longstanding views about strategy integration. It was widely regarded as a successful cross-party committee, which tried to fill the strategic planning vacuum left by the disbandment of the GLC. Most decisions were taken by consensus. LPAC lobbied central government on London's strategic planning issues and offered planning advice to the boroughs,

---

2 The government was committed to the introduction of a Public-Private Partnership (PPP) for London Underground, under which private companies would become responsible for maintenance and management of some parts of the system's infrastructure, while Ken Livingstone insisted that all parts of the system should remain under unified (public) management.

3 Not all members of the strategy team came from these three bodies: there were also some secondees and former civil servants from the Government Office for London and the Department of Environment, Transport and the Regions (DETR), as well as former employees of other local authorities.

and was itself a strong advocate of a new strategic London authority. It had already written a strategic-planning blueprint (*Endowment to the Mayor*) to hand to the Mayor when he took office. The *Endowment* was an attempt to integrate 'land use with transport, regeneration, economic and social policy and environmental matters' (LPAC, 2000), based on the European Spatial Development Perspective. So LPAC staff already had a 'joined-up' approach on arrival at the GLA, and hoped to implement it, and indeed pioneer it, in London. In addition to developing various strategies, the Strategy Directorate has direct responsibility for strategy integration. It was initially thought that three so-called 'cross-cutting' themes identified in the Act (sustainability, health and equalities) would provide a way to integrate the strategies. But Directorate staff were accustomed to working in an environment of political consensus, not one in which a new Mayor wanted to stamp his mark on London. So the Directorate's focus on comprehensive strategy meant that officers often found themselves tasked with Big Tent agenda items, and sometimes found that certain aspects of their work, such as the environmental policies, were treated as peripheral or ignored.

The different institutional cultures of the Mayor's Office and the Bureaucracy were to have a major influence on attempts to fulfil the co-ordination requirement of the new authority. If the GLA Act presented a rational process of policy formation and integration, this was far from obvious in practice. As a result of the differing cultures, conflicting views emerged between the power centres as to, first, the importance of the different strategies (both in relation to each other and in relation to the GLA's overall mission) and, second, the ways to integrate political priorities, the statutory needs of the GLA's work, and the policies of the different strategies. The rest of the chapter will explore these issues in more detail.

The relative importance of the strategies

While the GLA Act lays great emphasis on the development of eight mayoral strategies, rationally picked to reflect the areas of greatest strategic importance to London, it gave no guidance on the question of the prioritization of the strategies. In addition to the view that all strategies have equal importance, we have identified four different ways within the core GLA of viewing the importance of the strategies – according to their political significance, their amenability to direct implementation by the GLA itself, their statutory status and their integrative capacity.

The Mayor and his Office, unsurprisingly, ranked the strategies by their political significance. Unlike the bureaucracy, the Mayor's Office did not regard the strategies as important *per se* – they were important only insofar as they advanced the Mayor's agenda. As one observer within the GLA said, '[for the Mayor's Office] strategies are just one of the means of delivering the Mayor's manifesto. They are not the be-all-and-end-all'. The Transport Strategy was regarded as pre-eminent by the Mayor and his Office because transport was *the* political priority. The Mayor insisted that the draft Transport Strategy be published quickly and it was one of the earliest strategies to emerge, in January 2001. He had made a manifesto commitment to, 'consult widely about the best possible congestion charge scheme', which he was keen to implement during the middle of his term of office, and this required a broader contextual framework. The Mayor's Office initially saw the Transport Strategy as the foundation around which all strategies produced subsequently would be co-ordinated.

Related to political significance was the question of how much power the GLA had over each policy area – political debate and decision-making would centre most on the areas where the GLA could act. The Transport Strategy was important to the Mayor and his Office because of its political sensitivity – and it was particularly sensitive because it was an area where the Mayor could make real changes. The Mayor himself saw this clearly – he told the Assembly's Investigative Committee on the Environmental Strategies that his primary focus was on strategies over which he had financial and operational control (Minutes of Investigative Committee on Environment Strategies, 13 March 2001). In an interview in November 2000 we asked why there was such emphasis on transport; he replied:

> That's the only area where I've got real power; in everything else it's marginal. Where is there real power? Transport, SDS, influence over the police and fire and the LDA – the LDA in fact is minuscule – and then everything else...There will be quite an impact on waste eventually but nothing else is in that league. In the transport sphere, so long as Government continues to give me the money and cooperate with congestion charging, I've got the ability to turn it around.

While the GLA's ability to implement the strategies was of great interest to the Mayor's Office, it was a political factor to which the Act paid only scant attention. In Section 41 the Mayor was required to have regard to the resources available for the implementation of each strategy in preparing or revising them, but there was otherwise no recognition of the implications resulting from the fact that some of the strategies concerned policy areas over which the GLA had little influence.

Some of the strategies dealt with matters over which the GLA had operational control, but most covered areas where the GLA's involvement was confined to persuasion and partnership. The GLA had direct operational power over transport through Transport for London. Through the Spatial Development Strategy (the SDS – also known as *The London Plan*), the GLA could exercise significant control over borough unitary development plans, which must conform to the SDS. The SDS would also provide the framework for the Mayor's decisions about strategic planning applications (all planning applications for buildings over a certain size, or which breached UDP guidelines, were automatically referred by boroughs to the Mayor). With regard to economic development, one of the GLA functional bodies, the London Development Agency, had some limited direct operational power through its property holdings, and would also be responsible for distributing Single Regeneration Budget (SRB) funds in London. Most of the elements of the Economic Development Strategy, however, required action by the private sector or other public-sector bodies. The four statutory environmental strategies must be reinforced through the Transport, Spatial Development and

Economic Development Strategies, but ultimately require actions by other actors over which the GLA has no control (although the GLA did have certain highly circumscribed powers to direct London waste authorities).

Closely allied to the question of the 'implementability' of the strategies was the question of their statutory status. The GLA was required to produce eight strategies, but the only one that would have defined statutory force was the SDS, which would replace Regional Planning Guidance for London. All borough unitary development plans would be required to conform to the SDS once it had been through the formal requirement of the Examination in Public (EIP) and been adopted, a process not required of any of the other strategies. Officers working on the planning and development strategies together with the Deputy Mayor insisted that this demonstrated the legal superiority of the SDS, and argued that they needed more staff and time to ensure that the document fulfilled its complex statutory functions; the Mayor was, in the early days, deaf to this plea.

The SDS was clearly intended to have an integrating function. The Act (Section 334) required the SDS to express the spatial development aspects of all the mayoral strategies, while Government Office for London guidance on planning in London (GOL circular, June 2000) stated:

> The SDS offers the opportunity for an integrated approach to shaping the future pattern and direction of development in London. It should provide a common spatial framework for all the Mayor's strategies and policies, as well as for the land use policies in UDPs.

GLA planning officers emphasized the integrating function of the SDS, arguing that other mayoral strategies should be merely provisional pending its development.

The last possibility was to interpret the Act narrowly and regard all strategies as of equal importance. This appeared to be the view of those officers responsible for developing the environmental strategies. They argued against the prevailing view in the bureaucracy (outlined above) that the environmental strategies were less important than those dealing with planning.

While there were a number of views within the core GLA regarding the relative importance of the strategies, their political significance and implementability were the Mayor's main concerns during early strategy development. The Transport Strategy set the pace of strategy development in general, and in cases of conflict during the early period was regarded by the Mayor and his office as pre-eminent.

The need for a political vision statement to guide the GLA's work

The Greater London Authority Act was ambiguous about the relative importance of the strategies. It was also ambiguous about their overall aim – the set of objectives the strategies were meant to advance. The Act gave the GLA three principal and equal purposes: to secure economic and social development, and to improve the environment. The Act also stated that when working towards one of these goals, the GLA had also to consider the impact of its actions on the other two. Over time the GLA was meant, 'to secure a reasonable balance' between them (GLA Act, 1999, Sections 30-34; and see Figure 6.1).

This requirement to secure a reasonable balance over time reflected recognition that there were tensions among these three purposes. Where and how that balance would be struck was clearly a political choice. One way to try to achieve this 'balance' would have been through an explicit statement of the Mayor's objectives in these areas – a 'vision' document – to guide the strategies. In an attempt to bring some cohesion to the early strategy integration process, officers within the Strategy Directorate repeatedly asked the Mayor to issue a 'high-level vision'. Given Ken Livingstone's history as a strong advocate of social justice and his more recent overtures to the environment lobby, much was expected of him in terms of delivering a new kind of development strategy for London. While officers recognized that to some extent the 'vision' and 'objectives' were already set out in the Mayor's manifesto, published in early 2000, and the *State of London* report, published in August 2000, they felt they needed Livingstone's tacit commitments to be turned into something more concrete that would be sufficiently robust to 'inform strategy development'. One internal strategy-integration paper, dated September 2000 stated: 'Our vision should comprise: a healthy economy; a good quality of life; a sustainable future; and equality of opportunity'. This, it was argued, should be accompanied by a set of overarching objectives (which one officer did in fact attempt to draft).

It seemed that they would not have to wait long as the Mayor had announced to his advisory cabinet in June that he would publish a 'Prospectus' in November 2000. The report to the cabinet promised:

> The production of a London Prospectus at the end of the process [of stakeholder engagement], which will express the Mayor's vision for London, and provide a framework for the specific strategies, which will then be able to proceed with public consultation, and able [sic] to demonstrate their joined-up nature.

However, in the event the Prospectus was never published. The Mayor told us that his team had been too busy fighting the battle on funding for the Underground.

It could be argued that Livingstone's political priorities were set out in his manifesto and that no supplementary vision was necessary. However, his manifesto was not couched in terms of the three principal purposes of the GLA as laid down in the Act, and did not make explicit the trade-offs between them. Looking at the question from the Mayor's point of view, a fixed and definitive mission statement would have created something of a political straightjacket, leaving little political room for manoeuvre throughout the four-year mayoral term. We have already alluded to Livingstone's split agenda – short-term and 'Big Tent' – through which a broad coalition of support is maintained, and it might be argued that such a political strategy is necessary in an institution like the GLA where the scope for political action lies in brokering deals and building political alliances with a variety of external agencies. From a strategy officer's point of view, on the other hand, having a fixed set of objectives makes the task of policy development, co-ordination and integration all the easier. In the absence of a clear mayoral vision, officers attempted to supply their own maps for developing and co-ordinating the strategies. We discuss two modes of strategy integration that were attempted, both of which were controversial and eventually collided with the policy integration work of the Mayor's Office.

Mapping onto the Spatial Development Strategy

The first of these controversial modes we have termed 'mapping onto'. In this mode of integration, strategies were to be mapped onto, or made consistent with, a master strategy. This mode of co-ordination was evident in planning officers' attempts to bring the Transport and Economic Development strategies (which they regarded as shorter term and essentially operational in character) into line with their work on the SDS (the long term integrating strategy). As noted above, the SDS was initially developed by former LPAC staff, who arrived in the GLA with a very clear agenda as regards spatial development. From the outset they viewed the SDS as the overarching and linking strategy, which would itself represent a vision of how the GLA's three key purposes should be balanced. As we have already noted, the former LPAC officers, when drafting the *Endowment* document, clearly expected the SDS to be the principal mayoral strategy (or blueprint) with which the rest would have to conform. The *Endowment* offered advice to the Mayor on planning for housing, town centres, and sustainability, as well as on inter-regional and European collaboration.

In the summer of 2000, the SDS team started work on a mechanism to try to ensure the full integration of Spatial Development, Economic Development and Transport strategies in order that investment could begin to be dispersed away from the centre of London to inner- and outer-suburban London through increased transport accessibility. This mechanism, known as the Pan London Development Project (Agenda of Mayor's Advisory Cabinet, 18 July 2000), would essentially function as the co-ordinating blueprint until the SDS was published. The project was, however, eventually abandoned as the Strategy Directorate's lack of leverage over the transport and economic development strategies and the increasing control of the Mayor's Office over all strategies became apparent. The draft Economic Development Strategy was developed quickly and the Strategy Directorate was given little opportunity to integrate it with the Spatial Development and Transport strategies. The draft Economic Strategy was drawn up piecemeal, largely by external consultants working to an LDA brief and drawing on the previous work of the London Development Partnership; there was very little input from the core GLA. In contrast to the Transport Strategy (which the Mayor's Office had re-written after the Strategy Directorate had produced a version), the draft was accepted almost without change by the Mayor's Office. Ken Livingstone said to us: '...look at the economic strategy coming from the LDA. It's great because it's been drawn up by all these people who are running real businesses'.

The first, draft, SDS proposals were scheduled to be published in January 2001, but did not in fact appear until May 2001. Not until just before the initial publication date did the Mayor's Office start to take a close interest in the Strategy. Staff of the Mayor's Office felt the SDS proposals did not sufficiently relate to the Mayor's political priorities or promote London as a world city, while the primary concern of the strategy officers had been to establish a watertight legal document that would withstand any challenge and which would be consistent with the other transport and economic development strategies. Soon the strategy team was marginalized as the Mayor's Office, together with its newly appointed consultants, took control and organized the re-write of the proposals.

Drawing down the sustainability principles

The second of the controversial policy integration modes was evident in attempts by ex-LEU and other officers to get the Mayor to adopt a schedule of 'sustainable development principles' as the overall GLA policy template. Here there was no master strategy but rather a set of master principles. They wanted to co-ordinate strategies by bringing them all into line with a list of criteria in which sustainability was not confined to mere preservation of the physical environment, but rather informed all facets of the GLA's economic, environmental and social activities, and promoted a level of integration close to that envisaged in the Act. The list of principles went through some 17 drafts, being continually modified by officers and some Assembly members. The first draft covered social and economic sustainability as well as purely physical environmental matters. Officers invested much time and effort in encouraging the various components of the GLA family to adopt and commit to the principles, and initially their passage through the GLA was smooth. However, once their significance was brought to the attention of the Mayor's Office they became the subject of substantial revision, with the effect that their reach was largely confined to preservation of the physical environment.

Two serious attempts to achieve the social, economic and environmental synthesis in policy formation, which the Act seemed to require, were thus marginalized in favour of a more overtly political interpretation of the GLA's mission, which we have termed 'co-ordinating to the Mayor's manifesto'.

Bridging the cultural gap between the Mayor's Office and the bureaucracy

As we noted above, very early on in his mayoralty Ken Livingstone sought to reduce his dependence on the bureaucracy of the GLA by creating his own tight-knit office of trusted and loyal colleagues. Arguably this engendered a feeling of distrust between the Mayor's Office and the various groups absorbed into the GLA, and led to somewhat artificial, rather than organic links. Many observers commented that Ken Livingstone did not see himself as a manager of a large organization; that he was more comfortable as representative of his electorate than as leader of the staff of the GLA.

The first attempt to formalize communication between the Mayor's Office and the GLA bureaucracy was the Mayor's Management Board. This was a weekly meeting between Ken Livingstone and/or his chief of staff and the heads of the

GLA directorates. The Mayor's personal advisors, representing the Mayor in his absence, other officers and cabinet advisors were also invited to attend depending on what was being discussed. In the early days it was unclear what precisely constituted a mayoral decision, and increasingly the Mayor's Management Board came to be seen as the forum for the dissemination of Livingstone's decisions. A later mechanism for improving communication between the Mayor's Office and the rest of the GLA was the so-called 'white-boarding sessions', developed following the unacceptability to, and ultimate rejection by, the Mayor's Office of the strategy team's original draft Transport Strategy. White-boarding sessions were attended by one or several of the Mayor's senior advisors, depending on the strategy in question, and senior strategy officers. Strategy officers presented their emerging draft strategies to the Mayor's senior advisors, whose job it was to give clear political direction.

In these co-ordination forums, Mayor's Office staff assessed draft strategies in terms of how well they matched the priorities set out in the Mayor's manifesto, in which it is stated:

> The single most important priority for the Mayor and Greater London Authority will be to solve the crisis of London's transport system. For a city the size of London an efficient transport system is vital for both business and leisure (Ken Livingstone's *Manifesto for London*, undated, p.5).

In practice, this meant they judged them against the Transport Strategy – for them the 'master' strategy. A second important political priority was to assess them for business-friendliness or the extent to which they promoted London's world city role. Very soon after Livingstone was elected he commissioned a report from management consultants KPMG about the GLA's relations with the business community (GLA Mayor's Office, unpublished document, June 2000). This report set the tone for the Mayor's relationship with the business community (for further details see Thornley et al, 2002). Briefly, it said that early input into the development of the mayoral strategies was vital, and that joint working with the business community was essential to ensure London's increased prosperity. Livingstone also appointed John Ross (a long time associate of Livingstone) as his senior economic advisor, with a remit of liaison with the business community. Ross' influence over strategy development and co-ordination was undoubtedly far-reaching, and many interviewees commented that the Mayor would not adopt any strategy that Ross had not approved. In addition, a consultant from KPMG was employed in the Mayor's Office to carry out business-friendliness appraisals of all the emerging strategies. Business-friendliness appraisal, or world-city friendliness, was a significant strategy co-ordination tool for the Mayor's Office.

The integration of strategies undertaken within the Strategy Directorate would either be unravelled in cases of clash with the Mayor's political priorities, or strategy officers would attempt to retrofit the strategies according to the political steer given by the Mayor's personal advisors, in particular emphasizing transport and world-city priorities. Two examples are illustrative. During the period we examined, two strategies that were closely linked were the Air Quality and

Transport strategies. Officers worked hard to create synergy between the Air Quality and Transport strategies and to maximize the potential reduction in road traffic pollution; to this end the draft Air Quality Strategy included a low-emission zone roughly coterminous with the congestion charging zone. The release of the Air Quality Strategy was delayed so that it would not coincide with the draft Transport Strategy (published in January 2001). When the draft Air Quality Strategy finally emerged in March 2001, the commitment to a low-emission zone had been downgraded to a feasibility study. Later drafts of the Biodiversity Strategy were written, at the instigation of the Mayor's Office, to emphasize the economic and world city benefits of biodiversity in London, noting that:

> London's natural open space acts as a green magnet, attracting and keeping workers and enterprises in London. Greening also plays an integral role in the urban renaissance in new and existing infrastructure, the public realm, regeneration initiatives and other developments. The open spaces of London attract tourists, and the green economy provides jobs (The Mayor's Biodiversity Strategy, 30th January 2001, p.7).

The alignment of strategies with the Mayor's agenda is indicative of at least the notional integration of the three principal purposes of the GLA set by the Act. It appears, however, that the primary concern throughout was presentation rather than the achievement of real synthesis. Again, the overriding aim was to keep as many people as possible inside the Big Tent. This was also evident in the eventual publication of the draft proposals for the *London Plan* in May 2001, which superficially speaks to a vision that balances the social, economic and environmental. The stated objective is described as making London 'an exemplary and sustainable world city', and the goals – as stated in other mayoral strategies – are those of 'a prosperous city', 'an accessible city', 'a green city' and 'a city for people'. However, in some important respects social equity and the environment seem subordinate to, rather than balanced with, economic development. The very beginning of the document sets out the 'context, challenges and vision' for the *London Plan* and very starkly presents 'London's fundamental strategic choice': either revert to a policy of dispersing London's population and economic activity away from the centre, or accept and even promote the concentration of development in the centre. *The* central principle set out in this document is that of maintaining and enhancing London's world-city status in the face of potential attempts by other European cities (specifically Berlin and Paris) to usurp London's position.

Conclusions

What conclusions can we draw about the impact of the Greater London Authority on the formation and integration of policy for London from observations made during its first ten months? Clearly in any research on the establishment of a new organization there is much to say about specific personalities. In the case of the GLA, personality – particularly that of the incumbent Mayor, Ken Livingstone –

has dominated popular discussion. However, as we argue elsewhere (Rydin et al, 2002 and forthcoming), it is also possible to view the core GLA in terms of separate and fixed institutional cultures, obeying different logics in terms of world-views, resources, constraints and time horizons. The clash between these different cultures is all the greater when set in such an uncertain and unpredictable context of governance as that of the GLA.

The GLA Act lays down the challenge to develop a policy of economic development for London, which is 'green' and socially just, and provides the Mayor with a basic tool kit – eight mandatory strategies, strategic control of the key functional bodies and a skeletal budget – but how the experiment turns out in practice depends critically on the Mayor's ability to broker partnerships and deals with others. It is little wonder then that in such a context the Mayor, with an eye to the next election, is inclined to work somewhat opportunistically. His approach to policy development is political. It is perfectly understandable that his strategic focus is placed where he can make the most impact. He has no interest in setting out a fixed agenda, but rather requires flexibility in order to keep everybody – the business community, the voluntary sector, the boroughs and the environmental lobby – inside the Big Tent. Such an approach is nevertheless frustrating for strategy officers who see it as their remit to co-ordinate the strategies – which either have statutory force (as in the case of the SDS) or are meant to stand as policy guidelines for the boroughs and functional bodies – in a way which will realize the synthesis of economic, social and environmental development that the Act demands. To achieve that kind of deep policy integration – as opposed to the more superficial co-ordination of strategy to the Mayor's political agenda – requires a more deliberative and planned approach, and a rather clearer and more fixed strategic template.

There is much about the GLA that bears the hallmark of New Labour's general approach to the urban renaissance: high aspirations for humanized and environmentally sustainable urban growth, to be delivered through partnership, stealth and pragmatism. On the basis of the evidence outlined here, the problems of policy integration cannot be fully explained by the newness of the GLA as an organization. There are some old barriers to overcome concerning the relationship between the rationality of the legislation and the pragmatism of politics, perhaps heightened by the visible concentration of so much power in a single elected figure set within such an unpredictable context of governance. These old and persistent barriers to policy integration cannot simply be wished away by new initiatives like the GLA or Local Strategic Partnerships, and the future of an urban policy which relies so heavily on this kind of loose governance is surely questionable.

References

DETR (2000), *Our Towns and Cities: The Future – Delivering an Urban Renaissance*, HMSO, London.

Dowding, K., Dunleavy, P., King, D., Margetts, H. and Rydin, Y. (1999), 'Regime politics in London local government', *Urban Affairs Review*, vol. 34(4), pp. 515-45.

Hill, D. (2000), *Urban Policy and Politics in Britain*, Macmillan, Basingstoke.

House of Commons (1999), *Greater London Authority Act*, HMSO, London, and available online at: www.hmso.gov.uk/acts/acts1999/19990029.htm

LPAC (2000), *Endowment to the Mayor*, LPAC, London.

Newman, P. and Thornley, A. (1997), 'Fragmentation and centralisation in the governance of London: influencing the urban policy and planning agenda', *Urban Studies*, vol. 34(7), pp. 967-88.

Rhodes, R (2000), 'New Labour's Civil Service: summing-up joining-up', *Political Quarterly*, vol. 71(2), pp. 151-66.

Rydin, Y., Thornley, A., Scanlon, K. and West, K. (2002), *The GLA – A Clash of Organisational Cultures*, Discussion Paper No.6, Metropolitan and Urban Research Centre, London School of Economics, London, available at: www.lse.ac.uk/Depts/london/papers.htm

Rydin, Y., Thornley, A., Scanlon, K. and West, K. (forthcoming), 'The Greater London Authority – a case of conflict of cultures? Evidence from the planning and environmental policy domains', *Environment and Planning C*.

Thornley, A., Rydin, Y., Scanlon, K., and West, K. (2002), *The Greater London Authority: Interest Representation and the Strategic Agenda*, Discussion Paper No.8, Metropolitan and Urban Research Centre, London School of Economics, London, available at: www.lse.ac.uk/Depts/london/papers.htm

Travers, T. and Jones, G. (1997), *The New Government of London*, Joseph Rowntree Foundation, York.

West, K., Scanlon, K., Thornley, A. and Rydin, Y. (2003), 'The Greater London Authority: problems of strategy integration', *Policy and Politics*, vol. 31(4), pp. 479-96.

Chapter 7

Scottish Urban Policy: Continuity, Change and Uncertainty Post-Devolution

Ivan Turok

Introduction

Cities present the devolved Scottish government with some of its greatest challenges and opportunities. They contain the most intense concentrations of poverty and dereliction, but are also key drivers of economic growth and prosperity. Yet urban policy has not been high on the national agenda since devolution. There has been a Cities Review, a Community Regeneration Statement and separate national statements of social and economic policy, but nothing with the focus or status of an urban White Paper, an Urban Summit or a Cities Working Group of key government departments, core city authorities and development agencies championed by the Deputy Prime Minister (ODPM, 2003). As a new institution representing Scotland-wide interests, there is a desire to appear neutral in the treatment of different parts of the country and to rise above what might be construed as narrow territorial politics. There is also pressure to respond to well-organized rural interests and contested rural constituencies.

The thrust of Scottish Executive policy has been to prioritize popular issues of general concern for which it has clear responsibility, particularly health, education, crime and transport (Scottish Executive, 2003). They have typically been treated as distinctive and independent policy areas requiring better public service delivery and increased resources (improved schools and hospitals, more doctors, additional police on the streets, etc). There have been some attempts to connect the operation of these services at the local level through community planning arrangements and regeneration partnerships. However, there has been no overarching national concept of how these issues fit together and relate to the broader goals of social and economic progress. Mainstream resources are typically allocated through separate formula-driven funding streams in response to where the demand or population is, rather than a more strategic, integrated approach aimed at resolving underlying problems, such as poverty or slow growth.

Devolution has also brought a more transparent and inclusive style of policymaking, which has created opportunities for outsiders to influence decisions. The ability to lobby for particular projects has been of some benefit to the cities, particularly in the form of new transport schemes such as airport rail links, motorway extensions and new tramways. Devolution has also increased the amount of consultation and policy reviews undertaken. Some of these reviews have drawn attention to important causal relationships between problems of poor health, low educational attainment, crime, deprivation and unemployment. They have called for a more serious response to their uneven distribution, in recognition that selected areas face the greatest challenges all round. Some have also emphasized the opportunity for cities to improve Scotland's economic performance through their distinctive assets and institutions. These developments may be the first tentative steps towards a more joined-up urban policy, or they may turn out to be of limited significance. It is important to make some assessment of them, although it is too soon to reach a definitive conclusion.

Looking back over the history of urban policy in Scotland, two particular features of continuity stand out. First, despite repeated claims to be pursuing a comprehensive, co-ordinated approach, there has been a persistent and damaging failure to link regeneration schemes to wider economic, infrastructure and land-use planning policies operating at larger spatial scales. Within regeneration areas, there has been a tendency to focus on separate dimensions – people/social/community issues, place/physical/housing concerns or enterprise/business development – rather than a more strategic and integrated approach. Different policies have typically been the responsibility of separate organizations, which has sometimes reflected government misgivings about local authorities. Second, there has traditionally been an emphasis on housing as the single most important sector and a selective focus on residential neighbourhoods as the scale of action. This has reflected understandable pressures to respond to conspicuous local problems and immediate community concerns, but it has been to the neglect of other important issues and the wider geographical context of neighbourhoods. There have been several more positive developments recently, including emerging signs of a broader and more balanced view of cities and a better awareness of their distinctive challenges and contribution to the Scottish economy and society.

The purpose of this chapter is to review the changing character of urban policy in Scotland. It also seeks to identify the underlying ideas behind these policy developments and to relate them to the reality of conditions on the ground. The focus is on the Scottish Executive level of policy, justified by its control over resource allocation and consequent influence at the local level. Particular attention is paid to Glasgow because of its exceptional size within Scotland and the unique intensity of its socio-economic problems (Duguid, 1995; Kearns et al, 2000)[1]. The first section summarizes the development of urban policy prior to 1997, when Scotland had considerable administrative devolution, because of the important legacy of this period. Section two considers the main developments in urban policy and related areas since political devolution in 1999. The final section concludes with some thoughts on future prospects.

---

1 More than half (56%) of Glasgow City's wards are in the most deprived 10% of wards in Scotland (Social Disadvantage Research Centre, 2003).

Urban policy before 1997

The origins of Scottish urban policy need to be related back to the dispersal push led by the Scottish Office during the three post-war decades. Urban problems were seen in physical terms, including overcrowded dwellings and congestion. The solution was major de-concentration of population and jobs to surrounding New Towns and other overspill areas, and comprehensive clearance of run-down buildings[2]. This was partly a response to Glasgow's appalling slum housing and insufficient land to accommodate all the new development required. There was also a view within government that Glasgow was an uncompetitive economic location because of its unionised workforce, congested infrastructure and unresponsive local authority (Levitt, 1997 and 1999). The West of Scotland required areas with a 'new look', modern amenities and efficient administration to attract inward investment. As a result, major public investment in economic infrastructure, superior housing, modern schools and other facilities was targeted on separate 'growth areas' (the New Towns) under single-minded development corporations. The New Towns remained a special focus of policy until the mid-1990s, two decades after urban regeneration became a stated objective. The assumptions were that they offered the greatest economic potential and that city residents would either move or commute to work there. The weaknesses in this were shown much later – commuting from Glasgow to the New Towns never became significant (Webster, 1994).

Tensions between economic development and urban regeneration policies

The first sign of a policy shift came in the 1970s when it was realized that the rate of decline was well beyond expectations (Wannop, 1995). Glasgow desperately needed to improve its infrastructure, environment and housing[3]. This led to the Glasgow Eastern Area Renewal (GEAR) project. GEAR pioneered partnership working and revealed some of its limitations, including diffuse responsibility for

---

2 McCrone (1991) points out that Glasgow was one of the first cities in the world where population decline was a deliberate policy. This was a matter of great controversy with Glasgow Corporation, which was worried that it would create a momentum of decline (Levitt, 1997; Webster, 2002). Glasgow and other city authorities encouraged people to move from the most congested areas to large new council estates on the outskirts. Although the housing was an improvement on previous conditions, the emphasis was on quantity rather than quality and the peripheral estates grew up without many of the services required for sustainable communities, and with insufficient consideration given to the location of employment.

3 Glasgow lost 142,000 jobs between 1961 and 1981, more than a quarter (26%) of the 1961 total (Lever and Moore, 1986). Glasgow also lost a third of its population over the same period, compared with 10% in Edinburgh and 8% in Dundee (Scottish Executive, 2002b). Some 25,000 people were leaving Glasgow every year in the 1960s and early 1970s, mostly professionals and skilled manual workers (West Central Scotland Plan, 1974). Much of this was spontaneous as well as planned dispersal, with people moving out of the city to buy their own homes or for other residential preferences.

delivery and difficulties in policy integration. It involved the Scottish Development Agency (SDA), the local and regional authorities and two national housing organizations in a voluntary collaboration. The SDA was created to tackle economic decline in areas such as Clydeside, although it covered the whole of lowland Scotland. The government wanted SDA involvement in GEAR because of the local authority's limited powers and resources for economic development, and its historical focus on housing and population retention (Robertson, 1998).

GEAR was the largest of six SDA 'area projects' across the Central Belt. An important aim was to create jobs by upgrading the environment and infrastructure in order to retain and attract industry. This was a demanding process that the SDA was inadequately resourced for or dedicated to, including land assembly, decontamination, site preparation, and the provision of new roads and property. The SDA focused on building small workshops rather than larger premises or major infrastructure, so the economic impact was disappointing (McCrone, 1991). Thereafter it shifted its attention to fashionable high-tech sector initiatives and areas more attractive to private investors, such as city centres (Keating and Boyle, 1986). Housing renewal was more straightforward and the agencies retained their local focus, so it ultimately accounted for two-thirds of public investment in GEAR. This helped to modernize the stock and provide some new homes. It also improved the area's image but did little for jobs and incomes, which kept declining.

Meanwhile, the New Towns continued to benefit from their flagship status and attractive infrastructure for inward investors, which hampered urban renewal efforts (Lever and Moore, 1986). The UK Enterprise Zone programme during the 1980s and early 1990s did not help Glasgow either, since the city got none of the five Scottish Zones while surrounding districts got three. The government was effectively undermining the competitive position of the city and encouraging businesses to relocate, which caused thousands of local job losses (Strathclyde Regional Council, 1992; Turok et al, 2003). It took another decade for Glasgow agencies to gather sufficient support for a programme of six industrial sites and business parks in well-located parts of the city (EKOS, 2001).

A shift to social and community concerns

Regeneration policy shifted during the 1980s towards 'softer' social and community issues. This reflected a view that economic development was difficult to achieve within poorer areas but simpler at the wider regional level (Scottish Office, 1988; McCrone, 1991). The location or even total number of jobs was said to matter less than the ability of the unemployed to compete in the wider labour market, despite a lack of supporting analysis (Webster, 1994 and 2002). The shift was also related to government financial strictures and pressure on the SDA to reduce its property and environmental programmes in favour of business development (Lever and Moore, 1986). This was particularly unhelpful to Glasgow and Lanarkshire, which have the bulk of vacant and derelict land in Scotland (Bailey et al, 2002). The shift also reflected a view among some practitioners that renewal of 'bricks and mortar' did nothing for the core problems of poverty and deprivation.

A concern with urban social issues can be traced back over three decades to the perception that residual communities were not benefiting from post-war prosperity and slipping through the safety net of the welfare state. The Urban Programme provided assistance through improved support services of various kinds. This was widely criticized for attributing the causes of deprivation to the communities themselves (poor motivation, family breakdown and social disorganization) and not addressing the underlying problems of unemployment, poverty and inequality. Nevertheless, the approach became more prominent in the late 1980s, when Scottish urban policy was at its most distinctive from the rest of Britain. Physical and economic regeneration dominated south of the border via the Urban Development Corporations. They were better resourced and more focused than the SDA area projects. The Scottish Office response was *New Life for Urban Scotland*, which singled out four peripheral estates for broad-based partnership initiatives involving the community. In practice the focus was on housing, training and community support, in line with prevailing ideas and because it was easier to redirect these funding streams.

There was an explicit change of approach towards unemployment from job creation to supply side measures such as advice, guidance, training and job placement. They were less costly and implied that the cause was deficient personal skills and information rather than a lack of demand for labour, despite the growing shortage of jobs in the key urban areas. For instance, during the 1980s Glasgow lost 11% of all its jobs and more than a quarter of its manual jobs through deindustrialization (Turok and Edge, 1999). Dundee and other parts of Clydeside from North Lanarkshire to Inverclyde suffered similarly, resulting in a large rise in worklessness. Tens of thousands of people moved onto sickness benefits since there was no realistic prospect of finding work. These now disguise a real rate of unemployment in these areas of between 16% and 23% (Beatty et al, 2002).

There was also a renewed emphasis on active participation by the local community, partly to reduce their dependence on the state. 'The Government's central aim is to renew the self-confidence and initiative of local people and to help them to assume increased responsibility for their communities' (Scottish Office, 1988, p.11). The welfare state was perceived to have become part of the problem in encouraging dependency, rather than part of the solution to poverty. The idea of residents taking on more responsibility was reflected in initiatives to expand self-employment, community businesses, school boards, community-based housing associations and co-operatives.

Multi-agency partnerships were increasingly portrayed as *the* solution to urban deprivation. Eleven Smaller Urban Renewal Initiatives (SURIs) were established in poor council estates across Scotland. Their housing-led approach involved improving the quality and variety of homes, including private investment to expand owner occupation (Scottish Office, 1993). The initiative drew upon Glasgow's positive experience of renewing some of its older neighbourhoods through tenement rehabilitation, environmental upgrading and housing associations (Maclennan, 1987 and 1993; Bailey and Robertson, 1997). The small area approach was consistent with the idea of dealing with neighbourhood externalities coherently so as to limit the negative effects of physical decay and uncertainty, and to increase confidence for residents and investors through positive demonstration effects (Turok, 1992). This was appropriate if that was the extent of the problem, but not where the underlying issues were poverty or generalized low demand for housing. An evaluation of the SURIs found that they helped to improve housing but failed to address deeper economic and social problems (Kintrea et al, 1998).

Competitive bidding and co-ordination through partnership

In the mid-1990s the Scottish Office selected 12 Priority Partnership Areas (PPAs) across urban Scotland to add to the New Life schemes and SURIs. They borrowed the idea of competitive bidding from England's City Challenge by requiring councils to compete for three-year funding packages. This was intended to stimulate improved quality and value for money. In fact the opaque selection procedure was widely seen as unfair and brought the initiative into disrepute (Turok and Hopkins, 1998). There were suspicions of political interference because resources were shifted from the areas of greatest need towards marginal constituencies. This was arguably symptomatic of what could happen given limitations on transparency and accountability prior to devolution.

The steady withdrawal of responsibilities from local authorities to other agencies culminated in the abolition of the regional councils. They had provided an important city-region perspective for planning transport infrastructure and other major developments. Glasgow also suffered from the loss of resource redistribution following Strathclyde's abolition (Bailey et al, 1999). The regional councils had sponsored important experimental initiatives in community development, welfare rights and local economic development, even if some of them were not very successful (Turok, 2000). Strathclyde had also worked with other agencies in Glasgow to establish the Glasgow Regeneration Alliance. This was a citywide partnership intended to provide a coherent framework for the development of local initiatives.

Co-ordination became a key theme during this period: 'the problems of urban deprivation can best be tackled through a comprehensive, integrated, strategic approach which recognizes the linkages between the physical, economic and social aspects of disadvantage' (Scottish Office, 1995, p.3). Previous initiatives were acknowledged to be marginal to mainstream policies, treating the symptoms of deprivation, tackling issues piecemeal and offering quick fixes with doubtful sustainability (Scottish Office, 1993). Yet there was little agreement within the policy community about the relationships between physical, economic and social dimensions of deprivation. Lack of support for basic research over the years meant that the analytical frameworks and evidence base were thin. The rhetorical formula of a comprehensive, co-ordinated approach shifted responsibility onto local partnerships, without any guidance about the relative importance of, and links between, people, place and economic policies. The message was that if agencies worked together more closely in consultation with the community, neighbourhood deprivation could be removed.

The final evaluation of New Life illustrated some limitations of this. Despite their high profile, close collaboration, exceptional resources and community involvement, the partnerships failed to sustain a comprehensive approach (Tarling et al, 1999). Housing became the priority and accounted for two-thirds of expenditure. Much effort was also devoted to job advice and training. Poor educational attainment, ill-health, crime/community safety and economic development were neglected. Although the housing stock improved greatly, this failed to stabilize the population. People who managed to get jobs moved to better located parts of the city and were replaced by others in greater social need, so the employment rate and average incomes in two of the estates did not increase. In some cases, crime, drugs and anti-social households were merely displaced onto surrounding areas. The partnerships were unaware of or unable to respond to neighbourhood interactions and the dynamics of regeneration. They could do little about how their areas functioned within the wider urban system and the way housing allocation procedures concentrated the most deprived groups and reinforced segregation. They were operating in a strategic and spatial vacuum that undermined their effectiveness.

Urban policy in New Labour's Scotland

After Labour was elected in 1997 steps were taken to address two specific concerns. First, many of the deprived areas that failed in the competition for PPA funds were encouraged to apply again. Following a more transparent process most succeeded, and all the new and existing PPAs were renamed Social Inclusion Partnerships (SIPs). But expanding the number meant fewer resources for each, since there was no additional funding. The shortage of discretionary funds has continued to limit the impact of the SIPs because they have failed to exercise much leverage over mainstream budgets (Scottish Executive, 2002a; Tyler et al, 2002). The diversion of resources from the old Urban Programme to the SIPs also caused protests within deprived communities when the funding for time-limited projects expired and support services were closed down.

Second, it was acknowledged that deprived neighbourhoods cannot prosper in isolation. In a speech on regeneration, the new Secretary of State said he recognized that local partnerships depend on wider policies and developments elsewhere in their city (Dewar, 1998), although the full implications of this were not pursued. He did encourage the Glasgow Regeneration Alliance to be reconstituted as the Glasgow Alliance with an expanded membership to include Scottish Office officials. He provided some funding for a new Alliance strategy, but said it had to be based on the assumption that no additional funds would be provided for the city. The message was that Glasgow organizations had to deploy their existing resources more effectively by working together more closely. Edinburgh's equivalent – Capital City Partnership – was provided with similar support.

Within the first two years a series of new initiatives was launched to signal a higher priority to tackling 'social exclusion'. An inter-departmental Social

Exclusion Network was created among civil servants to co-ordinate responses. This was later widened to include representatives of organizations with experience of tackling deprivation and renamed the Social Inclusion Network. Its approach to social inclusion policy was informed by three principles: *co-ordination* because of the multi-faceted nature of the problem; *prevention* of deprivation as a preferable and more cost-effective approach to later palliatives; and *innovation* because of the complexity of the issues and need for new thinking (Scottish Office, 1998). Innovation and co-ordination were long-standing aspirations, while prevention was a newer idea, at least applied to people[4]. These themes were reflected in special initiatives to provide additional services to children, school leavers and parents on low incomes or living in deprived areas[5]. Some were UK programmes, reflecting the close connections between the Scottish Office and Westminster during this period. Most involved modest resources separate from mainstream budgets and intended to reflect new ministerial priorities.

Devolution, social justice and a new economic policy

Labour came to power on the back of considerable momentum for devolution. Public opinion strengthened during the 1980s and 1990s following a series of controversial policies introduced by the Conservatives despite their small representation in Scotland, such as the poll tax and privatization. Devolution was intended to strengthen Scottish self-government and to make the process of decision-making more legitimate, transparent and open to outside influence. This was an opportunity to place urban issues high on the core political agenda and to develop joined-up strategies to tackle the serious socio-economic challenges faced, given the wide responsibilities allocated to the Parliament and Executive under the devolution settlement. For instance, by investing to increase economic opportunities in the most deprived localities the Scottish Executive could make real inroads into poverty in a sustainable manner that was not reliant on continuing transfer payments. It had control over many of the important policy levers for urban regeneration, including transport, housing, planning, land, education and economic development. Yet, it lacked financial and administrative responsibility for welfare benefits and control over most aspects of taxation. This may have

4 The idea of prevention had been used to justify the selection of Wester Hailes as a New Life partnership estate in 1988. Wester Hailes was not in the list of Scotland's most deprived areas, but it was said by officials to be at risk of decline. It may be no coincidence that it was also in the constituency of the Secretary of State for Scotland at the time, Malcolm Rifkind.

5 For example, these included the Rough Sleepers Initiative to prevent and reduce homelessness, a Better Neighbourhood Services Fund to improve the quality of services in deprived areas, Alternatives to Exclusion to provide extra assistance for school children vulnerable to exclusion, Sure Start Scotland to support families with pre-nursery age children in areas of greatest need, a New Futures Fund to help equip the most disadvantaged young people for work, a New Opportunities Fund to support out-of-school-hours learning activities, Public Health Demonstration projects, a Listening to Communities initiative, Working for Communities Pathfinders, and New Community Schools to bring health and family welfare services together under one roof for children from poor backgrounds.

reduced the perceived pressure to reduce worklessness and the incentive to expand the economy, in the face of many other demands on the Executive. It also lacked control over aspects of labour market policy, such as the New Deal, that could otherwise have been tailored better to local circumstances. This may be one of the structural reasons why all sorts of other issues could and did end up receiving more attention. In addition, the diverse socio-economic circumstances of the cities, coupled with their historic rivalries, were not conducive to an alliance of urban interests, whereas rural concerns were more prominent[6]. Three first ministers since devolution, none of whom were/are reputed to be instinctive strategic thinkers, and many changes of ministerial responsibility, have also worked against the formulation of a clear vision for Scotland's socio-economic and spatial development (Ford and Casebow, 2002).

Social justice became the principal watchword of the Scottish Executive after devolution. It was defined as trying to create a fair and decent society by reducing inequalities in opportunity and tackling social disadvantage. This was interpreted mainly as improving the circumstances for people at key stages and transitions in the life cycle through better public services. This focus reflected a view that deprivation policies had over-emphasized place at the expense of people, and it was necessary to shift the balance (Scottish Executive, 1999). There were said to be more poor and excluded people living outside deprived neighbourhoods than within them. The new approach had four people-based priorities: giving every child the best start in life; equipping every young person to move into working life; giving every family the means to support itself, and every older person dignity and a decent quality of life. The fifth priority had a spatial dimension: to build stronger, inclusive communities, with an emphasis on increasing residents' satisfaction with services in poor neighbourhoods. The strategy said nothing about its implications for different parts of Scotland. It also said little about the uneven geography of economic and social opportunities, and the systematic effect on the living standards and life chances of people in all cohorts. For instance, Glasgow's employment rate was only 61% in 2001 compared with Dundee's 69%, Edinburgh's 78%, Aberdeen's 79% and the Scottish average of 74% (Office for National Statistics, 2002).

This could perhaps have been considered the responsibility of the new Framework for Economic Development (FEDS) (Scottish Executive, 2000). Its aim was to raise living standards by growing the Scottish economy in a durable way. The basic approach followed the new economic orthodoxy: increasing productivity and international competitiveness by improving the quality and quantity of output per worker and by reducing costs. This was to be achieved by

6 The Executive is governed by a coalition with strong rural representation by the Liberal Democrats. Rural constituencies are also the most closely contested between all three main political parties. It is no coincidence that the Executive has a dedicated Rural Affairs Minister and the Parliament has a powerful Rural Affairs Committee (Crichton, 2002). The Partnership Agreement signed after the 2003 election (Scottish Executive, 2003) contained a whole section devoted to rural concerns, but only a few bullet points specifically on cities or urban areas, despite the fact that 70% of Scotland's population live in urban areas.

increasing enterprise, R&D, innovation, skills and investment in plant and infrastructure. In addition, FEDS recognized the need to broaden economic opportunities to all parts of Scotland and all social groups. The confirmation that 'equity now matters as a principle of economic policy' (p.84) indicated a desire to influence the location of economic activity so as to reduce inequalities between places and people. This was partly for social justice, but also because balanced development was economically and environmentally beneficial in the long-term. FEDS cited the example of uneven growth across the central belt. This might constrain economic dynamism by creating shortages of skills and property and causing congestion and higher costs in overheated Edinburgh.

This was not a narrow growth agenda: the quality and form of growth were just as important as the rate. It also drew attention to employment as a key driver in reducing poverty and exclusion and strengthening communities, although the statement that the Executive was committed to 'an economy-led social justice agenda' is questionable from the emphasis on public services in the social justice strategy and elsewhere. FEDS was unusual in seeking to identify and make explicit the relationships between economic, social and spatial development objectives, including some of the tensions and trade-offs. It did not really spell out the implications for economic policy and public spending from making equity an important economic principle, but it was a step forward in honest joined-up thinking. It was also supported by substantial evidence and analysis, and acknowledged gaps in existing understanding. Finally, in discussing spatial issues the principal territorial unit referred to was the region. Cities or smaller urban areas did not feature, although FEDS recognized the need for better policy co-ordination at different spatial scales and argued for a stronger spatial dimension to Executive strategies.

FEDS was followed by Smart Successful Scotland (SSS), an important guidance statement to Scottish Enterprise (Scottish Executive, 2001a). SSS had a narrower emphasis on science and skills as the way to raise productivity and growth. It was influenced by knowledge economy ideas and stressed the importance of new ICT, e-commerce, innovation and commercialization of research in order to compete internationally. The concepts of human and social capital as drivers of economic regeneration were also very influential: 'Business growth and high skill levels come from confident communities which recognize personal achievement and advancement' (Scottish Executive, 2001a, p.7). SSS played down the spatial dimension of economic development policy and the challenge of wide geographical disparities. Cities barely featured at all (either as problems or as opportunities), except for the view that the key issue was disparities between neighbourhoods. The opportunity presented by the key knowledge assets of universities, research facilities, advanced skill-sets, specialized business services and broadband connections being located there was ignored. The role of infrastructure, property and place in enabling or constraining the conditions for wealth and job creation barely featured – human capital was considered the key. The response to unemployment everywhere was purely supply-side – to increase skills and employability. This was not the broad approach required for slack urban labour markets with a legacy of derelict land and environmental blight.

A parallel urban agenda

In parallel with these broad social and economic strategies, a variety of policy review groups were set up to analyse particular themes and to formulate recommendations. This was indicative of the more open and consultative style of decision-making that has followed devolution (Paterson, 2002). The reviews that related more or less directly to urban policy or had a spatial dimension were neighbourhood renewal, strategic planning, homelessness, social economy and cities. Their working methods, forms of evidence and impact on policy were highly variable. The homelessness group was one of the most effective in several respects. It established a prominent task force comprising mainly external experts and commissioned a programme of research on the gaps in knowledge and lessons from previous policies. One of the interesting empirical findings relevant to this chapter was that unemployment is a particularly strong driver of homelessness. Their reports had an important impact on legislation, service delivery and long-term strategy (Scottish Executive, 2001b). They helped to strengthen the legal rights of homeless people, establish a ten-year programme of action for preventing and tackling homelessness and create a regulatory regime for relevant public services.

The neighbourhood renewal review had a low profile and undertook nothing comparable to the intensive programme of analysis and policy development involving many external advisers and officials during the English Social Exclusion Unit's review of neighbourhood strategy. The outcome was the Community Regeneration Statement, a short document containing scant analysis of the nature or causes of the problem being addressed, and little reflection on many years of experience in Scotland (Scottish Executive, 2002a). The stated aspiration – to close the gap between poor communities and the rest of society – was ambitious, but bearing in mind the widening inequalities over the last two decades and the limited apparent impact of past policies (e.g. Kearns et al, 2000; Kenway et al, 2002; Social Disadvantage Research Centre, 2003), the proposals to achieve this were thin and undeveloped.

One of the two central ideas was to make core public services more effective at meeting the needs of deprived communities through a new process of community planning. This was said to represent an important policy shift away from special initiatives and area-based projects (such as the SIPs and others listed in Footnote 5). Many of them were considered unsuccessful because they treated neighbourhoods in isolation and neglected mainstream provision. Core providers had criticized their inflexibility and were reluctant to allow their own priorities to be diverted by marginal resources – the 'tail wagging the dog'. Community planning is somewhat ill-defined and aims to encourage collaboration by public, private and non-profit organizations at local authority level, with some echoes of the comprehensive, co-ordinated approach discussed previously. At present the emphasis seems to be on service delivery rather than development (Community Planning Task Force, 2003). Its suitability for targeting particular neighbourhoods and redistributing resources to enhance the life chances of the poor has not been tested. The Statement made no mention of how to overcome the traditional difficulties in bending mainstream public services or altering the complex housing market processes and allocation systems that reinforce segregation and marginalize the poor, especially in a context of scarce resources and fragmented governance. Interim community planning mechanisms such as the Glasgow Alliance have struggled to make a difference to core policies, at least according to a recent evaluation (Rocket Science, 2002).

The second idea was to increase the capacity of local communities to do more for themselves. It was described as equipping people to take advantage of opportunities and more responsibility for what happened within their areas. This theme dates back at least to the late-1980s, although it was now couched in the language of social capital. The mechanisms for strengthening community capacity and the specific benefits to be gained were not spelt out. There is also a genuine tension that was not mentioned between decentralising power to communities and strengthening collaborative planning mechanisms at local authority level. The uncertain balance envisaged between top-down and bottom-up procedures suggests some confusion about the real intention. More generally, in shifting from 'place' to 'people' concerns, the Statement neglected the importance of the environment, physical renewal and, above all, economic infrastructure (hence jobs and incomes) as key drivers of regeneration or brakes on success. Although briefly acknowledging the wider context of neighbourhoods, it ignored the disparities between different parts of Scotland and the greater all-round ability of relatively prosperous cities to improve conditions in their deprived localities compared with those exposed to extensive poverty, dereliction and stretched organizational capacity. Once again, it seems that neighbourhood regeneration is tending towards a limited, inward-looking approach, when English policy is developing a broader perspective (Hastings, 2003).

Ambiguities surrounding the cities review

A Review of Scotland's Cities was launched in 2001, two years after urban issues began to gather momentum in England with the Rogers Task Force. This was the first time there was a specific focus on cities as spatial units. It had a rather general remit to review the prospects for the economic, environmental and social development of Scotland's five cities and to identify Executive policies to improve them. Nevertheless, this gave scope for economic issues to feature alongside concerns about people and place, and for the consistency of Executive policies towards the cities to be considered. The Review was led by a small group of officials from the Executive's Policy Unit, rather than an independent task force, but drew on occasional contributions from a Sounding Board of external practitioners and an Academic Panel. It assembled whatever statistical evidence and previous research it could find on the state of Scotland's cities. This informed an extensive review of changes in the population, economy and labour market, housing and neighbourhoods, city centres, derelict land, transport connections, environmental waste, city governance and finance. Although the 'analysis' report that was released early in 2003 did not contain specific policy recommendations as such, embedded here and there in the text were various prompts to the Executive and other public organizations (Scottish Executive, 2002b).

For interested observers, the report was a useful compilation of information and insights, some of which could not have been obtained without an official review. It provided a wide-ranging evidence base documenting many trends and issues, rather than a systematic account of the drivers and dynamics of urban change. It showed an improvement in their recent economic performance with considerable variation: Edinburgh had done particularly well (assisted in part by the location of the Parliament) and Glasgow had turned around its employment trajectory, but Dundee was a source of concern on several counts. It also pointed to the cities' positive impacts on their wider regions, although fragmented governance and constrained boundaries impeded coherent development and management of the functional city-regions. Stronger alliances were therefore suggested between city core and suburban authorities. The redevelopment of derelict land and speedier provision of transport infrastructure were among the issues said to require more serious consideration, including dedicated delivery vehicles and more resources. More coherent city centre strategies were also supported, including culture, tourism, retailing and the public realm.

The report was formidable for policymakers to digest: 275 pages long, very diverse in content and no overall summary, index, chapter synopses or schema to guide readers through the lengthy exposition. A simple list of practical priorities and longer-term challenges would have been helpful, along with the issues requiring further analysis. The basic approach and tone of different sections were variable, comprising a mixture of fairly straightforward description of patterns and policies (e.g. transport), rather cursory discussion with little about policy (e.g. education and demographics), deeper analysis with more poignant policy messages (e.g. housing), and more discursive treatment with ambivalent policy implications (e.g. finance and labour market). This presumably reflected the uneven state of knowledge and the authors' understanding, combined with some policy sensitivities, since many of these issues are contested. The first and final chapters were much more assertive in pressing the Executive to take geography more seriously in its mainstream policies, and to recognize the cities' contribution to Scotland's economic, social and environmental development. These were important points to convey, although sceptics would have expected more robust analysis and evidence to be persuaded. Assistance with some of the tough choices facing the Executive might also have been useful, such as methods of deciding between competing territorial interests (e.g. rural areas, towns and cities; and cities facing strong growth pressures versus those with greater needs), and identifying the appropriate composition of economic and social policies to tackle urban poverty and exclusion.

Published at the same time was a slim action statement 'Building Better Cities' that was effectively the policy response (Scottish Executive, 2002c). It said the Executive had drawn two conclusions from the Review: cities are at the centre of Scotland's economic growth and dynamism; and each has an important role to play in the development of their surrounding region. The main announcement was a City Growth Fund of £90 million over three years for infrastructure to support economic development. It was allocated in a neutral way, essentially in proportion to the population of the core local authority, rather than some other measure of need or potential[7]. To secure their share, the city authorities were given four months to prepare a strategy and implementation plan (a City Vision) to justify the new investment. This had to be done in consultation with other local stakeholders and neighbouring authorities. The second announcement was a £20 million fund over three years to help tackle vacant and derelict land in Glasgow, Dundee and North Lanarkshire. A team led by the Executive would devise new delivery mechanisms for this. Further consultation was promised on vehicles to redevelop land and improve city centres.

The Review's publication in this form was a source of some ambiguity. A positive interpretation is that it marked the beginning of a process that could lead to a more concerted approach to planning and managing Scotland's cities. The Review could signal a need for functional departments of the Executive to take space and place more seriously and to devote more attention to the cities. It could prompt a more integrated vision at national level linking the agendas of economic growth with improved public services and stronger communities. After many years of neglect, the derelict land fund could demonstrate the value of up-front public investment in decontamination, site consolidation, etc. The analysis report could stimulate debate and encourage further research into the distinctive challenges and opportunities facing cities, thereby improving understanding for the longer-term. Perhaps most important, the City Vision process could lay the foundations for coherent strategic frameworks for each city-region which would spell out the roles and responsibilities of different public organizations at different levels, help to align local and national agendas in a way that has often been missing, and give local communities, non-profit making organizations and the private sector a tangible development plan to engage with. This is important for consistent sound judgements to be made about investment rather than ad hoc decisions based on projects[8].

An alternative interpretation is that this was a limited response to the many challenges facing cities, with few concrete outcomes. Although it is too soon to judge, the new funds could turn out to be separate one-off initiatives of the kind the Executive has said it is trying to limit in order to tackle issues more directly by making mainstream programmes more effective. No procedures were mentioned to ensure that a more comprehensive cities policy would be developed over time, particularly within the Executive (e.g. through a White Paper, a Cities Network or regular Forum of key interests). By requiring local organizations to prepare the

7 Of course this was to the disadvantage of under-bounded cities (particularly Glasgow and Dundee) and favoured those with a generous boundary (e.g. Stirling).

8 Tangible signs of a more positive approach to Scotland's cities in recent years include the announcement of a series of separate infrastructure projects: airport rail links to Edinburgh and Glasgow, a new tram network in Edinburgh, a city bypass in Aberdeen, completion of the M74 extension in Glasgow, completion of missing links in the Central Scotland road network, Glasgow's Housing Stock Transfer and Intermediate Technology Institutes in three of the cities (Scottish Executive, 2002c and 2003).

City Visions independently, the Executive may have passed on some of the responsibility from its own departments and agencies. It is not clear that the messages from the Review about the structural, financial and boundary problems hindering the cities had been absorbed, or that further investigations would be undertaken. Although the additional resources and their flexibility were welcomed locally, they need to be put into perspective in relation to the scale of what is required and the existing level of public investment in the cities from all sources, much of which is formula-driven and independently administered. There was no sign of new thinking on alternative instruments to boost public investment further, such as tax increment financing for derelict land or local retention of some of the revenues from growing the business tax base, as is happening in England.

According to participants, the process of preparing the City Visions was generally constructive, despite the time constraints. It prompted them to rise above their day-to-day concerns with delivering services and projects to consider the bigger picture of how their cities were changing, including the relationships between different activities and interactions with areas beyond their boundaries. They were encouraged to raise their aspirations and contemplate alternative possibilities for the future of their cities. In many places local politicians got interested and involved in strategic decisions for the first time. A useful dialogue and goodwill were also established across organizational and geographical boundaries in recognition of their interdependent interests. Local actors were concerned, however, that there might be little follow-through from key Executive departments and agencies to take the process forward and build upon the momentum achieved. They felt it would be helpful to have stronger leadership and commitment from the centre – perhaps a national champion for the cities. Otherwise, the City Visions might have a limited shelf life, having merely justified the extra funds. For a lasting impact they needed to be linked to core strategy and budgetary procedures at national level, as well as local mechanisms for planning and delivering development, including regional transport partnerships, structure plans, local economic forums and community plans.

Conclusion

Urban policy in Scotland has a patchy record. Many urban areas have experienced severe economic difficulties and a catalogue of serious social and environmental problems, some of which were exacerbated by wider government policies. For many years the support available under urban policy was very limited in scale and highly selective in where it was focused. Urban initiatives were divorced from mainstream service programmes and undermined by regional economic policies. Many urban projects in the 1980s and 1990s ended up addressing the symptoms of problems rather than tackling the causes or preventing future problems. Despite repeated claims to be pursuing a comprehensive, co-ordinated approach, the focus in practice was on housing, training and community support. Although selected households and neighbourhoods undoubtedly benefited, successive evaluations revealed a serious shortfall between the overall objective of sustainable regeneration and the practical achievements. Considering the enormous challenges faced in many of these areas, there was surprisingly little investment in analysis and evidence to improve understanding of the problems, to test assumptions about their causes and dynamics, and to learn robust lessons for future policies.

Differences are emerging post-devolution, reinforced by a different party being in power. The values of the new administration appear more sympathetic in principle to urban social problems and there is greater political will to make a difference. The whole policy process has also become more open and inclusive, allowing wider influences beyond the administration to be brought to bear. This has created a more fluid situation in which there are greater opportunities for policies to develop and for specific spending decisions to change. For instance, external pressure has brought about several commitments to major urban infrastructure projects that would have been less likely before. This greater willingness to invest in transport improvements, derelict land reclamation and other capital projects appears to be a significant development that could help to lay the foundations for increasing urban prosperity.

Yet it would be premature to say that the Executive has an urban policy, or has even fully recognized the distinctive challenges and opportunities of cities. Different national strategies and policy approaches co-exist, some of which have an explicit urban aspect, while others are neutral or indifferent to cities. The situation is not straightforward, indeed it is contradictory in various respects, and is evolving over time. The original statements of Scottish economic and social policy did not specify the implications for cities, although some public agencies seem to have become more supportive of a cities perspective subsequently. Other Executive departments seem to be sceptical of an emphasis on place and resistant to an integrated cities approach. There is a widespread feeling at the local level that stronger national leadership is needed to take forward the urban agenda. Below the national scale there is a variety of partnership arrangements being established or reformed at neighbourhood, local authority and city-region levels with overlapping remits, so there is some uncertainty about how decisions will be made and where the locus of power will lie. The ultimate balance between a community-based neighbourhood approach, a more corporatist council-wide procedure, and a functional city-region perspective is likely to vary between cities, so Scottish urban policy in future will probably look different in different areas. Whatever detailed local arrangements transpire, it seems inevitable that there will be enduring common concerns facing all cities that will require a serious and sustained response from higher authorities.

References

Bailey, N. and Robertson, D. (1997), 'Housing renewal, urban policy and gentrification', *Urban Studies*, vol. 34(4), pp. 561-78.

Bailey, N., Turok, I. and Docherty, I. (1999), *Edinburgh and Glasgow: Contrasts in Competitiveness and Cohesion*, Department of Urban Studies, University of Glasgow, Glasgow.

Bailey, N., Docherty, I. and Turok, I. (2002), 'Dimensions of city competitiveness: Edinburgh and Glasgow in a UK context', in I. Begg (ed), *Urban Competitiveness: Policies for Dynamic Cities*, The Policy Press, Bristol.

Beatty, C., Fothergill, S., Gore, T. and Green, A. (2002), *The Real Level of Unemployment 2002*, Sheffield Hallam University, Sheffield.

Community Planning Task Force (2003), *Final Report*, Scottish Executive, Edinburgh.

Crichton, T. (2002), 'Countryside alliances: rural Scotland', in G. Hassan and C. Warhurst (eds), *Anatomy of the New Scotland*, Mainstream, Edinburgh.

Dewar, D. (1998), Scottish Urban Regeneration Forum Inaugural Annual Lecture, Edinburgh, 8 May.

Duguid, G. (1995), *Deprived Areas in Scotland: Results of an Analysis of the 1991 Census*, Central Research Unit, The Scottish Office, Edinburgh.

EKOS (2001), *Review of the Strategic Sites Programme*, Scottish Enterprise Glasgow, Glasgow.

Ford, M. and Casebow, P. (2002), 'The civil service', in G. Hassan, G. and C. Warhurst (eds), *Anatomy of the New Scotland*, Mainstream, Edinburgh.

Hastings, A. (2003), 'Strategic, multi-level neighbourhood regeneration: an outward looking approach at last?', in R. Imrie and M. Raco (eds), *Urban Renaissance? New Labour, Community, and Urban Policy*, The Policy Press, Bristol.

Kearns, A., Gibb, K. and Mackay, D. (2000), 'Area deprivation in Scotland: a new assessment', *Urban Studies*, vol. 37(9), pp. 1535-59.

Keating, M. (1988), *The City that Refused to Die*, Aberdeen University Press, Aberdeen.

Keating, M. and Boyle, R. (1986), *Remaking Urban Scotland*, Edinburgh University Press, Edinburgh.

Kenway, P., Fuller, S., Rahman, M., Street, C. and Palmer, G. (2002), *Monitoring Poverty and Social Exclusion in Scotland*, Joseph Rowntree Foundation, York.

Kintrea, K., Pawson, H., Munro, M., Carley, M. and Lancaster, S (1998), *Interim Evaluation of Smaller Urban Renewal Initiatives*, Research Report 63, Scottish Homes, Edinburgh.

Lever, W. and Moore, C. (1986), *The City in Transition*, Clarendon Press, Oxford.

Levitt, I. (1997), 'New Towns, new Scotland, new ideology, 1937-57', *The Scottish Historical Review*, vol. 76(2), pp. 222-38.

Levitt, I. (1999), 'The Scottish Air Services, 1933-75 and the Scottish New Towns, 1943-75: a guide to the records at the National Archives of Scotland', *Scottish Archives*, vol. 5, pp. 67-82.

McCrone, G. (1991), 'Urban renewal: the Scottish experience', *Urban Studies*, vol. 28(6), pp. 919-38.

Maclennan, D. (1987), 'Rehabilitating older housing', in D. Donnison and A. Middleton (eds), *Regenerating the Inner City: Glasgow's Experience*, Routledge, London.

Maclennan, D. (1993), 'Spillovers, expectations and residents' beliefs in a housing revitalisation programme: Glasgow 1977-87', *Tijdschrift voor Economische en Social Geographie*, vol. 84(4), pp. 294-303.

ODPM (2003), *Cities, Regions and Competitiveness*, Second Report from the Working Group of Government Departments, the Core Cities and the Regional Development Agencies, ODPM, London.

Office for National Statistics (2002), *Annual Local Area Labour Force Survey 2001-02*, ONS, London.

Paterson, L. (2002), 'Civic democracy', in G. Hassan and C. Warhurst (eds), *Anatomy of the New Scotland*, Mainstream, Edinburgh.

Robertson, D. (1998), 'Pulling in opposite directions: the failure of post-war planning to regenerate Glasgow', *Planning Perspectives*, vol. 13, pp. 53-67.

Rocket Science (2002), *More Than the Sum of its Parts? An Evaluation of the Glasgow Alliance*, Glasgow Alliance, Glasgow.
Scottish Executive (1999), *Social Justice – A Scotland Where Everyone Matters*, Scottish Executive, Edinburgh.
Scottish Executive (2000), *The Way Forward: Framework for Economic Development in Scotland*, Scottish Executive, Edinburgh.
Scottish Executive (2001a), *A Smart, Successful Scotland*, Scottish Executive, Edinburgh.
Scottish Executive (2001b), *Helping Homeless People*, Scottish Executive, Edinburgh.
Scottish Executive (2002a), *Better Communities in Scotland: Closing the Gap*, Scottish Executive, Edinburgh.
Scottish Executive (2002b), *Review of Scotland's Cities: The Analysis*, Scottish Executive, Edinburgh.
Scottish Executive (2002c), *Building Better Cities*, Scottish Executive, Edinburgh.
Scottish Executive (2003), *A Partnership for a Better Scotland: Partnership Agreement*, Scottish Executive, Edinburgh.
Scottish Office (1988), *New Life for Urban Scotland*, The Scottish Office, Edinburgh.
Scottish Office (1993), *Progress in Partnership: Consultation Paper on the Future of Urban Regeneration Policy in Scotland*, The Scottish Office, Edinburgh.
Scottish Office (1995), *Programme for Partnership: Consultation Paper on Implementation Arrangements*, The Scottish Office, Edinburgh.
Scottish Office (1998), *Promoting Social Inclusion: The Strategic Framework*, The Scottish Office, Edinburgh.
Social Disadvantage Research Centre (2003), *The Scottish Indices of Deprivation 2003*, Scottish Executive, Edinburgh.
Strathclyde Regional Council (1992), *Survey of Industrial and Business Floorspace 1991*, Strathclyde Regional Council, Glasgow.
Tarling, R. et al (1999), *An Evaluation of the New Life for Urban Scotland Initiative*, Development Department Research Findings No. 70, Scottish Executive, Edinburgh.
Turok, I. (1992), 'Property-led urban regeneration: panacea or placebo?', *Environment and Planning A*, vol. 24(2), pp. 361-79.
Turok, I. (2000), *Inclusive Cities: Building Local Capacity for Development*, European Commission, Luxembourg.
Turok, I. et al (2003), *Twin Track Cities: Linking prosperity and cohesion in Glasgow and Edinburgh*, Department of Urban Studies, University of Glasgow.
Turok, I. and Bailey, N. (forthcoming), 'Glasgow's recent performance: unbalanced growth and its consequences', in D. Newlands (ed), *Divided Scotland?* Ashgate, Aldershot.
Turok, I. and Edge, N. (1999), *The Jobs Gap in Britain's Cities: Employment Loss and Labour Market Consequences*, The Policy Press, Bristol.
Turok, I. and Hopkins, N. (1998), 'Competition and area selection in Scotland's new urban policy', *Urban Studies*, vol. 35(11), pp. 2021-61.
Tyler, P. et al (2002), *National Evaluation of the Former Regeneration Programmes*, Development Department Research Findings, Scottish Executive, Edinburgh.
Wannop, U. (1995), *The Regional Imperative*, Jessica Kingsley, London.
Webster, D. (1994), *Home and Workplace in the Glasgow Conurbation*, Housing Department, Glasgow City Council, Glasgow.
Webster, D. (2000), 'Scottish social inclusion policy: a critical assessment', *Scottish Affairs*, vol. 30, pp. 30-50.
Webster, D. (2002), 'Urban regeneration under devolution: inheritance and prospects', *Fraser of Allander Institute Quarterly Economic Commentary*, vol. 27(4), pp. 40-6.
WCSP (1974), *West Central Scotland Plan: A Programme of Action*, West Central Scotland Plan Steering Committee, Glasgow.

Chapter 8

Governing the Cities Urban Renaiss

Rob Imrie

Introduction

> If places are for people, then people must help make the places (DETR, 2000a, p.2).

The conditions of life and living in cities are a perennial concern of government. Ever since Victorian urban reformers, such as Edwin Chadwick and Octavia Hill, and urban visionaries, such as Ebenezer Howard and Patrick Geddes, raised concerns about urban living, the population of cities has been a target for a panoply of policy measures. Such measures have ranged from sanitary reform and municipal housekeeping, to techniques of self-help, including the promotion of health, good hygiene, and the inculcation of habits of good parenting. As Cruikshank (1999, p.123), and others, suggest, the targets of these measures were those people perceived to be defective citizens, 'not for what they do or what they have been made into but for what they lack' (also, see Osborne and Rose, 1999). Thus, government, through the (self) activation of those characterized as the poor, the apathetic, and the feckless, became the basis for the revitalization of cities, a policy focus that continues to this day through the contours of New Labour's strategies for urban renaissance (see Imrie and Raco, 2003).

Such strategies emphasize the importance of partnerships between government and civil society, and the obligations of citizens to take responsibility for the content of their lives. As Tony Blair (Social Exclusion Unit (SEU), 2001, p.5) has suggested, 'unless the community is fully engaged in shaping and delivering regeneration, even the best plans on paper will fail to deliver in practice'. Defining, mobilising and institutionalising agencies and groups so that they can participate in their own governance, therefore, is a central element of policy-making. Thus, far from the state being cast as a coherent and calculating political subject, it is but one amongst many institutions, agencies, or groups which constitute, in Dean's (1999, p.72) terms, a 'plurality of diversity which shape how a field is to be governed'. The mentalities of government, or what Foucault (1977 and 1979) refers to as *governmentality*, become the critical focus of (policy) investigation in which the state is no more than a specific form of government.

This Foucauldian perspective, of state-society relations, provides valuable insights into the nature and logics of urban policy (see Cruikshank, 1999; Raco

, 2000; Raco, 2003). Foremost, it implies that an understanding of policy cannot be reduced to any particular source or mode/form of ntion, or to the study of different administrative agencies, and their interests actions. Rather, modes of intervention, and their particular organizational ms, are themselves to be explained. Foucault (1977 and 1979) enables analysts o note that relations of empowerment, so often claimed of urban policy, are always double edged, 'opening free space for the choices of individual actors whilst enwrapping these autonomized actors within new forms of control' (Rose, 1999, p.xxiii). In this regard, (urban) policy is neither apolitical nor amoral in content. In distinction, it is to be understood in terms of an underlying moral authority, or discourses that make (value) claims about the nature of state and society.

In this chapter, I develop the contention that New Labour's urban policies need to be understood as governmental rationalities, techniques and programmes that shape the conduct of urban populations, and the material and political spaces of urban governance. After Foucault, urban policy can be thought of as a form of bio-power in seeking to regulate life and its needs, particularly in relation to what Foucault (1979, p.9) refers to as 'the anti social bodies of the poor, deviant and unhealthy'. The next section briefly outlines the lineaments of governmentality, followed by an interpretation of the government of cities in the period from the late 19th century to the onset of New Labour's urban policies in the late 1990s. In particular, I focus on New Labour's policy emphasis on the re-activation of the active citizen through the context of community. I conclude by drawing out the broader relevance of using the concept of governmentality as a way of seeking to understand contemporary urban policy processes.

The lineaments of governmentality

The conduct of government in western societies is governed, in part, by its commitment to liberal values. Such values, as Foucault (1977) suggests, conceive of limits to political authority and the role of government in everyday life. Citizens, and civil society, are the fulcrum for choices and action in which government intervenes to ensure individuals' liberties, rights, and freedom. Interventions are based upon the cultivation of knowledge of the subject by government, and the use of experts and programmes through which to develop and administer policy. In particular, liberal rule seeks to facilitate what Foucault (1980, p.64) refers to as 'techniques of the self' or where, as Burchell (1996, p.20) suggests, a 'loosening of the connection between subjectification and subjection' occurs. Government, then, is the conduct of conduct or where indirect, non coercive, techniques are deployed by the state in order to guide and control individuals' behaviour, while insisting that such behaviour is the responsibility of individuals themselves.

Governmentality is the basis of political thought and action, or, as Foucault (1979, p.8) defines it, 'an ensemble formed by the institutions, procedures, analyses and reflections, the calculations and tactics, that allow the exercise of this very specific albeit complex form of power'. It is characterized by particular ways 'of thinking about the kinds of problems that can and should be addressed by various authorities' (Miller and Rose, 1990, p.2). These 'ways of thinking' are political rationalities or discourses that seek to direct the conduct of others or ourselves. Political rationalities are diffused throughout a panoply of institutions, agencies and groups and are underpinned by moral justifications which seek to describe the values and principals that government should be seeking to propagate (on this theme, see Rose and Miller, 1992). They are characterized by some description of the people or persons who are the subjects of government, such as parts of the population to be managed.

Political rationalities define the nature of subjects to be governed and, in doing so identify spheres of social life that are to be subject to government intervention. As Lemke (2001) notes, (urban) policy can be understood, in part, as Government defining a discursive field in which the exercise of power is rationalized. As suggested, particular forms of knowledge and expertise are deployed in order to identify problems and the courses of action required to solve them. This can occur through a variety of means, including the delineation of concepts, the specification of objects and boundaries, and the provision of arguments and justifications. This involves, what Miller and Rose (1990, p.1) refer to as, the deployment of 'writing, listing, numbering and computing that render a realm into discourse as a knowable, calculable and administrative object'. In this way, government is able to address problems by deploying particular strategies or courses of action (see Lemke, 2001, p.191).

Governmentality is also characterized by programmes of government or what Dean (1999, p.32) refers to as the intrinsically programmatic character of government. Programmatic behaviour is diverse and seeks to influence actors' adherence to routinized, bureaucratic and procedural mechanisms and modes of conduct. Rose and Miller (1992, p.181) conceive of government as a 'problematising' activity that seeks to reconcile the failures and difficulties of governing, from the inability to resolve urban unrest and tensions, to the threats of environmental destruction. Government, in seeking to respond to the 'problematics' of its subject matter, becomes programmatic through the context of White Papers, other official documents, committees of inquiry, etc., all of which seek to transform regimes of (government) practice. The programmatic nature of government offers the possibility of a panacea by calculative and normalising forms of intervention, that is, by recourse to 'rules, norms, and processes that can be acted upon and improved by authorities' (Rose and Miller, 1992, p.183).

The operation of programmes occurs through strategies, techniques, and procedures or what Foucault termed 'technologies of government'. Such technologies seek to deploy political rationalities and programmes of government through what Miller and Rose (1990, p.3) conceive of as 'the complex assemblage of diverse forces – legal, architectural, professional, administrative, financial, judgemental – such that aspects of the decisions and actions of individuals, groups, organizations, and populations come to be understood and regulated in relation to authoritative criteria'. The techniques of government are many and varied and are the practical aspects of government which constitute logistical and infrastructural powers, and subsume the moral and political shaping of conduct by performance criteria. Thus, such techniques of performance range from auditing to bench marking, and from the devolution of budgets to the introduction of cost centres, all of which seek to control domains of expertise by recourse to calculative regimes.

Governing the cities

Seeking to govern the cities is not a new or novel problem for government. As Rose (2000, p.95) suggests, 'the city, for at least two centuries, has been both a problem for government and a permanent incitement to government'. Others concur, with Cruikshank (1999) noting that the practical arts of liberal government, such as charities and philanthropic work, were an integral feature of the 19th century city (also, see Dean, 1999). This was a period of the 'discovery of evils' within the city and the emergence of the classificatory state. Representations of the city ranged widely from organic metaphors (and the pathologizing of people and place) to military and mechanical analogies. Thus, as Osborne and Rose (1999, p.739) suggest, 'from the 19th century the government of the city *becomes inseparable from the continuous activity of generating truths about the city*'. Such truths, throughout the 20th century, have given shape to a myriad of political rationalities and programmes of government in relation to the city.

These have tended to be underpinned, and characterized, by an enduring discourse about the nature of urbanism and the urban population. It conceives of the city as a place where part of the population is dependent on welfare, and where the 'evils of dependency' must be removed (on this theme, see Sennett, 2003). Throughout the last one hundred years, the conduct of conduct has been aimed at what Blair (SEU, 1998, p.1) refers to as the mission of the state 'to encourage work not dependency' by virtue of the application of strategies of self-sufficiency that inculcate good personal habits in deviant citizens. Thus, from the deployment of charity and care-giving in the late 19th century, to the current use of social entrepreneurs and community programmes, strategies of government in cities have revolved around those people that discourses have rendered as problems because of their (personal) failures to resolve their poverty, poor housing, social exclusion, and marginalization from society.

Such discourses underpinned the origins of modern urban policy in the period from 1968 to 1977. During this period, policy (initially launched and administrated by the Home Office) was concerned with social measures, primarily delivered through the Urban Programme and Community Development Programmes (see Atkinson and Moon, 1994; Edwards, 1997; Raco and Imrie, 2000). These programmes sought to tackle localized concentrations of poverty although they also served a wider governmental purpose of placating and controlling increasingly deprived and potentially restless urban populations. The subjectivities of urban populations were recast with those living in deprived neighbourhoods characterized as part of the problem, requiring the injection of resources and expertise from external sources. As Rose (1996, p.332) notes, such communities were delimited as zones that were subject to various forms of government inquiry

and investigation, including the classification of persona
behaviour, and their documentation and mapping.

This period was characterized by the 'rediscovery of
emergence of urban initiatives. These were channelled through
the lead organizations in developing and delivering services that
help and mutual aid in areas defined as being in poverty and
particular forms of deprivation. The terrain of government estab
improvement, comprehensive community programmes, and ...ity
development programmes, defined, in legal terms, the poor as a pro... and the
need for them to be conjoined with government experts and agencies in the fight against (their) poverty. This, then, was a period in which the inner city poor were (re)invented as a group with interests and powers, and who was enlisted as self help agents, through voluntary programmes, to enable 'government at a distance'. Such reinvention, however, did not really depart from pathological conceptions of the urban subject and, in this sense continuity was maintained with the past.

As Lemke (2001) notes, neo-liberalism is a political rationality that tries to render the social domain economic and to link a reduction in state services to an increase in personal responsibility and self-care. This was the broader context underpinning the shifting nature of urban policy from the late 1970s. It was a period (1977 to 1990) in which the pursuit of entrepreneurial rationales and programmes of government were paramount. Inner cities became new territories of government to be acted upon and transformed in ways that made them entrepreneurial and competitive. Discourses of community revolved around (the moral) notions of self-help and the activation of voluntary organizations and associations. New actors, primarily private sector players, became the focus of policy on the basis of their perceived expertise and resources and the ways in which these related to wider central government objectives.

The era saw the (re)surfacing of discourses of urban policy that sought to conceive of the individual as an active agent in their own economic governance, or through the enhancement of their own skills, capacities, and entrepreneurship. Urban policy was being shaped by the political rationality to normalize and naturalize, explicitly, the market, and, in doing so, to provide support for the emergence of flexible labour markets and public austerity. The art of government in this period was characterized by the denigration of the state, or what Peck (2001, p.446) refers to as neo-liberal states engineering their own reform and downsizing. This (re)moralization of urban policy played a significant symbolic and practical role in legitimating and exemplifying the merits of Thatcherite principles which eschewed the concept of 'Society' and sought to replace it by new subjectivities of entrepreneurialism and self-reliance.

However, the combination of property market failures in the early 1990s, and political pressure to redress the lack of community benefit from regeneration, led to a reappraisal of the *raison d'être* of urban policy, post 1990 (see Oatley, 1998; Colenutt, 1999; Imrie and Thomas, 1999). In particular, the period 1990 to 1997 saw a re-drawing of the dimensions of urban policy and the introduction of new forms of subjectivity, expertise and control. Directed, active citizenship, both collective and individual, came to play a growing role in policy-making and

…mentation procedures. Communities, as collectivities, were 're-discovered' in …rban policy and came to be characterized as both the diagnosis and the cure for socio-economic problems. Their absence from policy-making was, so it was argued, a factor in the decline of urban areas and hence their reinvigoration would enable policy agendas to be established and implemented by local people living and working in the areas concerned.

The reinvention of communities went hand in hand with the establishment of partnerships at the local level and new mechanisms of surveillance and control. As such, the period can be characterized as one in which specific forms of local partnership were promoted, from the top-down, in order to mobilize and control the actions of subjects in the pursuit of broader policy objectives (also, see Raco and Imrie, 2000; Atkinson, 2003; Raco, 2003). However, this did not necessarily involve the dilution of neo-liberal ideals, or the truncation of property-led regeneration. Rather, neo-liberalism, or the pursuit of individual freedom and choice through the context of the market, was being (re)activated through new social and organizational networks that sought, in part, to conjoin discourses of social justice and equity with the efficacy of the market. Amongst all of this, processes of government(ality) were, in Foucauldian terms, becoming more distant whilst, paradoxically, becoming more centralized.

Extending rights and responsibilities: urban policy under New Labour

New Labour has if anything heightened the centralizing political agenda since 1997. Blair's approach to the cities, as in other policy areas, is one of benign authoritarianism coupled with central-localist principles that seek to create the social, political, and organizational contexts for the modernization of the British state. Such modernization is based on a populist agenda that blames, in part, the inefficiencies and intransigence of public servants (and their rules, processes, and procedures) for preventing the development and delivery of social opportunity and wealth. The solution is to expand the scope of personal choice by permitting the extension of the mixed economy of welfare through the favoured route, that is, the (quasi) privatization of public services. The promise is the delivery of the liberal ideal of freedom of choice, unfettered by (central) government, and the restoration of power at a local scale that provides individuals with access to organizations that determine their quality of life.

The illusion of democratization and localism revolves around, and is bolstered by, the discourse of the active citizen, or the notion that 'for citizens to constitute the process of government depends upon them being able to play a full role in society' (Prior et al, 1995, p.72). The focus on the active citizen, in itself, is not original. It was, for example, part of the Thatcherite ideology for encouraging voluntary and community behaviour in the context of a reduced role for the state. However, the emergent tactics of government situate it at the centre of state-civil society relations in which citizens, playing an active role in the constitution and governance of society, offer a way forward in a context of growing social fragmentation, life opportunities, and expectations. Active citizens are defined, not

through consumerist power, or primarily as passive electors in repr
democratic elections, but as democratic agents, empowering themselves
their challenges to the activities of institutions and organizations which sh
everyday lives (see Hirst, 1994).

Many of the rationalities and technologies of government that characterized previous Conservative governments have been expanded by New Labour since 1997. These include new definitions of community, broader, more inclusive, local partnerships, and new methods of auditing, accounting and surveillance. Underlying the New Labour approach has been the extension of obligations and urban policy has focused on extending conditional rights to communities and citizens based upon the fulfilment of responsibilities. Following Rose (1996, p.352), one has seen the emergent forms of urban policy as part of 'advanced liberalism' or strategies which use 'citizens, individually and collectively, as ideally and potentially "active" in their own government'. Such strategies aim to produce self-managing citizens taking on more personal responsibility for their welfare while avoiding states of dependency (also, see Burchell, 1996; Cruikshank, 1999; Dean, 1999).

New Labour has highlighted the 'new deal' between government and citizens through a range of well-publicized speeches by ministers and follow-up policy documents and proposals. In particular, the language of a new moral order and subject has been evoked, based on the empowerment of the individual and the withdrawal of government (interference) from public life. In the Urban White Paper it is noted that 'government can offer a partnership to local people to rebuild a community, it must deliver basic services; but government can't do it for them' (DETR, 2000a, p.2). In addition it is suggested that 'government today is a partner not a master' (DETR, 2000a, p.2). Likewise, Mulgan (1998, p.200), notes that 'to the extent that powers and responsibilities can be passed down to smaller scales, politics and government can be freed to concentrate on what they alone can do...of thinking strategically, while leaving citizens and communities to govern themselves'. The inference is that too much government is a cause of the problems of cities.

However, as Lemke (2001) suggests, the neo-liberal agenda for the withdrawal of the state is a technique of government that seeks to reassert the power of central administration and its control of policy. In this sense, the apparent withdrawal of New Labour from direct control of urban policy is, arguably, connected to the emergence of indirect techniques for the control and subjection of urban subjects (Raco and Imrie, 2000; Imrie and Raco, 2003). For instance, for New Labour, neighbourhood decline has occurred because 'government failed to harness the knowledge and energy of local people, or empower them to develop their own solutions' (SEU, 2001). The remedy is, as the government has suggested, one whereby 'our policies, programmes and structures of governance are about engaging local people in a partnership for change and enabling communities to take a decisive role in their future' (DETR, 2000a, p.2).

The critical part of this passage is the emphasis on *our* policies and programmes. This reveals that any divesting of central control will be conditional, in that urban subjects, and the communities that they are part of, are held to be accountable (by central government) for their actions (see Atkinson, 2003; Imrie and Raco, 2003; Raco, 2003). Thus, as Blair (2001, p.1) has suggested, communities, for their development, depend on individuals' acceptance of duties and responsibilities that they, 'owe to society'. For Blair, 'respect for others, responsibilities to them, is an essential prerequisite of a strong and active community' (ibid.). Thus, the success of urban policy is premised on, as Blair suggests, 'opportunity and responsibility. Both are about people, their individual development and potential; giving them the chance to develop their potential; insisting on their duty to make the most of the chance they get...individual responsibility is the key to social order' (ibid.).

Core to New Labour's urban agenda is the gathering of information, or the evidence-base, to help particular discourses produce forms of 'truth' on its subject matter. Constituting the subjects, then, relies upon the development of knowledge, isolating and identifying certain defining characteristics of those that are to be empowered (see Rose, 1999). Indeed, New Labour's discourse, about the nature of the urban subject, seeks to construct, what Lemke (2001, p.203) refers to as, 'a social reality that it suggests already exists'. One example, in the context of urban policy, is the development of indices of deprivation which are, in Castel's (1991) terms, a particular kind of 'risk technology' (also, see Raco and Imrie, 2000). This, for Dean (1995), is a means of dividing populations into discrete categories, particularly those who are seen as capable of (self) managing risk, from those (i.e. the poor) who lack the personal qualities or attributes and who require, in turn, to be subjected to particular programmes of (urban) government.

Thus, the Indices of Deprivation (DETR, 2000b) identify six broad areas in which deprivation can be identified, ranging from income to housing (for an example, see Figure 8.1). These areas, or domains as the government entitles them, are further sub-divided into 33 indicators of deprivation, including categories such as 'access to a large food store', 'poor private sector dwellings', and 'working age adults with no qualification'. Data is collected at a ward level for each category and aggregated to produce a single figure, or index, of deprivation that is amenable to translation into policy. This enables policy-makers to identify what the DETR (2000b, p.16) refers to as 'hot spots of deprivation'. For the DETR (2000b, p.12), the target is 'at risk populations' characterized by deficits in social and material circumstances, or where there are deviations from a prescribed norm (of living and habitability). In turn, indicators permit the 'at risk' population to become 'known' to government and made amenable to management through the deployment of 'appropriate' policy.

Knowledge of the subjects of government has been a consuming feature of New Labour's urban agenda. Much of the government's 'knowing' or knowledge of urban subjects has been deployed in particular ways. For instance, it has been used to re-define the terms of reference for legitimate government intervention, and to render some phenomena, such as social inequality and its consequences, as somehow natural or even innate. In particular, the deployment of a specific language or discourse has been part of a political neutering process, or where New Labour has sought to re-direct the understanding of the causes of poverty from structural to individual determinants. Such discourses have also been important in

Adults in Income Support households (DSS) for 1998
Children in Income Support households (DSS) for 1998
Adults in Income Based Job Seekers Allowance households (DSS) for 1998
Children in Income Based Job Seekers Allowance households (DSS) for 1998
Adults in Family Credit households (DSS) for 1999
Children in Family Credit households (DSS) for 1999
Adults in Disability Working Allowance households (DSS) for 1999
Children in Disability Working Allowance households (DSS) for 1999
Non-earning, non-IS pensioner and disabled Council Tax Benefit recipients (DSS) apportioned to wards

Source: DETR, 2000b, p.7

Figure 8.1 Income deprivation – summary of indicators

changing the emphasis of debate. Thus, the Urban White Paper, and other documents, suggest that the 'absence of opportunity', not social inequality, gives rise to deprivation in cities. In this sense, I concur with Rose and Miller (1992, p.179) who note that language ought to be thought of 'as a kind of intellectual machinery or apparatus for rendering reality thinkable in such a way that it is amenable to political deliberations'.

Not surprisingly, the development of the government's 'evidence-base' has not displaced pathological conceptions of the poor. Indeed, conceptions of the nature of the (urban) subject to be governed are, for New Labour, not dissimilar to late 19th century ideas about 'the great unwashed'. As the Urban White Paper notes, it is the powerlessness of the poor that is the root cause of their poverty: 'too often local people feel powerless to influence what happens in the community' (DETR, 2000a, p.33). The poverty and deprivation of the urban poor is linked to the deficits of individuals and communities, that is, to the lack of resources and knowledge. In particular, the Urban White Paper points towards the inactions and incapacities, even apathy, of the poor as sources of deprivation. The solution is for subjects to be helped to help themselves through dialogical and tutelage processes, such as 'engaging communities more in turning around their neighbourhoods', and 'working collaboratively...to make joint working the norm' (DETR, 2000a, p.110). The prognosis is self help in that 'all areas need to take positive action to take control of their future in a changing world' (DETR, 2000a, p.35).

These exhortations are evident across the range of policy initiatives for tackling urban deprivation. For instance, cadres of community workers, akin to 19th century philanthropists, have been charged with tutoring individuals and communities in deprived areas. From advice about good parenting, to compulsory workfare programmes to inculcate 'good' working habits, deviant groups and/or individuals in cities are the target of what Rose (1996) refers to as the new regimes of self-help. These programmes appear to blame-the-victim in that they seek to respond to character defects or individual deficiencies. One example is the Community Finance and Learning Initiative, set up in 2001, which notes that financial exclusion is a source of deprivation that can be remedied by improving citizens' financial literacy (Oatley, 2002; also, see Imrie and Raco, 2003, p.24). While not unimportant, a focus on improving financial literacy is, potentially, to the detriment of changing broader, structural, relations, such as the unwillingness of bank's to provide credit to people living in certain neighbourhoods.

Self-activation, as the key to urban renaissance, is also occurring alongside programmes of government that have, at their core, the assessment and auditing of policy. New Labour's urban agenda comprises the expansion of policy target setting and achievement, characterized by a heightening of the surveillance of policy-makers and (self) active citizens through evaluation. Thus, Public Service Agreements – contracts between central government and local authorities to agree targets for improving the delivery of key services in return for greater operational freedom and financial rewards – are key to urban renaissance. Likewise, the Urban White Paper is suffused with the ideology of the 'evidence-base', of propagating a 'can-do' culture that seeks to identify 'what works', and where the development and attainment of performance indicators and targets, 'handed down' by central government, becomes the measure of urban policy success or failure (Wilks-Heeg, 2003). Govern(mentality), then, becomes institutionalized through discourses of evaluation.

In particular, the demise of the welfare state is, as Burchell (1996) suggests, being paralleled by the rise of 'performance government', in which multiple agencies seek, in their various ways, to administer to the plight of the poor. In this respect, particular techniques of government have surfaced including the Neighbourhood Renewal Unit, Community Strategies, Local Strategic Partnerships (LSPs), Social Entrepreneurs, and numerous partnerships and action zones of one type or another. Each, in their different ways, seeks to apply the knowledge of the urban poor in ways that are consistent with the political rationalities of advanced liberal thinking. That is, to cultivate new forms of professional expertise to shape and normalize the self-regulating capacities of people in deprived areas. Such expertise tends to take the form of experts who seek to advise, to direct or counsel, that is, benevolent expertism that places itself, allegedly, at the disposal of communities (Imrie, 1996; Wilks-Heeg, 2003).

The new expertism in urban policy conjures up Foucault's (1977) conception of pastoral power, or where the state's relationship to civil society is akin to that of a shepherd (the expert) to his or her flock of sheep (the urban subject). Indeed, urban subjects are increasingly dependent, for their welfare, on various agencies and, in Dean's (1999, p.76) terms, must, by necessity, seek out and obey 'the directions of pastoral agents'. This is evident across the terrain of urban policy, from the rule-based nature of the Single Regeneration Budget, which requires the deployment of expert knowledge in order to access funds, to the operations of LSPs, 'top-down' agencies albeit with community representation (see Edwards, 2003; Morrison, 2003; Wilks-Heeg, 2003). Such agencies are no more than the linking of political calculations in central government with actions elsewhere, through what Miller and Rose (1990, p.10) refer to as 'a delicate affiliation of a loose assemblage of agents and agencies into a functioning network'.

Conclusions

Foucault's concept of governmentality has received much attention and application in the social sciences yet, with some notable exceptions, has rarely been related to an understanding of urban policy processes (although, see Raco and Imrie, 2000; Atkinson, 2003)[1]. This is curious because the concept of governmentality provides researchers with a sophisticated series of analytical devices with which to dissect the complexities of government and public policy-making. It does so in ways that, potentially, avoid statist formulations or ignore the potency of multiple and overlapping sources of power. In particular, researchers' attention is drawn to conceptions of liberty and freedom, and to the variety of ways in which the ideals of liberal political rationalities become the driving forces of policy programmes. In this respect, the main contribution of the approach lies in its inter-linking of the mentalities, norms, aspirations and actions of members of the population with the objectives and techniques of (advanced liberal) government.

The focus on governmentality also directs analytical attention to the emergence of reflexive government seeking to manage risk, or where the deployment of audit, targets, and other technologies of performance are part of a broader political process that Dean (1999, p.193) refers to as the 'problematization, scrutiny, and reformation of government'. Thus, government itself is subjected to processes of 'governmentalization', whereby social and economic change is tackled, first and foremost, 'through the government of the mechanisms, techniques, and agencies of government themselves' (Dean, 1999, p.196). Not surprisingly, urban policy displays different aspects of this, from the dismantling of previous funding programmes, to the installation of new methods of surveillance, control, and evaluation (of the conduct of policy practitioners). The objective is nothing less than the development of transparent and accountable government (by virtue of the deployment of calculating and disciplinary measures).

Such concerns are paramount in government pronouncements and, as Tony Blair contemplates a third term of office, the rhetoric of modernization becomes ever more bound to a government(ality) that is seeking to secure the welfare of the

---

1 This chapter presents the bare bones of Foucault's concept of governmentality and interested readers will find much fuller accounts in the wonderful books by Cruikshank (1999) and Dean (1999). Also, see Raco (2003) for a good application of the governmentality thesis in relation to contemporary urban policy programmes.

population by recourse to heightened levels of 'government at a distance'. Thus, recent comments, by the Deputy Prime Minister, John Prescott, about the need to encourage a new localism by devolving power to regional assemblies, is part of New Labour's pursuit of freedom and liberty by recourse to drawing individuals, communities, organization, and other aggregations into what Dean (ibid.) refers to as the exercise of 'responsible autonomy' (see ODPM, 2003). Urban, and other, policies look set to continue as parts of a social and political project that will encourage such (delimited) autonomy, albeit within a framework that, as Dean (ibid.) suggests, encourages enterprising populations 'within contrived market regimes'.

Acknowledgements

I am grateful to Craig Johnstone and Mark Whitehead for their invitation to me to present a version of this chapter at the RGS-IBG Annual Conference at Queen's University, Belfast, in January 2002. I would like to thank them for their constructive comments on an earlier version of the chapter. I would also like to extend my thanks to Marian Hawkesworth who provided useful and insightful comments on the substance and style of the chapter.

References

Atkinson, R. and Moon, G. (1994), *Urban Policy in Britain*, Macmillan, Basingstoke.

Atkinson, R. (1999), 'Discourses of partnership and empowerment in contemporary British urban regeneration', *Urban Studies*, vol. 36, pp. 59-72.

Atkinson, R. (2003), 'Addressing urban social exclusion through community involvement in urban regeneration', in R. Imrie and M. Raco (eds), *Urban Renaissance? New Labour, Community, and Urban Policy*, The Policy Press, Bristol.

Blair, T. (2001), *The Government's Agenda for the Future*, speech delivered on February 8th, accessed at: www.number10.gov.uk.

Burchell, G. (1996), 'Liberal government and techniques of the self', in A. Barry, T. Osborne and N. Rose (eds), *Foucault and Political Reason: Liberalism, neo-liberalism, and rationalities of government*, UCL Press, London.

Castel, R. (1991) 'From dangerousness to risk', in G. Burchell, C. Gordon and P. Miller (eds), *The Foucault Effect: Studies in Governmentality*, Harvester Wheatsheaf, London.

Colenutt, B. (1999), 'New deal or no deal for people based regeneration', in R. Imrie and H. Thomas (eds), *British Urban Policy: An Evaluation of the Urban Development Corporations*, Sage, London.

Cruikshank, B. (1999), *The Will to Empower: democratic citizens and other subjects*, Cornell University Press, New York.

Dean, M. (1995), 'Governing the unemployed self in an active society', *Economy and Society*, vol. 24(4), pp. 559-83.

Dean, M. (1999), *Governmentality: Power and Rule in Modern Society*, Sage, London.

DETR (2000a), *Our Towns and Cities: The Future – delivering an urban renaissance*, DETR, London.

DETR (2000b), *Indices of Deprivation 2000*, DETR, London.

Edwards, C. (2003), 'Disability and the discourses of the Single Regeneration Budget', in R. Imrie and M. Raco (eds), *Urban Renaissance? New Labour, Community, and Urban Policy*, The Policy Press, Bristol.
Edwards, J. (1997), 'Urban policy: the victory of form over substance?', *Urban Studies*, vol. 35, pp. 825-843.
Foucault, M. (1977), *Discipline and Punish: the birth of the prison*, London, Allen Lane.
Foucault, M. (1979), 'Governmentality', *Ideology and Consciousness*, vol. 6, pp 5-21.
Foucault, M. (1980), 'Questions on geography', in C. Gordon (ed), *Power/knowledge: selected interviews and other writings*, Harvester Press, Brighton.
Hirst, P. (1994), *Associative Democracy: New Forms of Economic and Social Governance*, Polity Press, Cambridge.
Imrie, R. (1996), 'Transforming the social relations of research production in urban policy evaluation', *Environment and Planning A*, vol. 28(8), pp. 1445-64.
Imrie, R. and Raco, M. (2003), 'Community and the changing nature of urban policy', in R. Imrie and M. Raco (eds), *Urban Renaissance? New Labour, Community, and Urban Policy*, The Policy Press, Bristol.
Imrie, R. and Thomas, H. (1999), 'Urban policy and the urban development corporations', in R. Imrie and H. Thomas (eds), *British Urban Policy: An Evaluation of the Urban Development Corporations*, Sage, London.
Lemke, T. (2001), 'The birth of bio-politics: Michel Foucault's lecture at the Collège de France on neo-liberal governmentality', *Economy and Society*, vol. 30, pp. 190-207.
Miller, P. and Rose, N. (1990), 'Governing economic life', *Economy and Society*, vol. 19(1), pp. 1-31.
Morrison, Z. (2003), 'Cultural justice and addressing 'social exclusion': a case study of a Single Regeneration Budget Project in Blackbird Leys, Oxford', in R. Imrie and M. Raco (eds), *Urban Renaissance? New Labour, Community, and Urban Policy*, The Policy Press, Bristol.
Mulgan, G. (1998), *Connexity: Responsibility, freedom, business and power in the new century*, Vintage, London.
Oatley, N. (ed) (1998), *Cities, Economic Competition, and Urban Policy*, Paul Chapman, London.
Oatley, N. (2002), 'The Community Finance and Learning Initiative', *Local Economy*, vol. 17, pp. 163-9.
ODPM (2003), *Elected regional assemblies – another step closer*, Press Release, ODPM, London, 16th June.
Osborne, T. and Rose, N. (1999), 'Governing cities: notes on the spatialization of virtue', *Environment and Planning D: Society and Space*, vol. 17, pp. 737-60.
Peck, J. (2001), 'Neoliberalising states: thin policies/hard outcomes', *Progress in Human Geography*, vol. 25(3), pp. 445-55.
Prior, D., Stewart, J. and Walsh, K. (1995), *Citizenship: Rights and Community Participation*, Pitman Publishers, London.
Raco, M. (2003), 'Governmentality, subject-building, and the discourses and practices of devolution in the UK', *Transactions of the Institute of British Geographers*, vol. 28(1), pp. 75-95.
Raco, M. and Imrie, R. (2000), 'Governmentality and rights and responsibilities in urban policy', *Environment and Planning A*, vol. 32(12), pp. 2187-2204.
Rose, N. (1996), 'The death of the social? Re-figuring the territory of government', *Economy and Society*, vol. 25(3), pp. 327-356.
Rose, N. (1999), *The Powers of Freedom: Re-framing political thought*, Cambridge University Press, Cambridge.

Rose, N. (2000), 'Governing cities, governing citizens', in E. Isin (ed), *Democracy, Citizenship, and the Global City*, Routledge, London.

Rose, N. and Miller, P. (1992), 'Political power beyond the State: problematics of government', *British Journal of Sociology*, vol. 43, pp. 173-205.

Sennett, R. (2003), *Respect: the formation of character in an age of inequality*, Penguin, London.

SEU (1998), *Bringing Britain Together: A National Strategy for Neighbourhood Renewal*, Cabinet Office, London.

SEU (2001), *A New Commitment to Neighbourhood Renewal: National Strategy Action Plan*, Cabinet Office, London.

Taylor, P., Turok, I., and Hastings, A. (2001), 'Competitive bidding in urban regeneration: stimulus or disillusionment for the losers?', *Environment and Planning C: Government and Policy*, vol. 19, pp. 45-63.

Wilks-Heeg, S. (2003), 'Economy, equity or empowerment? New Labour, communities and urban policy evaluation', in R. Imrie and M. Raco (eds), *Urban Renaissance? New Labour, Community, and Urban Policy*, The Policy Press, Bristol.

Chapter 9

Neo-Liberalism, Crisis and the City: The Political Economy of New Labour's Urban Policy

Martin Jones and Kevin Ward[1]

Introduction

Since the New Labour government was elected in the summer of 1997 it has been at pains to point out how what it does, and how it does it, differs from its predecessor in office, the Conservatives. After eighteen years and three successive election victories, the defeat in May 1997 of the John Major-led Conservative Party was, at the very least, a vote for change (see Driver and Martell, 2002). As such, it was essential for New Labour to establish early on in their first term of office a discursive, symbolic and material distinctiveness in their approach to policymaking. And nowhere have the claims been bigger and bolder than in the realm of urban policy. While, for example, Gordon Brown had to stay true to Conservative spending programmes, those involved in the making of urban policy have had more freedom to re-think the government's approach to British cities. Although the likes of Richard Caborn and John Prescott have not seen through to completion their own particular brand of city-regionalism, and had initially to decide whether to maintain or end Conservative policies such as the Single Regeneration Budget Challenge Fund (SRBCF), they and their successors have also been able to roll-out a series of policies that constitute nothing less than a substantive remaking of the urban policy landscape (Johnstone and Whitehead, this volume).

Much of what New Labour has done since coming to power in 1997 has been delivered under the rubric of an urban renaissance, or as a means of achieving its realization. The notion of an 'urban renaissance' has become a shorthand way of communicating not just a change in policy terms but a more complex and multifaceted series of trends in societal lifestyles. New consuming habits, working-

1 The authors would like to thank the editors, Craig Johnstone and Mark Whitehead, for their useful comments on a first draft of this chapter and Neil Brenner, Bob Jessop, Mark Goodwin, Andy Jonas, Gordon MacLeod, Eugene McCann and Jamie Peck for conversations on matters of the state, governance and neo-liberalism over recent years. Usual disclaimers apply.

time arrangements, labour market practices, forms of political affiliations, architectural styles and urban governance arrangements have been rolled-together, integral, according to the government, to the constitution of an urban renaissance. In this way it is possible to interpret New Labour's attention to cities as being an important part of its 'Third Way' agenda (Hill, 2000). And yet, despite all the discursive claims made, and without denying some of the very real changes that have occurred in urban policy making, there is also much of what New Labour has done since 1997 that is strangely familiar, reminiscent of earlier attempts to address the 'urban problem'. Far from constituting an approach that sits somewhere between the Conservative's free-market approach and 'Old' Labour's more interventionist stance, we will argue in this chapter that New Labour's approach to British cities has distinct neo-liberal undertones, albeit couched in 'new language' (Fairclough, 2000). Heavy state intervention is justified in terms of 'freeing' market forces.

The purpose of this chapter, then, is to move beyond the claims made by those inside (and many outside of) the New Labour political machinery and to take a longer-run perspective on the most recent period of urban policymaking. It argues that contemporary urban injustices are in fact the expression of a much longer history of urban crisis-management that Conservative and Labour governments have wrestled with since the mid-1960s. Augmenting that work which evaluates current urban policy on its own terms, the chapter argues that *deep* policy analysis demands that we understand the *wider* logic at play in designing and implementing programmatic blueprints. In light of this claim, we situate contemporary urban policy within the wider context of the ongoing *neo-liberalization* of British cities and argue that it provides an insightful example of the ways in which state-market boundaries continue to be renegotiated in and through the delivery of a range of economic and social policies.

Theoretical preambles

Elsewhere we have set out how work on crisis theory might prove instructive in interpreting the recent history of British urban policy making (Jones and Ward, 2002a and 2002b). Specifically, we have used the work of Marxist geographer David Harvey (1982 and 1999) and his 'three cuts' theory of crisis to establish a theoretical framework with which to interpret the at first seemingly unrelated changes in the way British urban policy is designed, delivered and evaluated. From this standpoint we argue it is possible to develop his hugely insightful frame of analysis and to conceive of a 'fourth cut', that of a crisis of crisis-management, drawing on the work of Jurgen Habermas (1976) and especially Claus Offe (1984).

Common to the work of these two authors is a concern to reveal how the state constructs public policy problems that are more manageable politically than the economic and social problems facing key territories such as cities. To cut a long story short, the state can *temporarily* contain the contradictions inherent to capitalism, by switching economic and social crises into policy problems to be politically managed, but in doing so its interventions can sharpen such contradictions, which presents policymakers with new challenges. The state in advanced capitalism, then, has to address contradictions often caused by previous rounds of intervention and has 'its back to the wall and its front poised before a ditch' (Poulantzas, 1978, p.191). There are structural and strategic limits to the intervention of the capitalist state in the policy-making sphere. We argue that this analysis can provide us with a fine-grain and spatialized reading of 'crisis', and has four important implications for the state's current institutional architecture and modes of British urban policymaking[2].

- First, we suggest that crises are being *further* displaced, through a complex and contradictory process of state rescaling from the political sphere of the state and on to civil society's 'vulnerable groups' (such as the unemployed and the homeless), 'problem regions' through devolution, and more generally a complex mix of individuals, household and local states. Each one is then held accountable for their performance, in a social pathological sense, and made to shoulder responsibility. Perhaps the most high profile example of this trend is the various 'rights and responsibilities' campaigns, especially within welfare reform agendas, and the initiatives targeted at 'anti-social' behaviour (see Johnstone, this volume).
- Second, and related to this, regulatory experiments and crisis management tactics appear to accompany a number of contradictions and several ramifications are worth noting: there are problems of accountability and a blurring of policy responsibility (Jones and Ward, 1997); difficulties of co-ordination exist due to administrative inertia, *both* within and across different spatial scales, due to an emerging system of intergovernmental relations associated with 'multilevel governance' (Scharpf, 1997) or 'multi-level bargaining' (Poulantzas, 1978) and the bleeding of boundaries between market and state; conflicting time horizons are present between those formulating and those implementing policy initiatives (Jessop, 2000); and policy failure is frequently blamed on devolved institutional structures and their state managers and *not* central government (Cohn 1997; Jones 1999).
- Third, and building on the above, there is an exhaustion of policy repertories. Old policies are recycled and 'new' ones are borrowed from elsewhere through hyper policy transfer. Here, Offe (1996, p.52) makes an important distinction between 'institutional gardening' and 'institutional engineering' with the latter term capturing an institutional design open to policy influences from *external* forces. By contrast, 'gardening' implies working with the grain of path-dependency through home grown regulatory mechanisms. In the latter case, policy-making is not driven by the business cycle and/or the need to address sector-based crises: rather it is pushed along by the electoral cycle and the primacy of politics.

---

[2] A longer version of some of the arguments presented here can be found in our article 'Excavating the logic of British urban policy: Neoliberalism as the "crisis of crisis-management"', published in *Antipode*, 34 (3), pp. 473-94, 2002.

- Fourth, many of these regulatory strategies and their emerging urban contradictions are being presented as necessary requirements for securing a competitive advantage under globalization. Our interpretation of the entrepreneurial direction of contemporary urban policy suggests that the (il)logics and discourses of globalization represent a *further* 'scalar crisis displacement strategy' in and through which to legitimize the 'reshuffling of the hierarchy of spaces' (Lipietz, 1994, p.36).

So what might an analysis of British urban policy look like using this theoretical framework?

Reinterpreting British urban policy

It is our contention that three themes can be drawn out of recent British urban policy using our theoretical framework. First, we draw on recent urban policy developments to analyse the changing geographies of state regulation (or sites for crisis containment), paying attention to how spatial scale is manipulated in and through different policy frameworks. Second, we explain the ascendance of the competitive mode of policy intervention, as the state distributes resources through the introduction of the market (or 'market proxies') in the form of institutionalized inter-urban competitions. Third, we argue that the contemporary scalar emphasis on co-ordination and management (witness the growing usage of terms such as 'governance' and 'partnership') in urban policy reveals much about the state's construction of the problem as one not just of economic decline but also as one of failed management, through which the state appears to be engaged in the 'crisis of crisis-management' (Offe 1984).

The changing scalar geographies of the British state

The 1968 Urban Programme and 1969 Community Development Projects marked the first attempts by the British state to address geographically the wider Fordist-Keynesian crisis. Faced by disadvantaged communities and a serious deterioration of urban life, policy interventions became structured around the doctrine of 'social pathology'; individualized, localized, and joined-up community-based action in the face of wider economic forces that were leading to regional imbalance and urban decline (Atkinson and Moon, 1994). In effect, at this early stage in the evolution of the crisis tendencies of the British Keynesian welfare state, a 'rationality crisis' (Habermas, 1976) – relating to the inability of the state's administrative system to reconcile the imperatives received from the economic system – was being displaced on to strategically selected localities.

Since this time the 'urban' in policy formations has been in and out of political favour, as governments have emphasized different geographical scales through different periods of state involvement (Jonas and Ward, 2002a), so that, for example, the 1977 White Paper amounted to 'a major reformulation of the urban …issue so far as the state was concerned' (Rees and Lambert, 1985, p.139). And to a certain degree Rees and Lambert are right. However, and despite the shifts in the modes of intervention, state strategies to address the effects of widespread and systemic urban economic restructuring remained premised on the Keynesian welfare principle of redistribution up to the election of the Conservative government in 1979 – and even then it was a couple of years before they began to change the logic underpinning urban policy formation.

Initially the Conservative's critique was one of existing state involvement. As part of the Conservative's wider efforts to reduce public expenditure, urban policy was constructed as failing precisely because of the state's involvement in local economies. New Right thinking had the role for the state in the economy confined to one of maintaining the conditions for markets to function. Having de-stabilized the existing modes and rationalities of state involvement, the state began to roll out a number of 'nested hierarchical structures' (Harvey, 1999, pp.428-9) to manage the urban crisis. Each one represented a site for internalizing the contradictions of capital accumulation. Institutional creations such as Urban Development Corporations (UDCs) and Training and Enterprise Councils (TECs) were introduced to regulate urban property markets and urban labour markets (compare Cochrane, 1999; Jones, 1999). The particular institutional blueprint and policy form of each was not an unmediated response to economic restructuring; it was a politically constructed 'urban crisis' – a crisis of existing institutions and their spatial focus. And through a process of centrally orchestrated localism certain functions were devolved from the nation state downwards and delivered through an increasingly complex suite of flanking territorial alliances. New institutions were created to bypass the perceived bureaucratic modes of intervention associated with locally embedded and scale-dependent structures of local government. Through this strategy, the assumptions of how and for whom urban policy should be delivered were challenged, as the rationality for state involvement was systematically remade.

The growth in new urban-based institutions to deliver economic redevelopment marked a break from the Keynesian welfare settlement, where although local government acted as the dominant regulatory mechanism (Goodwin and Painter, 1996) its role was structured by the actions of the nation state. Viewed more broadly, this apparent restructuring of the systems of representation with the state apparatus (Jessop, 1990) was symptomatic of an altogether more complex series of shifts in the ways in which crisis was being managed through the rescaling of the state apparatus and the containment of conflict through instituting forms of representation. Across a range of policy areas the scale of intervention shifted, as the taken-for-granted primacy of the nation state was challenged and flanking mechanisms at the local level were introduced.

When it appeared that cities were continuing to suffer economically and socially the state again set about reorganizing the scale at which it regulated economic development, while maintaining a neo-liberal emphasis in the design of policy. Mirroring the logic underpinning the first wave of *after*-national changes in the contours of state activity, and with the progression of devolution across Western Europe in the 1990s, 'the region' emerged (perhaps more through a political practice of rescaling rationality crisis, than an underpinning territorial economic necessity) as *the* strategically important scale for the state to embed competitiveness within an increasingly global economy (Lovering, 1999; Jones, 2001; MacLeod and Jones, 2001). Hay's (1995) claims on crisis-management as a 'discursively mediated process' are important here; this round of rescaling involved the creation of regional 'myths' and the celebration of (somewhat isolated) 'success stories'. Accordingly, the creation of Regional Development Agencies (RDAs) in 1999 marked a substantial centrally prescribed *re-inscription* of the state's regional regulatory capacity. While the nation-state retained its orchestrating capabilities, the region (following on from the local) became constructed as the site at which to mediate successful economic restructuring.

In both waves of state scalar restructuring, then, the creation of new institutions was performed as part of the 'rolling back' of the welfare state and the 'rolling forward' of neo-liberal state forms and rule systems (Peck and Tickell, 2002). As part of the emergence of a neo-liberal urban policy, we suggest that the logic upon which the British state traditionally intervened – to address uneven economic development and of social inequalities – has been irrevocably altered. The state has rolled-forward a new programme, codifying and institutionalising its two defining principles – competition and the market.

Institutionalising inter-urban competition

A cornerstone of neo-liberalism has been the state's internalizing and subsequent creation in institutional form of inter-urban competition. This has been achieved by removing the (national) regulatory management of uneven development, and by encouraging more speculative forms of accumulation through the 'promotion of place' rather than meeting the needs of discrete territories (Harvey, 1989). This has often been enhanced by the marketization of the state apparatus, which has been made possible through the fragmentation of large units into so-called arms-length (or private) agencies (Harden, 1992; Clarke and Newman, 1997). As part of this filling in of the 'hollowed out' nation state (Jessop, 2002), the state set the parameters and established the rules to allow the formation *en masse* of 'territorial alliances' and 'local coalitions'. Places have been pitted against each other, forcing local coalitions to form and to mobilize around making bids for state funding for redevelopment.

So, in 1991 the British government announced a 'revolution in urban policy' (Department of the Environment (DoE), 1991). Launched with much razzamatazz, the first example of the new competitive logic underpinning the state's involvement in urban redevelopment was City Challenge. Initially only those cities and towns that had been eligible for state grants under the old Urban Programme were eligible to bid for City Challenge funding. In the first instance, then, the introduction of this new policy logic was about changing political behaviour amongst existing 'competitors'. The competition was tightly parameterized. More than simply a change in policy, the introduction of what became known as the Challenge Fund model marked the rolling-out of a whole new way of performing, of evaluating and even of talking about urban development. As Oatley (1998, p.14) explains, '[c]hallenge initiatives have focused on opportunities rather than problems'.

Illustrating the adoption of neo-liberal pro-market language by the state, this model has since evolved to become the defining mechanism through which the state distributes redevelopment money. Whether in terms of training – through TEC Challenge (where TECs compete against each other for extra revenues) or Sector Challenge (where some sectors were privileged over others for state monies) – the process through which issues/places are identified as needing state funds and how this expenditure is then evaluated has been realigned through *neo-liberalization*. Allocation has been marketized. This change in how resources are allocated is illustrative of the new logic that underscores the state's financing of urban redevelopment. Neo-liberal urban policy, then, inhabits 'not only institutions and places but also *the spaces in between*' (Peck and Tickell, 2002, p.387, emphasis original). Rules and mechanisms of inter-local competition rest on four principles, which together help to reproduce the neo-liberalization process:

- The introduction of the market (and the creation of 'market proxies' if no market exists) into the funding and the delivery of local state services;
- The incorporation into the state apparatus of members of local business communities in the regulation of redevelopment projects;
- The redesigning of the internal structure of the state through the formation of public-private partnerships to decide program goals, the best means of achieving them, the institutional configuration most suited to meet them and how their successes/failures should be evaluated;
- The creation of new institutions, combining business representatives with state officials to oversee and to deliver all forms of economic and social policy.

What underscores these different areas of programme re-design is the concern to introduce some notion of 'the market' into the state system, both through the formal resource allocation model in the case of Compulsory Competitive Tendering (CCT) and through the co-opting of business leaders, such as in the example of TECs and their institutional successors. In their wake, however, the changing geographies of state regulation and the institutionalization of inter-urban competition, has left a series of *unsolved* political and economic contradictions. In response the state has introduced a number of new institutions to co-ordinate the inter-urban competitions/scalar re-configurations, whilst at the same time choosing not to address the somewhat negative impacts of inter-urban competition.

In what sense a 'crisis of crisis-management'?

Building upon the above analysis, it is clear that the two tendencies in British urban policy constitute a significant effort by the state to, first, politically construct and, second, to institutionally regulate crisis at the urban scale, as opposed to acknowledging what could be considered the real crisis of cities – i.e. policies that seriously tackle structural economic problems. The construction of a 'new' scale of regulation, whether it be the 'local' or the 'regional', on which to begin to assemble neo-liberal regulatory mechanisms and the codification of inter-urban institutional competition, illustrates how the nation state apparatus continues to set the parameters for 'doing' urban redevelopment (Ward, 2001). And we would suggest that these endeavours are indicative of the ways in which a 'rationality crisis' has been created, by displacing economic crises of accumulation into problems for political and policy management, which, in turn, have to govern and to reconcile their *own* internal contradictions.

Repeatedly, then, the recent history of British urban policy can be read as being one in which the institutions and the programs *themselves*, and not the economy, become objects of regulation (cf. Goodwin and Painter, 1996), although this is not to argue that British cities do not suffer from real and deep-rooted economic and social issues. To understand and explain the demands on current urban policy, we feel it is necessary to examine how the political/policy sphere has been used as a means of managing (and mismanaging) ongoing urban economic difficulty.

In 1985 City Action Teams were formed to manage locally articulated national programmes. This though was not just a technocratic process: it was also a political one, ensuring the *melding* of local deliverables with the parameters set through national political strategies, which at the time revolved around the dismantling of a number of the central pillars of the Fordist-Keynesian settlement. It is not altogether surprising that these attempts to mobilize private sector expertise through the urban state apparatus were created in Birmingham, Liverpool, London, Manchester and Newcastle. These were (for the most part) large (Labour-led) urban city-regions and were those suffering most acutely the effects of economic restructuring. They were also where political resistance to Thatcherism was strongest (see Lansely et al., 1989). With the exception of the Community Development Projects, which were wound down in the late 1970s, this initiative constituted perhaps the first effort to regulate the *previous* years of state intervention, and in particular, to ensure that all programmes designed and introduced prior to the election of Thatcher in 1979 could be realigned, rationalized, or simply abolished. Rather than set about reorganizing the national level of policy design and implementation, the creation of city-based institutions had the advantage of effectively devolving the management of crisis *downwards*, not to local government – who were effectively bypassed – but instead to an elite group of state and business representatives.

The remit of City Action Teams was to minimize the overlap between different programs. Organized along the lines of the fast-action response teams favoured by contemporary businesses, the Teams were, by design, presented as the 'flexible' alternative to local government. They operated outside the formal local state machinery and it was argued could ring out so-called efficiency gains from existing programmes and, more systemically, influence urban development politics. A year later and eight Task Forces were rolled out across the English localities. This time around London acquired two Task Forces, with the other six being created in Birmingham, Bristol, Leeds, Leicester, Manchester and Middlesbrough. Again the emphasis was on the local co-ordination of national institutions and national state grants. Both City Action Teams and associated programmes, such as Enterprise Zones, which were local experiments in creating a de-regulation/anti-taxation space in which inward investment would relocate, came under the auspices of Task Forces.

After this period of experimentation in designing urban institutions to manage crisis, more recent state strategies have involved the creation of national institutions (such as Action for Cities) and national expenditure programmes (such as the Single Regeneration Budget) to manage the effects of, and contradictions of, *previous* periods of state intervention. In the first of these the state reaffirmed a dominant ideology that called for a more co-ordinated approach (and where the scope for local resistance was perhaps less). This concern was, in part, driven by the realization that neo-liberal urban policy had created a 'patchwork quilt of complexity and idiosyncrasy' (Audit Commission, 1989, p.4), a theme that would be returned to some fourteen years later (Johnstone and Whitehead, this volume). Instead of addressing this problem, late-Thatcherite state interventions were far from co-ordinated. For some critics, Action for Cities, and to an extent the Single Regeneration Budget, presented a 'rag-bag of policies with ill defined objectives' (Imrie and Thomas, 1999, p.39).

The national election of Labour in 1997 did not disrupt the neo-liberalization project that was underway in Britain's cities. Rather we would argue it simply led to its consolidation. However, during the first few formative months of the new Labour administration there were some signs of change: the Single Regeneration Budget was discredited as a strategy for 'ensuring co-ordination' (DETR, 1997a). It was though ultimately retained and modified to respond to contradictions created by a previous lack of community involvement in redevelopment. And even the more recent programmatic changes in city-region redevelopment governance, the creation of Regional Development Agencies (RDAs), have in their policy genes the 'effective and proper…co-ordinat[ion] of regional economic development' (DETR, 1997b. p.1).

However, to rationalize the policy messes and tangled hierarchies created by the RDAs, Labour created a Regional Co-ordination Unit, after a hard-hitting report concluded that 'better Ministerial and Whitehall *co-ordination* of policy initiatives and communication' was needed (Performance and Innovation Unit 2000, p.5, emphasis added). Such endeavours have been somewhat complicated by the continual national reorganization of the state apparatus, involving the abolition of the Department for Environment, Transport and the Regions (DETR) and its replacement with the Department for Transport, Local Government and the Regions (DTLR), which was subsequently replaced by a Department of Transport and the Office of the Deputy Prime Minister. As a consequence, city-region redevelopment is the responsibility of several branches of the state, which only fuels a crisis of crisis-management through further problems of co-ordination (Goodwin et al, 2002).

In turn, we would suggest that attempts by the state to regulate the problems invoked through its own contradictions, bound up within the crisis of crisis-management, are creating a landscape where policy-makers appear to be running out of 'new' repertoires and a 'circularity of policy responses' is emerging (Wilks-

Heeg, 1996). This trend is illustrative of 'identity crises' under advanced capitalism – a situation within the crisis of crisis-management, where state personnel are unable to secure the necessary policy innovation to produce visionary and meaningful frameworks and political legitimacy is questioned (cf. Habermas, 1976). This argument can be applied to the urban White Paper launched in November 2000 (DETR, 2000; see also Urban Task Force, 1999). Emphasis in the White Paper is placed on a 'new vision for urban living' and the need to make towns and cities 'places for people'. It predicts an emerging 'urban renaissance' that will 'benefit everyone', making towns and cities 'vibrant and successful' and offering a 'high quality life' and 'opportunity for all, not just a few'. Celebrating 'successful' developments in Western Europe, the White Paper focuses on the relationships between people and partnerships through new forms of urban leadership. And in doing so, 'the urban' is generally presented as an individualistic and all-round exciting place to be. In stark contrast to the 1977 White Paper, gone are references to poverty; instead the (postmodernist) 'urban idyll' is presented, with curiously no references to the inner city as a 'problem' (Hoskins and Tallon, this volume; see also Whitehead, 2003).

Yet this White Paper is far from 'revolutionary'; its policy genes are a document (with a similar title and content) published some 20 years ago (DoE, 1980) and key elements of the 'urban renaissance' are heavily reminiscent of the last urban White Paper, *Policy for the Inner Cities* (DoE, 1977). For Smith, '[t]his language of urban renaissance is not new…but it takes on far greater significance here' (2002, p.438). The future is, however, the past with fewer options. And despite continual emphasis placed on further *co-ordination* within this cultural mode of urban interventionism, no real attempt is either being made to rationalize the institutional/policy matrix of the city, or to address the endemic economic problems of Britain's cities.

Ending/beginnings

This chapter has sought to put some of New Labour's recent urban policy initiatives in their historical context. After a brief theoretical preamble, where we sought to set out the very basics of a framework for understanding the logic underpinning contemporary urban policy making, we moved on to demonstrate how the approach might illuminate our understandings of the way British cities are currently being redeveloped. Our contention is that crisis theory can help urban researchers to get at the underlying logic of many of the policy experiments that have shaped Britain's cities over the last four decades. The state *is* a key actor for *neo-liberalising* the city through its influence on the policy machinery and the policy-making process. Building on earlier work (Jones and Ward, 2002a and 2002b), we have made a number of further suggestive comments on how using what we refer to as a 'fourth-cut' crisis theory can provide rich accounts of the contemporary make-up of British urban policy.

Our empirical analysis seems to suggest that urban policies pursued by the state in Britain during the 1990s and early 21st century appear bound *by design* to intensify the internal contradictions of capital accumulation. And we have maintained throughout the chapter that Britain's cities are hosts to politically constructed urban problems, made real through urban policy experiments that appear to be responses to the socio-political and geographical contradictions of *previous* rounds of urban policy and not the underpinning contradictions of accumulation.

To end with a beginning: if we are in the midst of an 'urban renaissance', as is claimed, then in what ways is the type of 'urban renaissance' being pursued appropriate to the needs of the majority of Britain's cities? And what sort of 'subjects' are being constructed through the process of neo-liberalization and what does this mean for the relationship between city and citizen? The state's present approach to addressing urban injustices is prone to failure simply because no attempt is being made to regulate uneven development and neo-liberalism is unable to address the problems of those cities facing acute structural economic problems. As it is currently constituted, Labour's urban policy, by design, can only *increase* the processes of socio-spatial uneven development and territorial injustices occurring in Britain's cities.

References

Atkinson, R. and Moon, G. (1994), *Urban Policy in Britain: The City, the State and the Market*, Macmillan, Basingstoke.

Audit Commission (1989), *Urban Regeneration and Economic Development: The Local Government Dimension*, HMSO, London.

Clarke, J. and Newman, J. (1997), *The Managerial State: Power, Politics and Ideology in the Remaking of Social Welfare*, Sage, London.

Cochrane, A. (1999), 'Just another failed urban experiment? The legacy of the Urban Development Corporations', in R. Imrie and H. Thomas (eds), *British Urban Policy: An Evaluation of the Urban Development Corporations*, Sage, London.

Cohn, D. (1997), 'Creating crises and avoiding blame: The politics of public service reform and the new public management in Great Britain and the United States', *Administration and Society*, vol. 29, pp. 584-616.

DETR (1997a), *Regeneration Programmes – The Way Forward*, Discussion Paper, DETR, London.

DETR (1997b), *Building Partnerships for Prosperity: Sustainable Growth, Competitiveness and Employment in the English Regions*, DETR, London.

DETR (2000), *Our Towns and Cities: The Future – Delivering an Urban Renaissance*, DETR, London.

DoE (1977), *Policy for the Inner Cities*, Her Majesty's Stationery Office, London.

DoE (1980), *Urban Renaissance: A Better Life in Towns*, DoE, London.

DoE (1991), 'Michael Heseltine outlines new approach to urban regeneration'. Press Release 138, March 11th, DoE, London.

Driver, S. and Martell, L. (2002), *Blair's Britain*, Polity, Cambridge.

Fairclough, N. (2000), *New Labour, New Language*, Routledge, London.

Goodwin, M. and Painter, J. (1996), 'Local governance, the crises of Fordism and the changing geographies of regulation', *Transactions of the Institute of British Geographers*, vol. 21, pp. 635-48.

Goodwin, M., Jones, M., Jones, R., Pett, K. and Simpson, G. (2002), 'Devolution and economic governance in the UK: uneven geographies, uneven capacities?', *Local Economy*, vol. 17, pp. 200-15.

Habermas, J. (1976), *Legitimation Crisis*, Heinemann, London.

Harden, I. (1992), *The Contracting State*, Open University Press, Buckingham.

Harvey, D. (1982), *The Limits to Capital*, Blackwell, Oxford.

Harvey, D. (1989), 'From managerialism to entrepreneurialism: The transformation in urban governance in late capitalism', *Geografiska Annaler*, vol. 71b, pp. 3-17.

Harvey, D. (1999), *The Limits to Capital – New Edition*, Verso, London.

Hay, C. (1995), 'Re-stating the problem of regulation and re-regulating the local state', *Economy and Society*, vol. 24, pp. 387-407.

Hill, D. (2000), *Urban Policy and Politics in Britain*, Macmillan, Basingstoke.

Imrie, R. and Thomas, H. (1999), 'Assessing urban policy and the Urban Development Corporations', in R. Imrie and H. Thomas (eds), *British Urban Policy: An Evaluation of the Urban Development Corporations*, Sage, London.

Jessop, B. (1990), *State Theory: Putting Capitalist States in their Place*, Polity, Cambridge.

Jessop, B. (2000), 'Governance failure', in G. Stoker (ed), *The New Politics of British Local Governance*, Macmillan with the ESRC, London.

Jessop, B. (2002), *The Future of the Capitalist State*, Polity, Cambridge.

Jones, M. (1999), *New Institutional Spaces: Training and Enterprise Councils and the Remaking of Economic Governance*, Routledge with the Regional Studies Association, London.

Jones, M. (2001), 'The rise of the regional state in economic governance: "Partnerships for prosperity" or new scales of state power?', *Environment and Planning A*, vol. 33, pp. 1185-1211.

Jones, M. and Ward, K. (1997), 'Crisis and disorder in British local economic governance: Business Link and the Single Regeneration Budget', *Journal of Contingencies and Crisis Management*, vol. 5, pp. 154-65.

Jones, M. and Ward, K. (2002a), 'Excavating the logic of British urban policy: Neoliberalism as the "crisis of crisis-management"', *Antipode*, vol. 34, pp. 479-500.

Jones, M. and Ward, K. (2002b), *Urban Policy Under Capitalism: Towards a 'Fourth-Cut' Theory of Crisis*, SPA Working Paper no.50, School of Geography, University of Manchester, Manchester.

Lansley, S., Goss, S. and Wolmar, C. (1989), *Councils in Conflict: The Rise and Fall of the Municipal Left*, Macmillan, London.

Lipietz, A. (1994), 'The national and the regional: Their autonomy vis-à-vis the capitalist world crisis', in R. Palan and B. Gills (eds), *Transcending the State-Global Divide: A Neostructuralist Agenda in International Relations*, Lynne Rienner, London.

Lovering, J. (1999), 'Theory led by policy: The inadequacies of the 'new regionalism' (illustrated from the case of Wales)', *International Journal of Urban and Regional Research*, vol. 23(2), pp. 379-95.

MacLeod, G. and Jones, M. (2001), 'Renewing the geography of regions', *Environment and Planning D: Society and Space*, vol. 19, pp. 669-95.

Oatley, N. (1998), 'Cities, economic competition and urban policy', in N. Oatley (ed), *Cities, Economic Competition and Urban Policy*, Paul Chapman, London.

Offe, C. (1984), *Contradictions of the Welfare State*, Hutchinson, London.

Offe, C. (1996), *Modernity and the State: East, West*, Polity, Cambridge.

Peck, J. and Tickell, A. (2002), 'Neoliberalizing space', *Antipode*, vol. 34, pp. 380-404.

Performance and Innovation Unit (2000), *Reaching Out: The Role of Central Government at the Regional and Local Level*, Cabinet Office, London.

Poulantzas, N. (1978), *State, Power, Socialism*, New Left Books, London.

Rees, G. and Lambert, J. (1985), *Cities in Crisis: The Political Economy of Urban Development in Post-War Britain*, Edward Arnold, London.

Scharpf, F. (1997), 'The problem-solving capacity of multilevel governance', *Journal of European Public Policy*, vol. 4, pp. 520–38.

Smith, N. (2002), 'New globalism, new urbanism: Gentrification as global urban strategy', *Antipode*, vol. 34, pp. 427-50.

Urban Task Force (1999), *Towards an Urban Renaissance: Final Report*, E & FN Spon, London.

Ward, K. (2001), '"Doing" regeneration: evidence from England's three second cities' *Soundings*, vol. 17, pp. 22-24.

Whitehead, M. (2003), 'Love thy neighbourhood – rethinking the politics of scale and Walsall's struggle for neighbourhood democracy', *Environment and Planning A*, vol. 35, pp. 277-300.

Wilks-Heeg, S. (1996), 'Urban experiments limited revisited: Urban policy comes full circle?', *Urban Studies*, vol. 33, pp. 1263-79.

PART 2

BEYOND THE RENAISSANCE – ISSUES FOR THE FUTURE OF BRITISH URBAN POLICY

Chapter 10

Towards a 'Social Democratic' Policy Agenda for Cities[1]

Patsy Healey

Towards 'social democratic' cities

In this chapter, I argue that the initiatives of the Labour administration since 1997 have promoted, if in inchoate ways, an approach to urban policy and to planning which seeks to give a stronger profile to 'social' issues and which searches for a richer and more democratic relationship between the State and the citizen. These initiatives, with their rhetorical language of 'urban renaissance' and a 'third way' towards democratic governance, attempt to link the urban policy field and policy for land use and development, and re-cast the focus of urban policy from a concentration on 'problem areas' to a focus on the qualities of cities and their communities. But this re-awakening of a 'social democratic' agenda for cities, after two decades of neo-liberalism, is proceeding in a hesitant and fragmented way and in combination with conflicting concerns which continue to privilege the dominant policy discourses of the 1990s, those of economic competitiveness and environmental conservation (Vigar et al., 2000). Nor is it linked to contemporary understandings of the social life of cities and the way social deprivation and injustice arise in the complex dynamics of urban relations.

As discussed elsewhere in this book, the 1997 Administration inherited an urban policy field littered with initiatives aimed to address issues of poverty, deprivation and stock obsolescence in the context of progressively weakened and under-funded local governments. In contrast to the efforts in urban renewal in the 1960s, when planning was at the heart of the reconstruction of city centres and poor neighbourhoods, urban 'regeneration' policy and land use regulation policy (the 'planning system') proceeded as largely separate policy fields in the 1980s and 1990s. In neither urban policy nor planning was much attention paid to the city as a whole. Qualities of 'place' were addressed in urban policy primarily in terms of improving housing estates and 'regenerating' bits of 'obsolete' urban fabric. In the planning field, the preoccupation was to develop policy criteria to govern the release of sites for development, increasingly constrained by well-articulated

---

1 My thanks to Geoff Vigar, Ash Amin and the editors for helpful comments on an earlier draft.

environmental conservation lobbies. In both policy fields, there was an emphasis on wider consultation and involvement, drawing in residents, stakeholders from various sectors of society, and public participation generally. But these efforts were typically ad hoc exercises at the margins of the 'mainstream' of urban governance, with its emphasis on 'top-down' sectoral service delivery.

The New Labour project in this situation, though articulated incoherently and in often conflicting ways, has built on some of the practices emerging in urban regeneration initiatives in order to transform or 'modernize' mainstream urban governance. In this strategic and 'modernising' orientation, various initiatives have emphasized the re-valuing of 'the urban' in public policy, from 'problem' to 'opportunity'. There has been a new emphasis on social justice through the various policy initiatives to address processes of social exclusion. Quality of life in cities has been stressed to complement the earlier emphasis on the city as an economic asset. And there has been an attempt to take a more holistic view of cities and city regions, rather than the earlier focus on the 'problem' bits. In terms of governance process, a concern with 'customer satisfaction' has mingled with the promotion of citizen empowerment and a more active relationship between state and citizen. In all these developments, elements of a 'social democratic' agenda for the governance of place in dynamic and diverse urban contexts can be discerned. In government initiatives, this agenda tends to get expressed through discourses of 'overcoming social exclusion' (in the urban policy field), promoting 'community well-being' (in relation to local government management), and 'sustainable development' and 'design quality' (in the planning field). Organizationally, it is encapsulated in the search for 'joining up' policy initiatives and developing collaborative practices in which residents have a stronger voice. This 'social democratic' influence provides an impulse for the emergence of new urban governance policy discourses and practices, centred around concepts of a renaissance in the attractiveness and quality of urban life (Urban Task Force, 1999) and a 'third way' of governing democratic society (Giddens, 1998).

More coherent conceptions of what a 'social democratic' agenda for cities could mean can be found in academic 'manifestoes', for example (Healey, 1997; Sandercock, 1998 and 2000; Amin et al. 2000; Amin and Thrift 2002). In relation to the qualities of cities, these contributions understand a city in relational and social constructivist terms. They focus on the diversity and mixity of city life (Amin and Thrift, 2002) and the challenge of accepting difference and conflict while finding ways to 'co-exist in shared spaces' (Healey, 1997). Understood in this way, a focus on the 'social' is not just about distributional equity and access to good quality services for material welfare. It is also about the formation and expression of multiple identities, and about how to combine a concern for providing home environments which sustain human flourishing in diverse ways with an openness to the opportunities of the many networks and webs of relations which traverse the space of the city (Amin et al., 2000). It emphasizes an appreciation of the value of having many strangers as neighbours in the shared spaces of urban life (Sandercock, 2000). In this conception, place quality is about much more than physical design. It is about the social qualities and values of the different nodes and networks, the places and flows of urban life.

This conception of the 'good city' connects to ideals of an urban governance which recognizes the value of diversity and mixity, 'cities of the many not the few' (Amin et al., 2000), and the multiple views of what a city and the locales within it may signify (Healey, 2002). While reviving mid-twentieth century concerns with social 'need' and 'justice', these ideas also stress the importance of the diversity of identities and the 'politics of recognition' in a society where multiple cultures co-exist (Parekh, 2000). This conception leads on to a concern with developing deliberative or 'dialogic' democratic governance forms in which understanding and voice for the diverse 'many' can find expression. These ideals stress the importance of improving the 'sociability' of urban life (Amin et al., 2000; Amin and Thrift, 2002), encouraging openness and connectivity, and generating a public realm or public sphere of political argument and morally-aware action, grounded in a richness of social expression and forms of radical critique, but yet capable of collective action to sustain an inclusive democracy and fairly-distributed material welfare and opportunity[2].

This project is itself a very general ideal. It involves innovation not merely in the specific areas of urban policy and planning discourse, but also in legislative initiatives to secure rights to voice and justice which operate in a trans-scalar way. Translating such a project into concrete policies and practices involves developing its meaning into the specific concerns, experiences and struggles of particular cities and their governance contexts. This is a tough challenge for a highly centralized governance culture – such as that which exists in Britain – in which place qualities and their diversity have traditionally been given little systematic attention. In theory, the 'urban policy' and 'town and country planning' policy fields have been arenas where place qualities are supposed to be addressed. Since the 1960s, both fields have retreated from attempts to conceptualize urban dynamics. Urban policy has focused on 'problem areas', zones of high social deprivation, or physical stock obsolescence. Planning policy has focused on generalized policy criteria for judging development applications and on building new 'pieces' of the city through master-planning schemes. Cities, their people and the complex daily life relations between people and places within and beyond the city, have slipped out of focus, to be weakly and uncertainly replaced by some marketing image or generalized ambition in the 'vision statements' which became fashionable in urban policy and planning in the 1990s.

In any case, government initiatives in urban policy and planning since 1997 contain within them contradictory emphases. In urban policy, which is driven primarily by the manipulation of funding flows, innovative programmes are repeatedly tied down with public sector accounting practices which require precise specification of aims, targets and achievements (Stewart, 2002). There is also a

---

2 This public realm of rich and diverse dialogic encounter would not be characterized by the formation of a monological 'consensus'. Instead, it would provide space for active critique in different forms, and mechanisms to challenge and test what emerge as dominant policy discourses and practices in ways which reflexively shift these governance practices so that the 'many', and in particularly those who have traditionally been on the margins of dominant governance cultures, can find that their needs, values and voice are attended to.

continual tension between a social agenda aimed to release resources for economic activity (expanding the size of a skilled labour market, for example) and social objectives aimed to improve the quality of daily life experience and human flourishing for diverse people in diverse places. In planning policy, the mantra of 'sustainable development' is supposed to link together economic, social and environmental objectives in a 'balanced' approach to development. But in practice, the well-articulated policy discourse of balancing economic development demands for land with environmental defence of landscape still dominates the interpretation of 'sustainable development' at the expense of concerns for social justice (Vigar et al., 2000; Owens and Cowell, 2002).

How then are the various impulses of transformation encouraged by the New Labour administration working out as practices? What prospect do they hold of generating new forms of social democratic policy discourse and practice in Britain's cities? How far do they build a capacity to 'see' the city and its multiple relations and dynamics in ways which can reduce injustice, build connectivity and synergy, and reduce environmental damage? And how are the urban policy and planning fields, both focused on place qualities and both involved in building new forms of participative process, to relate to each other in this endeavour? In this brief chapter, I review the relation between the initiatives in the urban policy and planning fields in relation to these questions. Through this, I identify three deficiencies in their evolution under the New Labour mantle. In conclusion, I propose an alternative 'New Vision for Urban Living' to promote a more powerful social emphasis both in the content and the process of urban policy and planning.

Re-shaping urban policy

The 1997 New Labour administration set in train three initiatives which have increasingly shaped urban governance in England. The first aimed to transform local government (see DETR, 1998a and the Local Government Act, 2000). In response to widespread critique of the competence and management of local authorities, but yet informed by a strong and influential local government lobby, local authorities were to be given more financial and regulatory 'freedoms and flexibilities' in return for 'good performance'. In this Report, and in later developments, the emphasis is on an uneasy combination of efficiency measures and responsive interaction with communities, guided by an overall purpose for local authorities of promoting 'economic, social and environmental well-being'.

The second initiative has been the work of the Social Exclusion Unit (SEU), a policy unit originally based in the Cabinet Office and now located within ODPM, which has provided sophisticated analyses of the causes of poverty and marginalization experienced by people in areas of concentrated poverty (SEU, 1998, 2000 and 2001). This has lead, firstly, to policies devised to focus the attention of service delivery departments nationally and locally on a 'joined up' approach to overcoming exclusion, aimed to 'narrow the gap' between the 'poorest performing' neighbourhoods and the rest (DETR, 2000a, p.110). Secondly, it has encouraged a whole series of measures aimed to provide substantial resources to achieve this, ranging from the experimental New Deal for Communities programme to the Neighbourhood Renewal Fund. The intention is for communities to define their own projects and objectives, rather than have these defined for them by local authority officials and politicians. The third initiative has been an attempt to focus on the city as a whole and the 'urban experience', expressed in *Towards an Urban Renaissance*, the 1999 report of the Urban Task Force chaired by the architect Lord Rogers. This aimed to replace the persistent association in public policy with the urban as 'problem', with a view of the positive qualities of urban life. It also aimed to challenge the regulatory culture which had overtaken the planning system and to promote a more positive and pro-active approach to urban development, underpinned by a stronger appreciation of design quality.

For a while, these three initiatives proceeded largely separately from each other, until the Urban White Paper (DETR, 2000a) sought to bring them together. But they encountered each other as they filtered through into three areas of policy delivery: local government management; the focus of 'urban regeneration' funding; and the planning system. The first emphasized a search for joined-up thinking, more attention to community voice organized on an area basis, and the development of community strategies to integrate the overall local authority effort, produced in conjunction with partnerships of stakeholders (Local Strategic Partnerships), including citizens (DETR, 2000b and 2001). This overlapped with the consolidation of the different urban regeneration measures of the 1990s into a single funding source, the Single Regeneration Budget and the later Neighbourhood Renewal Fund. Both funds were accessed through the development of an urban regeneration strategy or 'vision' by local partnerships. Meanwhile, the planning system was being encouraged to 'modernize'. This in part re-iterated an inherited pre-occupation with decision speed, but also placed a new emphasis on strategic plans, at the regional and local level, focused around the objective of promoting 'sustainable development' (DETR, 1998b). By late 2001, these ideas had been developed into proposals for Regional Spatial Strategies and Local Development Frameworks (DTLR, 2001). The 2000 Urban White Paper and the 2002 Planning Green Paper both make explicit links between the three agendas of modernising local government, overcoming social exclusion and developing some kind of overview of the city/local authority area and its qualities.

In the next section, I assess the extent to which these initiatives have carried forward the 'social democratic' ideals articulated in the previous section. Already, there are many critiques of the government's approach, as well as confusions, tensions and struggles of interpretation in local practices (see other chapters in this book). Nevertheless, the initiatives are having significant impacts on local authority agendas and practices. There is a great deal of experimentation underway and signs of some kind of 'cultural change', as sought by the 1998 *Modern Local Government* paper (DETR, 1998a). But at issue is how far these experiments and emergent governance practices embody a 'social democratic' agenda. To explore this in more detail, I examine the rhetoric of the Urban White Paper, *Our Towns and Cities* (DETR, 2000a), and the Planning Green Paper, *Planning: Delivering a Fundamental Change* (DTLR, 2001), and their relation to evolving practices.

Political rhetorics and policy struggles

The Urban White Paper represents an attitude of policy integration in search of a concept of the 'urban'. Lacking a coherent conception of urban dynamics and the multiple meanings and experiences of urban life, it collects together material from the *Modern Local Government*, *Social Exclusion* and *Urban Renaissance* initiatives and wraps a general rhetoric around many of the sectoral policy discourses and specific interventions already underway or under discussion. The Planning Green Paper develops some of the directions indicated in the Urban White Paper along with others arising from discussions and criticisms of the planning system itself.

The 'new vision' of the Urban White Paper encapsulates both the government's ambitions for 'towns and cities, and the dilemmas within it (see Figure 10.1). The 'urban' is conceptualized into three types – 'towns, cities, and suburbs', an inheritance to be proud of:

> We have famous historical and cultural centres; dynamic commercial areas; pleasant suburbs; and seats of learning and research that command respect the world over. We want to build on success (DETR, 2000a, p.7).

As places, towns and cities should be 'attractive' and 'well-kept', understood in terms of attraction to investors, quality of the physical stock and reductions in pollution and congestion. An 'urban renaissance' (meaning: concentrating development in existing urban areas rather than building on 'greenfield sites') will help to protect the countryside. This rhetoric is familiar from planning policy discourse, with its attempt to combine economic development and environmental conservation objectives. The social agenda finds expression in two ways, through the emphasis on quality services, and through community involvement in 'shaping the future' and serving 'people's needs'. 'Community', 'people' and 'local people' are used as interchangeable terms. 'Local people are [to be] in the driving seat' of policy development, through 'participative democracy' which is 'inclusive' (p.8).

Achieving this vision is to be lubricated with additional government resources, through New Deal for Communities and the Neighbourhood Renewal Fund, etc. But the primary mechanism will be partnership and leadership, harnessing the 'energy and effort' of an array of agencies, government levels, business and community organizations (para. 5, p.8). Through such partnership, somehow an integrated approach will emerge which will:

> bring together economic, social and environmental measures...to enable people and places to achieve their economic potential; bring social justice and equality of opportunity; and create places where people want to live and work. These issues are interdependent and cannot be looked at in isolation. For instance, there are close links between housing, health and education. This is why moving towards more mixed and sustainable communities is important to many of our plans for improving the quality of urban life (DETR 2000a, p.8).

A New Vision for Urban Living

Our vision is of towns, cities and suburbs which offer a high quality of life and opportunity for all, not just the few. We want to see:

- **people shaping the future** of their community, supported by strong and truly representative local leaders;

- people living in **attractive, and well kept towns and cities** which use space and buildings well;

- good design and planning which makes it practical to live in a **more environmentally sustainable** way, with less noise, pollution and traffic congestion;

- towns and cities able to **create and share prosperity**, investing to help all their citizens reach their full potential; and

- **good quality services** – health, education, housing, transport, finance, shopping leisure and protection from crime – that meet the needs of people and businesses wherever they are.

The urban renaissance with benefit everyone, making towns and cities vibrant and successful, and protecting the countryside from development pressure.

Source: Adapted from DETR, 2000, p.7

Figure 10.1 A 'new vision' for cities

In theory, then, it is up to 'local people' in some combination to generate a specific understanding of their cities, to exercise 'local choice', reflecting the distinctive qualities of individual localities. But at the same time, access to national and regional urban regeneration funds will be driven by national government's conceptions of 'best practice' in 'modern local government' through which local authorities are to access the 'freedoms and flexibilities' for exercising such 'local choice'[3].

The Urban White Paper may perhaps be best understood as a policy 'collage', drawing bits of social democratic rhetoric from parts of the New Labour policy vocabulary, pasted in alongside a physicalist urban design view of cities, an old set of ideas about containing urban sprawl, economic conceptions of the value of 'attractive cities' and specific sectoral policy agendas. Its value lies in what it attempts. It seeks to focus on cities as such rather than merely deprived

3 Only 22 of local authorities reviewed in late 2002 achieved a rating of 'excellent' from the Audit Commission, the 'grade' which released the promised 'freedoms and flexibilities'.

neighbourhoods. It seeks to promote a positive view of cities. It emphasizes a governance mode in which citizens are actively involved. It stresses the importance of the connections between policy issues. And it nods in the direction of inclusivity and 'mixity'. But it has little to say about the multiple communities and identities of city life, or what it takes to generate qualities of openness and inclusivity in cities, or about creating a rich and critical public realm of argument about what a city and its parts and dimensions could become. It lacks not just a well-developed concept of urban dynamics, but shows little of the complex, overlapping, intersecting and conflicting social worlds of urban life. The 'social' is understood primarily in the welfare state language of 'needs' and the new rhetoric of social exclusion and marginalization. If a well-developed practice of participative local governance were to emerge, a richer meaning of the 'social' might develop, as people engaged in struggle over their different values, interests and understandings of the urban. But despite the rhetoric of 'people' shaping their own collective future, a very specific mode of governance is promoted, which emphasises building new partnership arenas for articulating policy, and policy delivery governed by specific performance criteria. There is no necessary connection between such a mode and fostering the 'sociability' of urban life and a rich public realm of argumentation about the quality of urban life. Citizens are being invited to join a governance game and play an active part in it, but without much opportunity to shape the rules of the game.

There is much in the Urban White Paper which involves implementation through the plans and regulatory power of the planning system, with its focus on the location of development. 'Urban renaissance [is to be] at the heart of the planning system' (DETR, 2000a, p.9). The Planning Green Paper (DTLR, 2001) seeks a 'fundamental change' in the planning system. The present system is criticised as being complex, slow, uncertain, and operating with limited community engagement. The reasons given for these problems are attributed largely to the formal procedures and distribution of competences. There is no discussion of the inherent challenge of combining multiple objectives and policy goals as they impact on particular places and territories. Nor is there an assessment of the kind of governance processes needed to give voice to all sections of the community in an open, transparent way, while reducing the transaction costs for different kinds of people undertaking development projects in different situations.

The Green Paper focuses largely on a few formal parts of the planning system, rather than these wider issues. Yet it is these wider issues which will determine how the changes proposed for the planning system will evolve in practice. Changes are proposed to the system of plans, to make them simpler and more strategic. The longstanding preoccupation with decision speed is combined with measures to simplify compulsory purchase arrangements. There are requirements for stakeholder involvement in regional plans and community involvement in local development frameworks, which are to be linked to local authority community strategies. Reflecting the long experience of a policy system in which many people from all walks of life get involved from time to time, there are references to ensuring that the system is 'open and transparent', trusted by 'the community', and susceptible to community influence (e.g. para. 5.52, p.43). But when it comes to 'understanding diversity', the Green Paper admits to intellectual defeat (see Figure 10.2). 'Diversity' is interpreted in terms of a governance landscape of organized groups, each promoting a particular interest and struggling to be heard. Potentially excluded groups are asked to come forward to add their voice to the array of pressures.

Understanding Diversity

Planners working on the ground have a good appreciation of the impact of planning policies on the needs of different groups in the community, including ethnic and religious minorities, the elderly and the disabled.

At all levels of the planning system, special attention is paid to the elderly and disabled people whose needs are particularly apparent. There may be other groups that have been less engaged in considering whether there are planning policies that impinge particularly on them.

We invite black, ethnic minority and other groups to respond to this consultation and let us know whether there are aspects of the planning system considered in this Green Paper on which they have a particular viewpoint.

Source: Adapted from DTLR, 2001, p.46

Figure 10.2 The Planning Green Paper 2001: approach to diversity

Despite its title, there is little 'fundamental' proposed in the Planning Green Paper. It nevertheless attracted a large response of 15,000 comments from a wide range of groups, an indication of the strength of popular interest in a system which government had been treating for many years as a minor regulatory activity. The proposals in the Paper were interpreted by many as an attempt to meet business objections that the system 'holds up development'. The focus on speed is moderated, many argue, by only token acknowledgment of the role of community voice. The proposals in the Green Paper were rolled forward into a new *Planning and Compulsory Purchase Bill* in December 2002[4].

Planning systems routinely have to 'balance' economic, social and environmental interests and values in developing policies and plans and in making specific regulatory decisions. This balancing act is continually criticized by parties who object to its process and content. The experience of continual conflict, often interpreted by business lobbies as 'delay' and 'interference', gives evidence of the great difficulty of achieving an enduring approach to 'economic, social and

4 This articulates a new, but very generalized, purpose for the planning system (sustainable development), but many of the difficult or controversial proposals were left out of the Bill to ensure that it passed through Parliament reasonably quickly. In the end, the Bill was delayed until the 2003-2004 Parliamentary session, and did not reach the statute books until 2004.

environmental well-being', or any version of 'sustainable development'. The Green Paper contains no concept of what it means to pay attention to the spatiality of urban relations and the qualities of places. The treatment of the social dimension of cities is collapsed into a role for 'community voice', and recognition of the need to consider the social impacts of development decisions on specific groups which get to have political identity. Social democratic rhetoric seems drowned in the Green Paper by a pre-occupation with procedural reform designed to reduce bureaucratic burdens.

Despite introductory rhetorics, both papers are weak on articulating an understanding of urban dynamics. They reflect a limited conception of the 'social' and an undeveloped notion of the participatory governance which they espouse. They lack a conception of contemporary urban dynamics or of the social life of cities and how people value, use and appreciate the relations and places of the city and its many locales. They lack a notion of active urban governance in which collaboration and critique intertwine to expand the sociability of urban life and promote involvement in rich dialogue about policy agendas and practices for cities and the qualities of places within them.

It could be argued that this does not matter so long as the ambition to promote 'local choice' is realized. This puts the focus on local efforts to emphasize social justice and participatory governance. There can be no doubt that such efforts are underway in many cities and towns in England. Some of these are strategic initiatives to build new agendas and practices at the level of the city, or even city region, or local authority area. Others are developing around particular area initiatives, notably in regeneration areas, and sectoral programmes, for example health, education and Local Agenda 21 initiatives. There is increasing discussion of how to 'mainstream' what has been learnt from particular initiatives and sectors to the whole local authority and the wider governance culture. But building new governance capacities and creating momentum around new agendas is never an easy process. Many key actors report continual struggle to maintain the momentum for governance change. They are also continually frustrated by the way that national government initiatives operate. The rhetoric and the funding may be welcome, and may serve to promote the advance of new agendas and practices. But they come packaged with performance criteria and accounting rules which frustrate their intentions. 'Local choice' evaporates when faced with the requirements of centrally-defined auditing and targetry. Community involvement in urban policy and planning tends to lose interest when faced with a weight of nationally-articulated regulations ('planning policy guidance') and performance targets. Defining the rules of the game rather than just playing the game as defined requires a strength of collective commitment and leadership that it has been hard to build in the context of the weak powers and political position of British local government.

In this context, the agendas and practices which evolve depend on the way existing local power bases interact with the power behind the urban policy and planning initiatives at the national level and the wider initiatives to modernize local government, develop regional government and increase spending in sectoral programmes. This is leading to considerable variation across the country. Yet overall, the likelihood is that economic and environmental 'well-being' will get much more attention than social 'well-being', and that concepts of 'social well-being' will struggle to move beyond a 'needs' and 'groups' agenda. Valuable though this is, it does not encompass what it means to live in and get access to the complex, dynamic and multi-dimensional places of the city. The sectoral programmes will deliver more funding to health and education services, but with only limited attention to how this affects citizens' daily life experiences in cities. There may be an urban renaissance, but its benefits could well flow to the 'few' not the 'many'.

The social life of cities

In summary, the 'social' in urban policy and planning needs to be articulated with more depth to give it a stronger voice in the struggle over defining a 'balance' between the economic, environmental and social dimensions of 'well-being' and 'sustainable development'. More attention needs to be given in urban policy and planning to the meaning of the 'social', to the interrelation between the social and the spatial in the 'places' of the city, and to the development of a richly discursive public realm in which the relative importance of economic, social and environmental dimensions of 'well-being' and 'sustainable development' can be discussed, made more specific and probed, tested and critiqued. What this might involve is sketched out in Figure 10.3 as an alternative 'new "social democratic" vision for urban living', drawing on the ideas presented earlier in this chapter.

Of course, such a vision remains a very general statement. But it provides criteria by which to judge current urban policy and planning agendas and practices. Many of these initiatives remain appropriate in this 'alternative' policy programme. Beyond the current agendas, Figure 10.3 emphasizes the importance of recognising the diversity and mixity of urban life as a critical factor in promoting 'well-being' in cities. It also stresses the significance of developing both a much more participative governance culture, grounded in strong local government powers and well-formed and distributed rights to involvement in making policy claims, and in policy development and delivery. Finally, Figure 10.3 is not naïve in the promotion of 'local choice'. It recognizes the potential for local elites to capture control of governance cultures and operate in mono-cultural ways at the material and cultural expense of the diverse cultural communities living within a local government's formal jurisdiction. The role of the arenas of higher tiers of government is crucial here, providing a wider spatial scale within which distributive justice and claims to special protection can be considered.

But changing government competences and legislating for rights and duties will not of itself lead to urban policy and planning agendas and practices which reflect the spirit of this alternative new vision. To bring it about requires a new kind of consciousness and a different mode of practice for all those involved in urban governance. It involves major transformations in urban governance cultures and the practices and discourses embedded within them. Signs of what these might look like can be found in many of the innovations and experiments currently

A New 'Social Democratic' Vision for Urban Living

• Cities as locales imagined as complex webs of relations, traversing many social worlds and spatial scales, intertwining to promote synergy and a capacity to co-exist in shared spaces.

• Social life in cities composed of multiple social worlds, confident internally and engaging with the many others in open and respectful ways, creating and moulding the places and flows of urban life.

• Democratic life in cities characterized by a diversity of voices, a spread of power to challenge and to generate collective action, and a governance culture of active involvement in collective debate and critique.

• An urban politics structured by people's rights to material welfare and to democratic voice.

• A strong local government institution, with significant financial and legislative power, held in check by citizens' rights and a culture of active critique as well as periodic elections.

• Local choice encouraged and held in check by EU, national and regional specification of rights and duties which promotes social justice, by research to inform local debates and by resource flows to balance general and specific distributional inequities.

Figure 10.3 An alternative 'new vision' for urban living

underway in Britain's cities. But although these flicker brightly for a moment, they often fade through lack of institutional support. If social well-being and democratic governance are really to be promoted, then governance initiatives need to be evaluated in terms of their contribution to the 'social democratic' project, not merely in relation to their contribution to economic competitiveness, and environmental conservation. It is time that urban policy and planning developed once again a strong 'social' voice.

References

Amin, A., Massey, D. and Thrift, N. (2000), *Cities for the Many not the Few*, The Policy Press, Bristol.

Amin, A. and Thrift, N. (2002), *Cities: Reimagining the Urban*, Polity Press, Cambridge.

DETR (1998a), *Modern Local Government: In Touch with People*, DETR, London.

DETR (1998b), *Planning for the Communities of the Future*, HMSO, London.

DETR (2000a), *Our Towns and Cities: the Future - Delivering an Urban Renaissance*, HMSO, London.

DETR (2000b), *Preparing Community Strategies*, DETR, London.

DETR (2001), *Local Strategic Partnerships: Government Guidance*, DETR, London.

DTLR (2001), *Planning: Delivering a Fundamental Change*, DTLR, Wetherby.

Giddens, A. (1998), *The Third Way: the Renewal of Social Democracy*, Polity Press, Cambridge.

Healey, P. (1997), *Collaborative Planning: Shaping Places in Fragmented Societies*, Macmillan, Basingstoke.

Healey, P. (2002), 'On creating the "city" as a collective resource', *Urban Studies*, vol. 39(10), pp. 1777-92.

Owens, S. and Cowell, R. (2002), *Land and Limits: Interpreting Sustainability in the Planning Process*, London, Routledge.

Parekh, B. (2000), *Rethinking Multiculturalism: Cultural Diversity and Political Theory*, Palgrave, Basingstoke.

Sandercock, L. (1998), *Towards Cosmopolis*, John Wiley, Chichester.

Sandercock, L. (2000), 'When strangers become neighbours: managing cities of difference', *Planning Theory and Practice*, vol. 1(1), pp. 13-30.

SEU (1998), *National Strategy for Neighbourhood Renewal*, Cabinet Office, London.

SEU (2000), *A National Strategy for Neighbourhood Renewal: a Framework for Consultation*, HMSO, London.

SEU (2001), *A New Commitment to Neighbourhood Regeneration: The Action Plan*, HMSO, London.

Stewart, M. (2002), 'Compliance and collaboration in urban governance', in G. Cars, P. Healey, A. Madanipour and C. de Magalhaes (eds), *Urban Governance, Institutional Capacity and Social Milieux*, Ashgate, Aldershot.

Urban Task Force (1999), *Towards an Urban Renaissance*, E & FN Spon, London.

Vigar, G., Healey, P., Hull, A. and Davoudi, S. (2002), *Planning, Governance and Spatial Strategy in Britain*, Macmillan, Basingstoke.

Chapter 11

The Scaling of 'Urban' Policy: Neighbourhood, City or Region?

Mark Goodwin

Introduction

I want to begin this chapter by asking what might appear to be a somewhat foolish question; in what sense is urban policy actually urban? Despite the tautological nature of its construction, I want to contend that this is a fundamental question for those concerned with the future of urban policy. For it is only by exploring and unpacking the answer to this that we will gain an appropriate sense of the direction that urban policy should be heading. The chapter attempts this task by initially outlining the key scales at which New Labour's urban policy is currently delivered. One thread in the broader ideologies which underpin these policies is the claim that New Labour is *renewing* or *reinventing* social democracy. In the words of Tony Blair, the 'Third Way' pursued by his governments 'is not a third way between conservative and social democratic philosophy. It is social democracy renewed'. (Blair, 2001; see also Driver and Martell, 1998). The chapter takes this claim at face value, and problematizes the scale at which current urban policies work by exploring the urban policies of the more traditional brand of social democracy, as represented by the post-war Labour government of Clement Atlee. Finally, the chapter utilizes this retrospective to suggest a number of issues which still remain to be tackled if we are to look forward and set out a vision for urban policy in the new millennium.

The scaling of New Labour's urban policy

Even a cursory glance at the other chapters in this book will have revealed something of the complexity of contemporary urban policy. Indeed, given the detail provided elsewhere in the book I will limit myself to a discussion of the broad parameters of New Labour's urban policy. In Chapter 1 of this volume Johnstone and Whitehead quote a government regeneration minister who characterized this complexity as something akin to a bowl of spaghetti. What I want to stress here is that this metaphor not only describes a diversity of strategies and policy arenas, but also refers to the different scales and spaces over which these policies operate. Very few, if any, of these policy initiatives operate at the level of the city as a whole. Many are restricted to very small pockets within the city – often operating at the level of an individual housing estate or neighbourhood (Whitehead, 2003). The proliferation of various 'action zones' is an example of this. Education Action Zones, Health Action Zones, Sport Action Zones and Youth Music Action Zones are all based on the principle of giving additional resources to specified areas of particular need. So are the various 'neighbourhood' initiatives, such as Neighbourhood Management, Neighbourhood Nursery Centres and Neighbourhood Wardens. In other instances New Labour has targeted the delivery of its major initiatives, such as the Single Regeneration Budget, the Neighbourhood Renewal Fund and New Deal for Communities, by aiming at the most deprived areas.

Although the delivery of some of these initiatives lies outside cities (the Neighbourhood Renewal Fund for instance covers parts of Cornwall, West Cumbria and some semi-rural areas of the former Durham and Northumbria coalfields), when we focus on urban areas the overall picture is one where urban policy is actually concentrated in a few small areas, often located in the major conurbations. The vast majority of urban Britain, and the bulk of those who live in urban areas, have neither seen, nor benefited from, any urban policy at all. These policies are urban to the extent that they are delivered and experienced in some parts of some cities. But by definition they are not comprehensive, do not engage with the bulk of the urban population and only operate in selected (and restricted) zones and neighbourhoods which have been specially chosen to receive additional funding.

These localized initiatives have tended to focus on social and welfare issues. In the economic sphere New Labour has relied on regional scale agencies to formulate and deliver its 'urban' policies. While this might read like a non sequitur, it is because the government has channelled most of its economic regeneration initiatives through the Regional Development Agencies (RDAs). Their establishment in 1999 marked the construction of the 'region' as the site and scale through which to pursue economic regeneration. According to the White Paper *Our Towns and Cities: The Future* (DETR, 2000) each of the nine RDAs lies 'at the heart of the government's agenda for promoting sustainable regional economic growth, enterprise and regeneration' (para.5.22). This is in contrast to preceding Conservative administrations which had sought to deliver economic regeneration through locally based schemes – such as Enterprise Zones, Urban Development Corporations and City Challenge Schemes (Duncan and Goodwin, 1988; Atkinson and Moon, 1994). In its 2000 Spending Review the government announced that the RDAs would have a strengthened role as 'strategic leaders' of economic development. Subsequently, the separate budgets they received from the DETR, the DfEE and the DTI were brought together in a single budget to allow more flexibility in RDA spending. As part of the formation of this 'Single Pot' the resources of the Single Regeneration Budget – previously the largest single source of urban regeneration funding – were also transferred to the RDAs. The 2000 White Paper makes few references to any economic initiatives at the urban level – the section on Facilitating Economic Success (para.5.32ff) largely refers to generic national policies concerned with skills training, entrepreneurship, business support and investment. In the main these services and facilities are equally available in urban and non-urban areas alike, and there is nothing specifically 'urban' about them.

The RDAs, however, are not the only regional agency with an interest in urban policy. The 2000 White Paper includes a section on 'working together at all levels', which significantly highlights neighbourhood action, regional action and national action, with no mention at all of any role for the urban level. The paragraph on regional action (3.32) states that:

> Government Offices for the Regions will have a new and enhanced responsibilityfor joining-up regional Government activities. They will work closely with the business-led Regional Development Agencies, which will have a key role in driving forward economic and physical change. Together with Regional Chambers, Regional Planning Bodies and the Regional Cultural Consortia, they will provide the strategic context for towns and cities.

Hence there are a number of different regional actors which together are charged with setting the strategic policy context for urban areas. There is of course no guarantee that the interests of these agencies will coincide, or that their strategic views on urban development will harmonize. Indeed they are more than likely not to – there have been several cases, for instance, where RDAs have clashed with Regional Planning Bodies over the best location for urban growth. The former, charged with promoting investment and employment (and having to do so by meeting specified growth targets within an appropriate timescale) tend to favour the concentration of development in and around economically buoyant areas. The latter, charged with preventing congestion and promoting transport flows, tend to want to spread development across the region more evenly. In these circumstances it can be difficult for urban areas to know from which agency they should take the strategic lead. There is also a clear split between the economic and the social aspects of regeneration. The government's flagship scheme for social regeneration, New Deal for Communities, and other programmes of the Neighbourhood Renewal Unit operate through the regional Government Offices, whereas the Single Regeneration Budget and other economic programmes operate largely through the RDAs.

The White Paper recognizes the potential problems caused by operating 'urban' policies at the local, regional and national scale, but implies that these can be overcome through proper co-ordination and co-operation. It states, for instance, (para.3.30) that:

> What happens at the local level depends to a significant extent on what is happening elsewhere in the region and nationally and vice versa. In particular the conurbations and major cities have an impact that stretches well beyond their administrative boundaries and influences the entire region. Policies and programmes need to reflect this. To get the best possible result we need to recognize the different roles which different places play and co-ordinate action at the neighbourhood, local, regional and national levels so that we all pull together rather than against one another.

Further on, the White Paper concludes that, 'it is essential that action at the national, regional, local and neighbourhood level is closely co-ordinated and mutually reinforcing' (para.5.13). This is, however, likely to prove far more difficult to achieve in practice than on paper. This is not just because of the inherent difficulties involved in co-ordinating such complex arrangements across a whole series of policy initiatives operating at different scales, but also because the ideological, political and economic parameters within which New Labour is working militate against such co-ordination and co-operation. It is instructive to illustrate this with reference to the ways in which the very first social democratic Labour administration tackled its own set of urban problems. Looking back some 50 years can help to understand the way urban policies are always politically constructed within certain ideological and economic frameworks – and the way these frameworks in turn lead to the adoption of particular scales of activity.

The scaling of Old Labour's urban policies

In August 2003 the New Labour government became Labour's longest continuously serving administration in history. At the same time Tony Blair passed Clement Atlee's record of six years and 92 days in 10 Downing Street from 1945-51. Blair is extremely conscious of this achievement, and of the place occupied in the annals of the Labour Party by the 1945 government which established the welfare state. He has gone on record calling Atlee's administration 'the greatest peacetime government' of the century (Driver and Martell, 1998, p.74). This after all was the government which created the National Health Service and implemented Beveridge's National Insurance Scheme. By the end of its term the coal, rail, cable and wireless, civil aviation, electricity, gas, coal, iron and steel industries had also been brought into public ownership. What is equally important for the purposes of this chapter is that the Atlee government pursued a very distinctive agenda concerning urban and regional change. In discussing this agenda I want to highlight the difference between the urban policies which emerged from the post-war version of social democracy, and those which are the product of the reinvented version which characterizes the policies of the Blair governments. In other words I want to make explicit the contrast between 'First Way' urban policy and Third Way urban policy.

The Atlee government came to power at the end of the Second World War faced with a major task of urban reconstruction – caused not just by the effects of German bombs, but also by the virtual cessation of any building activity for some six years. Moreover it was also inheriting the legacy of considerable urban problems which had begun to manifest themselves before the war started, but which could not be tackled until it ended. The Great Depression of the early 1930s and the differential economic and spatial growth which followed, resulted in a profoundly uneven urban system within Britain. On the one hand the older industrial towns and cities of Northeast and Northwest England, Scotland and Wales were wracked with mass unemployment and economic decline. These were suffering from unemployment rates of over 50%, and were the places which launched the hunger marches and the unemployment crusades. In these areas, urban was associated with decline and deprivation. On the other hand, the inter-war years had also witnessed considerable economic growth around the new 'lighter' consumer based industries of Southeast England and the Midlands. These areas saw a population expansion coupled with accompanying problems of housing supply, transport infrastructure and urban sprawl. This juxtaposition of growth and decline had thus caused considerable urban problems – both for those urban areas which were expanding and also for those which were contracting (Rees and Lambert, 1985; Hall, 1996). These problems had become so great by the end of the inter-war period that the Conservative government of Neville Chamberlain established a Royal Commission on the Distribution of the Industrial Population. Its report was published in 1940 and endorsed regional balance in the distribution of employment, planned metropolitan decentralization and the extension of planned urban redevelopment (Ward, 1994; see also Cherry, 1996). The following year Lord Reith, head of the war-time Ministry of Works and Buildings set up the Uthwatt Committee on Betterment and Compensation to advise the government on the relationship between the state and the land market, and the Scott Committee on Land Utilization in Rural Areas to advise on broader rural and regional aspects of planning policies. Together, these three reports, coupled with the effects of the Blitz, created what Ward has described as 'a huge momentum for planning and reconstruction issues' (1994, pp.89-90).

Even before the war had ended, this momentum had lead to considerable activity around urban and regional issues. The Town and Country Planning Act 1944, otherwise known as the 'Blitz and Blight' Act, gave compulsory purchase powers to local authorities to facilitate the wholesale replanning of war damaged and obsolescent areas. As Ward points out, this 'marked the formal beginnings of positive planning' (1994, p.94). The *Control of Land Use White Paper* of 1944 was followed by the *Employment Policy White Paper* in 1945. The latter led directly to the Distribution of Industry Act in 1945 which allowed financial investment to firms locating in Development Areas, provided for the development of factories and key worker housing and established negative controls to prevent industrial development in designated areas. 1945 had also witnessed the publication of Abercrombie's *Greater London Plan, 1944*, which 'forcefully articulated' (Ward, 1994, p.97) the strategic concepts of regional balance and urban decentralization, containment and redevelopment. By focusing on the entire metropolitan region the plan was able to consider a broad range of planning problems and solutions – most radically, perhaps, recommending the planned decentralization of over a million people from inner London to an outer ring of new and expanded towns.

It is important not to lose sight of the scalar narratives (Swyngedouw, 1997) which helped to construct, and in turn were reinforced by, this plethora of wartime reports and plans. They were all essentially premised on the idea of nationally controlled intervention occurring at the urban and regional scale. The urban was the centre of attention – whether in terms of preventing sprawl, decentralizing inner city populations or redeveloping slums and bomb-damaged areas – but it was recognized that the urban could only be tackled by delivering a co-ordinated and coherent set of policies at a regional and even a national scale. The policies were to be put very firmly in place following the end of the war and the 1945 General Election, which delivered a landslide victory for Atlee's Labour Party. The Distribution of Industry Act was already in legislation. Atlee's government built on this by passing the New Towns Act in 1946 which provided for the building of new towns by public development corporations; the Housing Act, also in 1946, which raised subsidies for the building of public housing and ensured that four out of every five houses built in Britain during the life of the government was a council house; the Town and Country Planning Act of 1947 which gave Counties and County Boroughs a duty to regulate nearly all land development; and the 1949 National Parks and Access to the Countryside Act, which in addition to establishing National Parks also gave planning authorities the power to run countryside parks. These were followed in 1952, after the fall of the government by the Town Development Act, which enabled large cities to negotiate with smaller towns to take 'overspill' population.

The main criteria behind this legislative system were clearly spelt out by Lewis Silkin, the Minister for Town and Country Planning, in the following manner:

> [T]he objectives of town and country planning...are to secure a proper balance between competing demands for land, so that all the land of the country is used in the best interests of the whole people...[Land will be needed for] the housing programme, including the clearance of slums and the rebuilding of blitzed areas, the redevelopment of obsolete and badly laid out areas, the dispersal of population and industry from our large, overcrowded cities to new towns...On the other hand town and country planning must preserve land from development. A high level of agricultural production is vital. More land must be kept for forestry...And it is important to safeguard the beauty of the countryside and coastline [in order to] enable more people to enjoy them...these conflicting demands for land must be dovetailed together. If each is considered in isolation the common interest is bound to suffer. Housing must be located in relation to industry that workers are not compelled to make long, tiring and expensive journeys to and from work. Nor must our already large towns be permitted to sprawl, and expand, so as to eat up the adjacent rural areas and make access to the countryside and to the amenities in the centre of the town more difficult...the continued drift from the countryside must be arrested (cited in Rees and Lambert, 1985, pp.64-5).

This passage is worth quoting at length as it is so instructive not just on the intentions of the Atlee Government but also on the scale at which these were to be pursued. Notions of the 'common interest' may seem quaint now, but in the post-war period they were the cornerstones of a political ideology which underpinned the creation of the welfare state. This was a government committed to full employment, to redistributive public spending and to a Keynesian economy centred on macro-economic demand management. Driver and Martell (1998, p.34) conclude that, 'it was a government motivated by socialist ideals, elected on a landslide, intent on real effective reforms in the interests of the people as it perceived them'.

Its urban and regional policies were a key component of this programme – for the ideology espoused by Atlee was not simply one nation social democracy in a social and economic sense. It was also one nation in the literal sense – of evening out spatial differentials in terms of employment, housing, transport and other civic amenities. Uneven geographical development was linked to uneven social development, and the aim was to reduce both by using 'all the land in the best interests of the whole people'. Moreover this was to be achieved through a comprehensive programme of policies aimed at reducing spatial disparity. As Silkin explained in his speech, if any element of urban and regional development was considered in isolation the 'common interest is bound to suffer'. To a certain extent Atlee's government could logically attempt to meet this ideal. For as Jessop explains (2002a, pp.58-61), the form and functions of the type of state it established should not just be described as a Keynesian Welfare State, but crucially should be conceptualized as a Keynesian Welfare *National* State. The 'National' here is critically important, and signifies the principal scale at which social and economic policies were developed, and to which they referred. Jessop points out that, 'the institutional and discursive 'naturalization' of the national economy and national state was linked (within Atlantic Fordism) to the relative closure of post-war economies undergoing reconstruction on the basis of mass production and mass consumption' (2002a, p.60). Thus key macro-economic levers, such as interest rates and the money supply, were controlled and adjusted nationally. In other words it was possible for industrial and sectoral policies to be pursued at the national level, within a relatively closed economic space. Firms, for instance, could be directed to locate in specific parts of the country, as they were not liable to move production to Europe, or be closed by a multi-national headquarters in New York. In turn, the impact of employment growth on housing need could be forecast, and then planned for. Jessop concludes that 'in particular, economic and social policies at the urban and regional level were orchestrated in top-down fashion by the national state and primarily concerned with equalizing economic and social conditions within [the] national econom[y]' (2002a, p.60).

The result, as we have seen, was a set of integrated policies which had a definite vision of the 'urban' at their core. This was a vision which saw the city as an integrated whole (although made up of distinct communities and neighbourhoods), with the city in turn being integrated into its wider regional setting. It was also a vision which was based on a particular understanding of the nature of the urban problem, and hence of solutions to it. The problems for cities were socially and politically constructed as essentially physical in nature – overcrowding, sprawl, poor housing and derelict land. The responses were also physical – urban containment, new and overspill towns, inner-urban redevelopment and regional balance. There was an implicit assumption that in tackling these physical problems, one could also 'solve' any economic and social concerns – such as unemployment and poverty. There were obvious flaws in this argument, but the detail of whether these policies worked or not is not my main concern in this chapter (although see Hall et al, 1973; Rees and Lambert, 1985; Ward, 1994 for assessments). The reason for exploring these policies is rather to draw out the link between the way that urban policies are always constructed within broader political and ideological frameworks, and the scales at which such policies are pursued. I will now turn in the next section to examine the implications of this link for the urban policies of New Labour. For as we have seen, the urban policies of Third Way social democracy are rather different from those of 'First Way' social democracy.

Urban policy or policy which impacts upon urban areas?

In speaking to journalists in the week that he became the Labour Party's longest continuously serving Prime Minister, Tony Blair made the observation that 'modern social democracy is what today's Labour Party is about and must continue to be about' (Blair, 2003). The contrast between traditional and modern social democracy is in many ways exemplified in the sphere of urban policy. As we have seen, traditional social democracy, working through the Keynesian Welfare National State, constructed the urban as a specific object of policy – and developed a series of legislative interventions at different, yet integrated, scales to address what it saw as an interlinked set of urban problems. In contrast, this chapter has pointed out that modern social democracy, in the guise of New Labour, is adopting an inconsistent and fragmented approach to the urban – with few, if any, of its policy initiatives being conducted at the urban scale. Indeed, even its self-proclaimed 'urban' policies are delivered largely at the regional, electoral ward or neighbourhood level, and following publication of the 2000 Urban White Paper, the Office of the Deputy Prime Minister listed ninety six separate programmes which were of relevance to urban policy[1]. These cover the areas of business and investment, communities, crime and community safety, education and training, environment, health and well-being, homes and housing, land and planning, leisure and sport, and transport and traffic. Put simply, it is very difficult to discern a coherent urban policy within such complexity. Cochrane (2003, p.223) concludes that, 'in principle, it appears at times as if almost any aspect of public policy could become part of urban policy'.

Yet in many ways this complexity is entirely within keeping with New Labour's broader political philosophy. Jessop (2002a, ch.7) suggests that there has been a tendency for a shift away from the Keynesian Welfare National State towards a state form which he labels as the Schumpeterian Workfare Postnational Regime (SWPR). This new state form is Schumpeterian (derived from the ideas of the economist Schumpeter) in the sense that it promotes innovation and flexibility in order to strengthen the competitiveness of relatively open economies. It is workfarist in that it subordinates social policy to economic policy, thereby putting downward pressure on the 'social wage' and attacking welfare rights. It is post-national because the privileged space of the nation state as the organizer and referent of social and economic policy is replaced by the increased significance of other scales of activity. And it can be conceptualized as a regime given the tendential shift away from state intervention (to tackle market failure) and more towards public-private partnerships and other self-organizing governance networks

---

1 The relevant lists can be accessed at: www.odpm.gov.uk/stellent/groups/odpm_control/documents/contentservertemplate/odpm_index.hcst?n=2914&l=2

(to tackle state and market failure). This picture, of course, is used as a heuristic device and in practice individual state forms will all vary to some degree from this ideal-type. But the broad structure within which New Labour is delivering its urban policies is clearly discernible.

Of particular concern in this chapter are the scalar implications of such a shift. These of course are linked to the way in which New Labour has constructed particular sets of 'problems' for its policies to tackle. Firstly, the region has been privileged as the most appropriate space through which to promote economic competitiveness (Jones and Ward, this volume), and the problem couched in terms of promoting regional economic competitiveness. When the Regional Development Agencies were first announced in 1997, the Department of Environment, Transport and the Regions (DETR) claimed that they would provide 'new opportunities in the English regions to enable them to punch their weight in the global market place' (DETR, 1997). Here we see a confirmation of the need for relatively open economies to compete globally in a market driven system – but the institutional scale felt most appropriate to do this is the region. A key issue here is the relationship between the RDAs and the major cities within them. How does the North West Development Agency, for instance, allocate resources and opportunities between Liverpool and Manchester, and how does Yorkshire Forward, the RDA covering Yorkshire and Humberside, decide on investment across Leeds, Sheffield, Bradford and Hull? And what happens if the decisions taken by the RDAs do not chime with the wishes of city councils, which might have other investment priorities focused around the needs of their local electorates? These concerns are not constructed as problems by central government. Cities might be seen as the engines of economic growth, and centres of innovation in a new knowledge-driven economy (see Jessop, 2002b; Peck and Tickell, 2002), but under New Labour the key institutional agencies charged with promoting competitiveness are regional in scale.

Many of the local initiatives, based at the neighbourhood level and delivered via partnerships, also derive from New Labour's broader political ideology. The Blair governments' pursuance of neo-liberal policies via the SWPR is given a particular inflection by their reliance on the philosophy of the 'Third Way' (Giddens, 1998 and 2000; Johnstone and Whitehead, this volume). A belief in 'community' lies at the heart of New Labour's version of the Third Way. According to Driver and Martell (2000) it is possible to identify four key themes in Tony Blair's speeches and writings on the Third Way – equal worth, opportunity for all, responsibility and community. As they point out, notions of responsibility are linked closely to those of community:

> In a decent society, individuals should not simply claim rights from the state but should also accept their individual responsibilities and duties as citizens, parents and members of communities. A third way should promote the value of 'community' by supporting the structures and institutions of civil society...which ground 'responsibility' in meaningful social relationships (ibid., p.151).

Crucially, partnerships enable the themes of responsibility and community to be brought together and put into practice. The problem here is one of encouraging citizen participation, and delivering policies at a scale which can facilitate this. Even in opposition, New Labour was emphasising the sharing of powers *and* responsibilities between local government and the communities they served. The Commission for Social Justice, for instance, suggested in 1994 that:

> the aim [of policy] must be to build among local people the capacities and institutions which enable them to take more responsibility for shaping their own futures...small and local initiatives, based on a partnership of public, private and voluntary sectors, are the essential foundation of lasting empowerment (cited in Raco and Imrie, 2000, p.2192).

Echoing this some seven years later, the government's new guidance on Local Strategic Partnerships states that:

> Involving local people and communities is vital for the successful development and implementation of community strategies and local neighbourhood renewal strategies, and key to achieving lasting improvements (DETR, 2001, p.13).

The stress then is on small-scale local initiatives, which can be delivered through partnerships in order to allow members of local communities to fulfil their responsibilities as active citizens. The result, as we saw earlier, has been a whole plethora of local action zones and partnership agencies, all targeted at particular parts of specific cities. There are, however, signs that these partnerships find it difficult to fully engage local populations and that they suffer from problems of accountability and representation (Glendinning et al, 2002).

Somewhat ironically then, the urban is actually the missing scale in the delivery of New Labour's urban policy. Even its recent drive to promote *Sustainable Communities* (ODPM, 2003) by underpinning (with £610 million) the building of new towns in Southeast England, which at first sight appears to engage with the notion of the city as a whole, suffers from a lack of integration with wider regional infrastructures. The key element of these proposals is to use the private sector to expand housing development around Milton Keynes, Cambridge-Stansted, Ashford and the Thames Gateway (Blitz and Tricks, 2003). The plan is for over 250,000 new houses to be constructed in the Southeast, with 120,000 in the Thames Gateway alone. The concerns here centre on the poor provision of other services, especially transport, and the increasing imbalance such government investment is likely to cause between the Southeast and other regions. In contrast to the regional balance pursued by the post-war Labour government, the concentration of yet more investment and infrastructure in the Southeast can almost be said to be a counter-regional policy. There are also reports of residents in the initial developments having to wait for a month for a doctors appointment, and as one of them put it;

> It's pleasant enough living here but all those promises that were made have not materialized. They were going to build shops, schools, play areas; but there's no

> facilities for children at all. They're only interested in building the houses, because that's where the money is (cited in Blitz and Tricks, 2003).

While improvements to services are likely to be made over time, the overwhelming feeling at present is of unplanned and market-led growth, which will inevitably suffer from a lack of co-ordination within regional infrastructure and the provision of local facilities. The signs are that this latest policy development might solve housing shortages in the Southeast, but only at the expense of congestion and poor services in this region and reduced investment elsewhere.

Concluding comments

The problem of co-ordinating a cohesive urban policy across all scales – from the local to the regional and including the urban – thus looks set to continue. The argument in this chapter has been that this is not unexpected, given the wider political philosophies which are underpinning New Labour's policy development. The government's claim is that these philosophies are renewing social democracy – as Tony Blair (2001) put it, 'The third way was always intended to renew and modernize progressive politics, not find a …compromise between left and right'. In the urban policy field, however, the actions of New Labour have done little to 'renew' the activities of Atlee's original social democratic administration. Indeed, they seem far removed from each other – in terms of both the content of the policies and the scale at which they operate. In contrast to the urban policies of the 'First Way', New Labour's policies have a distinct vacuum at the urban level – those which are economically orientated tend to be pitched at the regional scale, whilst those which are more socially focused are normally delivered at the neighbourhood level. Whilst there are signs that the lack of co-ordination has been recognized and is beginning to be tackled through initiatives such as Local Strategic Partnerships and the Regional Co-ordination Unit, these do not have a specifically urban focus. There is still a great danger that in the plethora of 'urban' initiatives put forward by New Labour, the urban is the one scale that is not being addressed.

References

Atkinson, R. and Moon, G. (1994), *Urban Policy in Britain*, Macmillan, Basingstoke.

Blair, T. (2001), 'Third way, phase two', *Prospect Magazine*, March, accessed at www.angelfire.com/hi3/pearly/htmls2/tony2.html

Blair, T. (2003), 'The Blair Milestone: Statements', accessed at: http://uk.news.yahoo.com/030801/143/e5h6q.html

Blitz, R., and Tricks, H. (2003), 'Gateway to growth', *Financial Times*, 2nd August, p.11.

Cherry, G. (1996), *Town Planning in Britain Since 1900: the Rise and Fall of the Planning Ideal*, Blackwell, Oxford.

Cochrane, A. (2003), 'The new urban policy; towards empowerment or incorporation? The practice of urban policy', in R. Imrie and M. Raco (eds), *Urban Renaissance? New Labour, Community and Urban Policy*, The Policy Press, Bristol.

DETR (1997), 'Regions invited to have their say', *Press Notice 214/97*, DETR, London.
DETR (2000), *Our Towns and Cities: The Future – Delivering an Urban Renaissance*, HMSO, London.
DETR (2001), *Local Strategic Partnerships: Government Guidance*, HMSO, London.
Driver, S. and Martell, L. (1998), *New Labour: Politics After Thatcherism*, Polity Press, Cambridge.
Driver, S. and Martell, L (2000), 'Left, Right and the third way', *Policy & Politics*, vol. 28(2), pp. 147-61.
Duncan, S. and Goodwin, M. (1988), *The Local State and Uneven Development*, Polity Press, Cambridge.
Giddens, A. (1998), *The Third Way: The Renewal of Social Democracy*, Polity Press, Cambridge.
Giddens, A. (2000), *The Third Way and its Critics*, Polity Press, Cambridge.
Glendinning, C., Powell, M. and Rummery, K. (2002), *Partnerships, New Labour and the Governance of Welfare*, The Policy Press, Bristol.
Hall, P. (1996), *Cities of Tomorrow*, Blackwell, Oxford.
Hall, P., Thomas, R., Gracey, H. and Drewett, R. (1973), *The Containment of Urban England*, Allen and Unwin, London.
Jessop, B. (2002a), *The Future of the Capitalist State*, Polity Press, Cambridge.
Jessop, B. (2002b), 'Liberalism, neoliberalism and urban governance: a state-theoretical perspective', in N. Brenner and N. Theodore (eds), *Spaces of Neoliberalism*, Blackwell, Oxford.
ODPM (2003), *Sustainable Communities*: *Building for the Future*, HMSO, London.
Peck, J. and Tickell, A. (2002), 'Neoliberalizing space', in N. Brenner and N. Theodore (eds), *Spaces of Neoliberalism*, Blackwell, Oxford.
Rees, G. and Lambert, J. (1985), *Cities in Crisis*, Edward Arnold, London.
Raco, M. and Imrie, R. (2000), 'Governmentality and rights and responsibilities in urban policy', *Environment and Planning A*, vol. 32, pp. 2187-2204.
Swyngedouw, E. (1997), 'Neither global nor local: 'glocalisation' and the politics of scale', in K. Cox (ed), *Spaces of Globalisation*, Guilford Press, New York.
Ward, S. (1994), *Planning and Urban Change*, Paul Chapman, London.
Whitehead, M. (2003) 'Love thy neighbourhood – rethinking the politics of scale and Walsall's struggle for neighbourhood democracy', *Environment and Planning A*, vol. 35, pp. 277-300.

Chapter 12

Knowing the City? 21st Century Urban Policy and the Introduction of Local Strategic Partnerships

Michael Keith

Introduction

In many ways the notion of the Local Strategic Partnership (LSP) represents the most radically redistributive moment of the 1997 Labour Government. At its heart is a notion of spatial justice that is as disarmingly simple to articulate as it is beguilingly difficult to conceptualize[1]. The notion that a basic level of services should structure the life chances of even the poorest communities is one that harks back to the founding principles of the welfare state. The suggestion that it should be possible to articulate such minimal standards in terms of a series of life chances that should enhance the prospects of some of the most disadvantaged is similarly laudable. The translation of such a suggestion into specified *floor targets* may smack more than a little of the positivist fallacies of the worst excesses of New Public Management but it is still an appeal to both achieve social change and capture a manner in which it might be objectively demonstrable.

So at a time when the notion of targets appear to be diminishing in the minds of Labour ministers looking to a possible third term it might be appropriate to consider the conceptual provenance of Local Strategic Partnerships as well as their chances of success. Where does the LSP fit within the post-1945 attempts to identify particular innovations in spatial governance? Is it possible to consider LSPs as a particular form of urban policy as the contributions to this volume might

---

1 In 2000 the government published a *Framework for Neighbourhood Renewal*, which outlined the manner in which local government would be obliged to create Local Strategic Partnerships that would be expected to address the most intense patterns of socio-economic deprivation in the towns and cities of England through processes of neighbourhood renewal. In particular the government set a goal of key floor targets for basic service provision. The aspiration was that no neighbourhood in Britain should fall below such basic standards. Community Strategies were to be drawn up by local stakeholders to remedy any shortfalls. In areas of particular need, allocations of neighbourhood renewal funding have been made from 2000 to 2005 to encourage joint working between public, private and community sectors to promote change. For fuller details see Social Exclusion Unit (2000).

suggest? More pointedly, how does the territory of the city figure in the structures of power that reconfigure the relations between state institutions and contemporary urbanism?

This chapter is written from the perspective of an individual whose interests are twofold, both those of an academic researcher in the field and as somebody who has chaired one LSP in London over a period of three years[2]. Immanuel Kant demanded a proper scepticism that should inform intellectual inquiry. In contrast, for Voltaire's protagonist Pangloss in *Candide* all was for the best in the best of all possible worlds. At times both the position of critic and the position of publicist provide reassuringly straightforward takes on social policy change. In contrast to these extremes of *academic cynic with clean hands* or *ideological faith and evangelistic revisionism* this chapter attempts to consider some of the incommensurabilities of LSPs constructively. The chapter is consequently written in the spirit of practical engagement, a sense of the pragmatically principled nostrum of having the courage to change the things one can, the strength to accept those one cannot, and the wisdom to know the difference between the two.

Reinventing local state legitimacy?

The origin of LSPs in part needs to be set in a wider debate about the very nature of local government that configures the entire relationship between local and central state power. Within a certain genre of semi-academic/semi-technocratic writing, the 1980s and 1990s in the United Kingdom were seen as bad times for local authorities (see Commission for Local Democracy, 1995; King and Stoker, 1996; Stoker, 2000). A pervasive metaphoric trope represents this era through a narrative that describes the *confiscation* of local government powers by the various *arrogations* of centralising government. This particular narrative played in a melancholy fashion through much of these two decades, cataloguing the systematic removal of one discretion after another from the democratically elected organs of local government. A partial but not exhaustive sample of such a trend of twenty years from 1977-97 might cite: inhibiting the right to intervene in local economies (through restrictions on the right of local authorities to set up arms length companies), curbs on abilities to set the local tax base (through capping regimes), the restrictions on educational interference (through local management of schools), regulations of intervention in the conduct of civil society (through measures such as Clause 28 prohibiting the promotion of gay lifestyles) and limitations on the right to perform the role of social landlord (through right to buy, restrictions on new house building and the promotion of the role of housing associations).

Faced with a need to reinvent itself the most influential lobbyists and local government policy wonks began to fight back in the early 1990s. Among several initiatives one of the more influential was the Commission for Local Democracy

2 The author has been from 2001 to the present the chair of the LSP in the London Borough of Tower Hamlets. The views represented in this article are his alone and are not representative of this partnership in any way.

(1995), which produced work through the early 1990s to its conclusion in 1995. The Commission was chaired initially by Brian Redhead and then, after his death, by Simon Jenkins.

The Commission neither founded nor concluded the debate about the nature and workings of local government. Yet it was both influential in its own right and notable for both the quality of the submissions that were made and the number of its central propositions that subsequently were adopted in whole or in part by the major reforms of the local authority structure adopted by the first Blair administration between 1997 and 2002. A key dynamic that runs to the heart of its ruminations was the fact that local government is in the United Kingdom a creature of statute. Most straightforwardly, the structures of the state at a local level were conventionally allowed to do nothing unless there was statutory justification for them doing so. In this context many – most notably Professor John Stewart from the Institute of Local Government in Birmingham – had long argued for the need to allow local government new powers to register a new legitimacy (Stewart, 1995). Stewart (amongst others) argued that local government should be allowed a new freedom. Rather than being constrained by statute to doing things that were delegated to it from the central state, local government should be able to do anything at all as long as it was not explicitly prohibited from doing so by central government decree. Seemingly extremely simple, this notion of a 'default power' radically restructures the manner which we might think about the constitution of *the polis* at a sub-national level.

Firstly, and most importantly it questions exactly what is government (and more particularly local government) for? In the banal nature of its exercise it is easy to naturalize the changing functional basis of state power under capitalist modernity. A crude and caricatured description of the history of local government across the industrialising globe might typologize the functional concerns of the local state (Rhodes and Wright, 1987). Local governmental power has focused on both *forms of provision* and *regimes of regulation*. Both have tended to emerge as responses to specific crises of demography and morality that the state feels most appropriate to address in a register of the local. Consequently some forms and powers of local government are common to 'western democracies', others more idiosyncratic.

In Britain the industrial excesses of mortality and environmental deterioration commonly demanded a specifically local response to the public health issues of sanitation from the early 19th century onwards. A concern with the warring feudalism of the Jago in East London prompted the London County Council to initiate one of the earliest experiments in state provision of social housing. This resulted in the creation of the Boundary Estate, still standing just to the north of Brick Lane. The provision of homes for *needy* people – reinforced by the legitimacy crises of two world wars – resulted in the accumulation of increasing amounts of local state-run forms of residence from that point until the landmark individualism of Thatcher's Right to Buy legislation began to decimate this socially-owned stock. Until relatively recently in the post war decades there was no such thing as a Social Services Department in a local authority. It emerged with the twin concerns of a specifically post-war notion of social responsibility and a particularly post-Keynesian understanding of an expanding welfare state. Similarly, the tales through which locally-elected councillors came to run geographically discrete education systems arguably owe as much to the imperatives to reproduce a disciplined and literate labour force sensitive to local conditions as it does to any capture of power by local democratic structures. And – in some ways most interesting of all – the obscurely Christian genealogies of languages of renewal and departmental functions of urban regeneration barely existed before the fashion for the reinvention of post-industrial spaces and places of the late 1980s and early 1990s.

Similarly, the *regimes of regulation* reflect particular moral crises as much as the outcomes of conflictual struggles for localized or centralized governmental power. It is possible to read the governmentalities of the control of drinking, enjoyment, sex and food (if these are indeed discrete indulgences) through an iconographic evolution of moral powers that regulated the liberal self of industrial capitalism (Valverde, 2003). The seemingly obscure and hidden histories of land use planning might similarly display the changing notions of governmental common sense about the post-Durkheimian functional nature of the metropolis. So in both forms of provision and regimes of regulation it is imperative to historicize the nature of reform within the perhaps more than banal question. Just what is local government for?

None of the above is stated from a position of hostility or cynicism over the possible answer to such a question. It is instead the case that we need to understand the histories of how both the subjects and the objects of local governmental power are invented, defined and regulated. Such histories explain both the commonalities and the differences between local government regimes in Britain and the rest of the world. More significantly such differences contextualize the meaning of urban policy and urban regeneration. The city becomes both a subject that narrates imperatives of governmentality and an object to be governed. At its heart we need always to remember the Humpty Dumpty-like way[3] in which the imagined and real cities that are the focus of urban policy are the subject of continual reinvention and contestation. The city that informed Peter Shore's introduction of inner city policy in the late 1970s is not necessarily the same city that sits at the heart of Lord Richard Rogers-invoked urbanism and urban renaissance.

It is in this context that the turning away from the notion of statute was so important. If organizations below the level of the nation state were given a default power of well-being they could potentially define the meaning of the cities they were serving and governing. And so if central government was to embark on an adventure through which the prerogative of local government power was to be inverted from a licence to do explicit things to a licence to do anything except

---

3 In *Through the Looking Glass* Alice suggests to Humpty Dumpty that he misuses the word 'glory'. '"...glory doesn't mean a nice knock down argument" Alice objected. "When I use a word," Humpty-Dumpty said in a rather scornful tone, "it means just what I chose it to mean, nothing more, nothing less." "The question is," said Alice, "whether you can make words mean so many different things." "The question is," said Humpty Dumpty, "who is to be master – that's all."' (Carroll, 1865/1978, p.171).

those things that were prohibited, then it would need to be set within a certain sense of humility about the instability that characterizes the remit of local governmental powers from their very inception.

The default power was introduced. It became a central plank of the Local Government Act of 2000. But it was introduced within a conditional license. The long argued default power was qualified by the setting of a *new branding of the local state*. Within the reforms of the act – and much of the subsequent writing of the New Local Government Network[4] – local authorities were to be transformed from being principally *providers of services* to being principally *creatures of influence* and the major stakeholders amongst many in a locality. The default power could be exercised as long as it related to politics that were congruent with a Community Plan that set out a major strategy for the locality that was agreed by key stakeholders that were drawn together in Local Strategic Partnerships.

This inflection in local representative democracy is significant. Numerous reforms from the late 1980s onwards that had generated litanies of *partnerships* at times began to look like pluralist state theory institutionalized after the fact. A look at the ESRC Local Government programme of the mid-1990s is revealing in this (see particularly Stoker, 2000). There is a sense in which the refashioning of local government (driven by the licensed return to local democracy after two decades of drift in the opposite direction) was structured by the normative imperatives that supported new pluralist state theory. In this context social theory did not so much explain the world of local government as reshape it in its own image. Not so much the city made comprehensible when Robert Dahl (1961) comes to town as the city remapped when new pluralist state theory was institutionalized in Britain. This may or may not prove to be felicitous. A series of partnerships in economic development, social welfare, crime prevention, public health and social housing came to characterize the local authorities of the late 1990s. So in one sense LSPs represented some kind of *uber partnership*; an attempt to capture the end logic of this new pluralism.

LSPs are also an aspect of the post-1997 attempt to generate both constitutional change and, with it, increased levels of regional autonomy. This has sometimes been described as a form of *new localism*[5]. The creation of Regional Development Agencies, a Scottish Parliament, a National Assembly for Wales, a new institutional architecture of London government and regional assemblies all pointed to a wish (at least a rhetoric) of decentralising power from Whitehall and Westminster.

But the LSPs were also mediated through the language of social exclusion. Here again language is important in shaping the objects of government and the subjects of the city. There is not the space here to provide suitable analytical consideration of the import of the shift from a language of *inequality* and injustice to a more European notion of *exclusion* (Lister, 1998a and 1998b). Suffice to say

---

4 See the New Local Government Network literature on their website: http://www.nlgn.org.uk/nlgn.php

5 An increasingly prolific literature exists on the new localism but for a helpful introduction see Corry and Stoker (2002).

that one strand of the genesis of social reform ran from John Smith's attempt to develop a reforming agenda for the late 20th century when he was leader of the Labour Party. His Commission for Social Justice (1994) (with research run by a young David Milliband) began to put together a broader vision for a Party aspiring to power. The genesis of many of the more social democratic measures that have emerged since 1997 can be seen in the final report of the Commission. But most importantly the conventional tension on the Left between the conflict-laden languages of social inequality and the electoral imperatives of economic pragmatism are elided through a language of social exclusion. Within a broader concern of state legitimacy LSPs were to be established (and governed by) the new central government's Social Exclusion Unit, with its mandate translated through Regional Offices of national government[6]. In this context the LSPs were to carry the burden of New Labour's commitments to a more inclusive society. In this sense it is worth exploring further the degree to which the pluralism of the LSPs facilitates the transformation of urban policy through the default power of well-being as it is currently articulated.

Most visions of social justice – from the pragmatic to the Utopian – contain within them a certain sense of contradiction, or at least a series of constitutive tensions. Such contradictions are properly the subject of the debates of political theory. In this context it would be nothing new to suggest that the social policy interventions of the Blair years will in part be shaped by the contradictions that they contain. As Andrew Gamble (1994) has demonstrated, Thatcherism built a coalition of interests that was very successful at winning elections through harnessing moral conservatism, economic liberalism and social nationalism. The incommensurability of these forces was made visible at their moments of greatest tension, most dramatically when nationalist anti-European sentiment clashed with the imperatives of finance capital. Likewise Blair's populism has attempted to subsume social democratic reformism, constitutional innovation, economic liberalism and moral conservatism. The new localism is so important to such a political project because it in part subsumes the potential incommensurability of these imperatives. However, in doing so it reproduces at a local level the tensions that are manifested between them.

Such is the inevitable product of both the dialectics of reform and the will to power. It does not traduce the efforts of many people working across very many LSPs to suggest that the workings of this particular innovation will in this way similarly be structured by the incommensurabilities of its design. In the case of

---

6 LSP monitoring, the disbursement of Neighbourhood Renewal and New Deal for Communities funds, and the accreditation of partnerships, Neighbourhood Renewal Strategies and Community Plans remains (in 2004) with regional Government Offices rather than with the Regional Development Agencies, through which many other 'urban regeneration' programmes are now channelled. This creates a further tension in the co-ordination of 'social' programmes of social inclusion that are disbursed and monitored by the proxy arms of central government and 'economic' programmes that are controlled by Regional Development Agencies (for further discussion see Goodwin, this volume; Johnstone and Whitehead, this volume).

contemporary urban policy it is the argument here that the particular contradictions of the LSP design process are in this fashion directly related to the discursive construction of a notion of social exclusion within (firstly) current Labour thinking around the crisis of legitimacy of the local state and (secondly) within government practice that tries to *regovern the city*. Such contradictions are not necessarily pernicious. They are instead near universal features of social policy innovation. After all, as the introduction to this chapter observed, LSPs represent in many ways fundamentally one of the more redistributive moments of policy reform in the post-1997 government of Britain.

It is in this spirit that it is worth considering in a little more detail where some of the tensions within the workings of the LSP process might arise. What follows is written partly from the subjective position of an author that has for three years chaired an LSP and continues to do so. However, these comments are based much less on this biographical role than on the various research projects based at the Centre for Urban and Community Research that have taken democratic participation, community politics, neighbourhood renewal and urban regeneration as their subject[7].

Tensions in the formation and operation of LSPs

There are, I would argue, five crucial tensions that have emerged from the formation and operation of the LSPs now established in English towns and cities. These tensions all relate to the manner in which, in responding to forms of urban inequality, social policy generally (and urban policy in particular) constructs the city to be governed through its institutional form and deliberative processes.

Participatory v representative democracy

One strand of thinking around notions of social exclusion represents the phenomenon in terms of certain distinctive features of provision that relate to a calculus of geographical risk; less chance of a job, less long to live, more chance of being a victim of crime, less chance of finding a decent doctor. A second strand of its definition highlights the impacts such cartographies have on the people that are mapped by them. In particular *the exclusion* from labour markets, social networks and civil society is diagnostically taken (or asserted or assumed) to be a feature of exclusion itself. The logic of such a stance suggests that participation is not merely a product of social *inclusion* but also a social good in its own right that should be promoted. Consequently – frequently translated through a language of social capital – a causal connection is commonly made between low rates of participation (in elections, voluntary organizations, 'bowling clubs') and high rates of social exclusion. In much policy discussion this leads to the conclusion that local participation in the local government decision-making process, and likewise the running of local schools, hospitals or housing estates, is a social good to be promoted. Within the model of LSPs, enhanced democratic power for local

7 For further details of completed and ongoing research see www.goldsmiths.ac.uk/cucr

councils (representative democracy) is promoted alongside enhanced forms of participatory democracy. In part this emerges in occasionally hubristic tensions between local councillors and voluntary organizations, each keen to promote the legitimacy of their representative status. But more significantly the tensions between participatory democracy and representative democracy run deeper than this. They speak to very different models of the democratic.

Co-ordinating v command models of accountability

In part, LSPs address the self-evident need to co-ordinate service provision at the local level. The now clichéd lexicon of *joined-up* and *seamless* public services is nowhere more clearly illustrated than in grim moments of its failure such as when an old woman in the East End of London (who survived the camps and the holocaust) is burnt out of her home by a gang of young men (that the police fail to catch), is discharged from hospital on a Friday night by NHS social workers (who have failed to make sure that she has somewhere to stay the night) and so arrives at the local council housing office where the local authority's social workers fail to find her respite care[8].

But such a lack of co-ordination might also prompt a questioning of the responsibility for such a failure. Of course here – as elsewhere – it is everybody's fault except the poor individual who is in need of support. Yet such a worry pervades the very architecture of partnership. Because the more that powers are pooled between agencies in the city the more difficult it is to define accountability. There is a very real tension between partnership governance and notions of responsibility; two laudable goals that are not always reconcilable.

Strategic v consensual models of decision-making

In the welter of literatures that focus on the nature of the spaces through which urban policy is realized there tends to be relatively little consideration of the temporalities of the city. Most straightforwardly the interests of the locality in the long, medium and short terms are not always clearly reconcilable. The notion of rebuilding a sink estate in the inner city in order to rehouse people that may die early because the overcrowded conditions lead not only to problems of anti-social behaviour but also to pronounced concentrations of ill health and mortality may appear an unalloyed good. But such medium term gains may come at the price of short-term losses. Families may be broken up by the process of decanting the estate and rehousing, leaseholders that have taken up their right to buy (RTB) at a high discount may not realize the full capital potential of their newly acquired property, potential purchasers may lose their right to buy by being rehoused on a housing association estate with no RTB, young children may be forced to move schools.

Similarly, the need for major new infrastructure – a new hospital, a new railway line, a new property development with jobs on a derelict piece of land –

---

8 See the East London Advertiser of 23rd October 2003 for a slightly inaccurate detailed account of this true case.

may all foreground a calculus of long term collective gain and short term disruptions of environment, amenity and preference. The temporalities of social progress may be measured in aggregate yet are lived individually. The time horizons of urban policy need to be considered alongside its spatialities. In such a context the ability to harness a consensual model of change through LSPs is not perhaps as straightforward as some of the prescriptive good practice might suggest. Politics is about settling such agonistic debates (Mouffe, 2000) and is not always susceptible to consensus. The structure of the LSP potentially subsumes such a tension, demanding strategic intervention at the local level but implying a consensual model of deliberative democracy.

Social inclusion v service quality

The sociology of risk has highlighted the variable metrics against which different policy interventions might be measured. In such circumstances the credentialized knowledges of the police service to police, the health service to determine health provision and the health and safety inspectors to determine the risks of social congress create a tension between specific forms of technocratic expertise and particular realizations of participatory democracy. This particular tension is common to all forms of deliberative democracy but may surface vividly in the contemporary city over the relative (cash) value for money of extra police constables or neighbourhood wardens, the right to be funded for alternative forms of medical therapy or the right to hold a street party. This is compounded when in each case the model of neighbourhood-based democratic structure may clash with alternative scales of democratic accountability; the local authority or the interests of the city as a whole. In late 1980s and early 1990s London, forms of neighbourhood local democracy became momentarily fashionable (notably in Islington and Tower Hamlets) until the nimbyism of one neighbourhood against another began to surface (see also Whitehead, this volume). In Tower Hamlets the racial geographies of neighbourhood democracy translated into a form of racist Bantustans with a white East of the borough limiting the housing choices (and housing demand) of the overcrowded west of the borough around Spitalfields and Whitechapel. Such 'localism' promoted division and resulted in the Commission for Racial Equality taking action against the local authority's creation of seven (geographically discrete) separate registers of housing need and the BNP coming to power on the Isle of Dogs on a racially coded ticket of 'Island Homes for Island People' (see Keith, 1995). The spatial decentralization of power is not unproblematic.

Knowable v unknowable notions of the city

Perhaps most interestingly for studies of contemporary urbanism the notion of the LSP contains within it a model of the local as largely knowable and controllable. It is refreshing in its reflection on the aspirations for social justice that are explicit in the notion that nobody should suffer worse forms of basic service provision because of where they live. The territory of the city that is covered by the partnership and the Community Strategy (or Community Plan) is to be mapped through baseline statistics, developed at the small scale through neighbourhood action planning and regulated through regimes of neighbourhood management. Yet such a valorization of the knowable nature of city life contrasts starkly with a genre of writing about the city that sees it as fundamentally elusive. This has both political (ethical) and policy implications. A city that valorizes the urban as a meeting place of strangers is quite simply not reconcilable with a communitarian city that privileges an anthropological ethical matrix. In policy terms the city that prioritizes the individual's rights to find their own way through the journey from home to school to job is not quite the same as one that polices the behaviours of domesticity, prescribes the school to which a child is allocated and regulates workfare.

Again such a tension is most lucidly illustrated by example. The role of faith communities in civil society is demonstrably powerful in the inner cities across the United Kingdom. However, the ethical plausibility of Catholic, Jewish and Islamic education is commonly a product of historical struggle as much as it is a straightforward reflection of demographic presence. The issue of geographical scale again amplifies such dilemmas. The right to 'plan' the city speaks directly to the plausibility of the (frequently noble) notion of social engineering that underscores a reformist social democratic agenda. And yet the creation of structural land-use planning at regional level (for example the London Plan of the new mayoral system) may prioritize a different model of the future than the Unitary Development Plans of individual local authorities (such as the London boroughs). The exercise of *planning* as such is in a sense a case of epistemological arrogance, a claim to know what can and should happen next in particular city spaces (see Keith, 2003 for a fuller exploration of some of these issues). But geography determines the optics through which interest may be represented differently; the material interests of the city as a whole do not necessarily coincide with those of any of its constitutive parts. Both the plausibility of the knowledge claims of the plan and the field of vision that it takes as its object make visible very different notions of urbanism.

Conclusion

The tensions that subsist within the creation of Local Strategic Partnerships are not always unhealthy. However they are constitutive features of the democratic process rather than incidental features of poor design. Their existence will promote different forms of (momentary) reconciliation and different forms of (antagonistic) confrontation. Moreover, the five tensions listed here create dynamics that are both internal to themselves and that are relative to one another. An optic that renders the city visible in terms of its ability to co-ordinate the quality of public service provision is very different from one that measures the degree to which a model of participatory democracy is promoted. Heretically, it may be the case that the strategic co-ordination of the big battalions of health, police and local government is not easily reconciled with a model that promotes participatory deliberation. And this might prompt us to ask the citizens of the city whether the models of the latter are quite as celebratory as they sometimes appear. Aphoristically perhaps it might prompt us to ask if we really all do want to live in Porto Allegre[9]?

References

Carroll, L. (1865/1978), *Through the Looking Glass*, Methuen, London.

Commission for Local Democracy (1995), *Taking Charge: The rebirth of local democracy*, Municipal Journal Books, London.

Commission on Social Justice (1994), *Social Justice - Strategies for National Renewal*, IPPR, London.

Corry, D. and Stoker, G. (2002), *New Localism*, New Local Government Network, London.

Dahl, R. (1961), *Who Governs?*, Yale University Press, New Haven, Conn.

Fung, A. and Wright, E. (2003), *Deepening Democracy: institutional innovations in empowered participatory governance (Real Utopias Project)*, Verso, London.

Gamble, A. (1994), *The Free Economy and The Strong State: the politics of Thatcherism*, Macmillan, Basingstoke.

Keith, M. (1995), 'Making the street visible? Placing racial violence in context', *New Community*, vol. 21(4), pp.551-65.

Keith, M. (2003), *Between Postcolonial Melancholia and the Allure of the Cosmopolitan*, AA Files 49, Architectural Association, London.

Keith, M. (2004), *After the Cosmopolitan*, Routledge, London.

King, D. and Stoker, G. (eds) (1996), *Rethinking Local Democracy*, Macmillan, Basingstoke.

Lister, R. (1998a) 'From equality to social inclusion', *Critical Social Policy*, vol. 18(5), pp.215-25

Lister, R. (1998b), *Social Exclusion and New Labour*, Macmillan, Basingstoke.

Mouffe, C. (2000), *The Democratic Paradox*, Verso, London.

Rhodes, R. and Wright, V. (1987), *Territorial Politics in Western Europe*, Cass, London.

Sandercock, L. (1997), *Towards Cosmopolis*, Wiley, Chichester.

Social Exclusion Unit (2000), *National Strategy for Neighbourhood Renewal: a framework for consultation*, Cabinet Office, London.

Stewart, J. (1995), *Innovation in Democratic Practice*, INJOGOV, Birmingham.

Stoker, G. (2000), *The New Politics of British Local Governance*, Macmillan, Basingstoke

Valverde, M. (2003), *Law's Dream of a Common Knowledge*, Princeton University Press, Princeton.

---

9 The Porto Allegre model of participatory democracy has become increasingly well referenced as a model of best practice. I am not questioning the validity of such citations but do wonder about the degree of celebration in the light of many years first hand experience of forms of participatory democracy that privilege populist intolerance in multicultural city settings. For exploration of the Porto Allegre model see Sandercock (1997) or Fung and Wright (2003).

Chapter 13

Gender, Place and Renaissance

Sue Brownill

Introduction

The failure of past regeneration policy to engage with gender relations and inequalities is well documented (see, for example, May, 1997; Brownill and Darke, 1998; Alsop et al, 2001; Women's Design Service (WDS), 2002). With the advent of a 'new regeneration narrative' (Morgan, 2002) with its stress on the creation of an inclusive urban society and revitalized, liveable, sustainable, urban space, an important question must be how gender fits into the storyline. Does this new tale of the city have the potential and intent to engage with gender relations and inequalities in the urban environment in ways in which its predecessors did not? And, what are the potential impacts on those same gender relations on the vision it is portraying?

This chapter addresses these and other questions in a number of ways. Firstly, it examines the gender implications of the language and discourse associated with current urban policy statements and in, particular, their emphasis on issues of exclusion and community. Secondly, it reflects on possible scenarios for the complex and dynamic interactions between gender, place and renaissance that potentially flow from the vision of revitalized urban areas put forward in these policies. Finally, this chapter examines some different ways of seeing the relationship between gender and regeneration and outlines their possible implications for policy. The chapter will reveal the gap that exists between the rhetoric of New Labour policies aimed at addressing gender inequalities in the urban environment and the reality on the ground. But it will also underline the contradictory potential contained within the vision of sustainable, revitalized cities that is at its heart. Before looking at these contradictions in more detail however, existing discussions on gender and regeneration are explored.

In writing this chapter I will be drawing not only on policy documents and accounts of research but also the experience of a group which has been trying for a number of years to put gender on the regeneration agenda in the UK. Organized through Oxfam as part of its UK anti-poverty programme, the ReGender group brings together projects, individuals and organizations who are trying to engender regeneration on the ground and to lobby all levels of government to prioritize gender in their regeneration programmes and strategies. Figures 13.1, 13.2 and 13.3 provide a summary of three of the projects that are linked to ReGender which will be referred to in the chapter.

West Midlands Gender and Regeneration Project: began in 1998 and brought together voluntary groups in the area aiming to:

- Strengthen the commitment to an 'inclusive' approach to regeneration which incorporates a gender dimension;
- Draw on the research that highlights the absence of women from many regeneration initiatives;
- Promote positive action to address gender differences within regeneration programmes.

The initial strategy was to organise a number of awareness raising events for practitioners and policy makers. This was unsuccessful. The strategy therefore shifted to one of a survey to map the involvement of organisations in gender and regeneration and to identify why agencies and practitioners did or did not prioritise gender in regeneration. The poor response rate to the survey confirmed the invisibility of gender in regeneration. The next phase focused on the development of some practical tools to facilitate the development of a gender perspective in regeneration. This led to the production of a gender mainstreaming toolkit (Bennett et al, 2000a and 2000b).

Figure 13.1 Examples of gender and regeneration projects 1: West Midlands Gender and Regeneration Project

Gender and regeneration

The relationship between gender and regeneration can be approached from a number of directions and there are therefore a variety of perspectives to draw upon when thinking about gender and the urban renaissance. Much work has centred on regeneration policy itself, drawing attention to its general failure to acknowledge gender as a strategic regeneration issue (May, 1997; Brownill and Darke, 1998; Alsop et al, 2001; WDS, 2002). This work has also sought to counter the invisibility of gender by showing empirically how and why gender is central not marginal to urban policy. Thus Jane Darke and I (Brownill and Darke, 1998) argue that men and women's experience of living in regeneration areas is different and they therefore have different routes to regeneration which should be reflected in policy. May (1997) concentrates on the gendered nature of poverty and exclusion and the concentration of women in poverty in regeneration areas. The Local Government Information Unit (LGIU) (1998) shows how key regeneration issues such as community safety, transport and employment creation are affected by women's differential use and experience of urban areas, and puts forward a policy agenda for regeneration schemes based on this.

While not theoretically explicit and in places failing to distinguish between gender and women, this work can be seen to draw on the stream of feminist urban research which seeks to explore the connections between gender relations and

The Women's Design Service ran a three-year project between 1999 and 2001 looking at the role of women in urban regeneration in London. It aimed to build the capacity of women to influence the decisions and policies of their regeneration partnership boards and to develop good practice guidance. It focused on the involvement of specific groups of women including elderly women, disabled women, ethnic minority women and women on low incomes. Work was carried out in three case studies in varying parts of London. Volunteer women rather than existing groups from these areas worked with project workers on a variety of issues including:

- Community consultation exercises where local women undertook surveys in their areas of women's perceptions of and needs from regeneration. This resulted in increased skills for the women involved and better information for policy-makers.

- Community health and safety audits looking at the impact of the built environment on safety and well-being and the drawing up of schemes to address the issues identified.

- An audit of women's centres to enable women to design their own within one of the areas.

- Networking within the area.

- Raising the skills and capacity of individual women to participate in the ongoing regeneration of their areas.

From this experience a checklist and other guidelines have been produced to promote gender within regeneration (WDS 2002) but difficulties have been encountered in sustaining this work after the funding expired.

Figure 13.2 Examples of gender and regeneration projects 2: Women's Design Service

space (Mackenzie 1989; McDowell 1993a and 1993b; Massey 1994). This work has noted how the spatial organization of urban space into spheres of work, home, leisure etc. both mirrors and reinforces the division of roles between the sexes. Research has also highlighted the ways in which women are disadvantaged in the city and their experience marginalized (Little et al 1988; Darke et al 2000). Against this, Wilson (1991) argues that the city can provide opportunities for women and can be the place within which gender relations can be transformed. Recent work on gender and gentrification (see Bondi, 1999; Lees, 2000) has sought to explore these tensions between opportunity and oppression that the city presents and will be returned to later in the chapter.

Objective 1 South Yorkshire is funded through European Structural Funds. The programme runs between 2000 and 2006 and involves £700m in EU funding and £1.8b overall. To meet the EU mainstreaming requirements a number of initiatives have taken place including;

- A crosscutting themes team whose role is to embed gender equality as an issue in all aspects of the funding process.

- A Gender Task Group made up of independent individuals which meet to scrutinize and co-ordinate activity throughout the programme.

- A number of positive action projects to tackle labour market segregation, to promote work-life balance in employment practice, to advance gender balance in decision-making and projects targeting disengaged men.

- A gender manager to oversee positive action projects and the progress on mainstreaming.

- A gender champion to promote understanding among programme staff, partners and applicants.

- Research and monitoring e.g. a gender profile of the labour market.

In addition a number of events have been organised across the region to bring women and women's organisations together. Finally separate from Objective 1, the South Yorkshire Women's Development Trust was launched in April 2002 to provide a voice for women across the region, to provide links between different projects and organizations and to look to sustain activity through accessing funding and sharing resources and expertise. SYWDT co-ordinates a number of projects including training in leadership and technology, and community regeneration (Objective 1 South Yorkshire, 2003).

Figure 13.3 Examples of gender and regeneration projects 3: Objective 1 South Yorkshire

Other research on gender and regeneration has examined the conceptualization of women and men within the 'urban problem' as defined by policymakers. In previous work, for example, I have discussed how women's role in 'areas of deprivation' has been problematized (Brownill, 2000). There has been a long-standing trend in urban policy, which, as we will see later, is continued by New Labour policies, of seeing women's role as mothers, and especially as 'bad' or single parents as indicators of and key contributors to the poverty and social malaise that urban policy is trying to tackle. Thus policy has not always been gender blind, but has sought to stigmatize women and the areas in which they live on the basis of their deviation from the nuclear family ideal and assumptions about their 'proper' role in urban communities. This is repeated when the role of young men is looked at with a focus on their involvement in crime and urban disorder.

More recently some alternative ideas on gender and regeneration have developed within both theory and practice. Organizations and projects on the ground have increasingly been exploring gender mainstreaming as a strategy for getting gender on the regeneration agenda. Developed largely within the EU, gender mainstreaming refers to the hardwiring of gender into all aspects of the policy process – analysis, programme development, implementation, evaluation and decision-making – rather than relying on separate equalities policies or units to deliver (European Commission, 1996; Gilroy and Booth, 1999).

But gender mainstreaming is largely a tool and needs to be driven by a theoretical perspective on the relationships between gender and the urban environment. Recent work has explored the ways in which the geography or infrastructure of everyday life could perhaps provide the link between gender and the environment (Gilroy and Booth, 1999; Horelli, 2000). Drawing on earlier ideas of utopian urban landscapes (for example, Hayden, 1981), this approach starts from the perspective of the lived experience of men, women and children in cities. The emphasis is on the patterns of everyday life – caring, schooling, getting to work and the structures into which they fit. Inevitably, the 'physical environment is also closely woven into the repetitions that form the spine of the routines of everyday life' (Horelli, 2000, p.38). It argues that the segregation of spheres in the urban environment – public and private, production and reproduction – that are, themselves, so imbued with gender relations, need to be broken down. This is as much to do with the recognition of the way in which contemporary urban living for both women and men is based on attempts to combine increased and multiple roles, as it is with a desire to focus solely on the implications for women's roles of the elision between the segregation of urban space with the sexual division of labour. 'What is needed now, in practical terms, are spaces which do not constrain multiple roles' (Gilroy and Booth, 1999, p.308). Providing the infrastructure for this therefore becomes the prime focus of local development and the organising principle for urban space. The implications of this approach for the mixed use, compact and sustainable urban forms of the renaissance will be returned to later in the chapter.

Having set out, albeit briefly, some of the ways of thinking through the relationships between gender and regeneration and the policy implications of these, the chapter will now go on to look at how this relationship is manifested in the latest round of urban policy, beginning with the language and discourse of regeneration.

The place of gender in the discourse of renaissance

The language and discourse of urban policy in the UK is receiving particular attention at present (for example, Imrie and Raco, 2003). Some have noted how the proliferation of words such as exclusion, capacity building, social capital and renaissance are part of the professionalization of the regeneration process, excluding those who fail to understand the jargon (Centre for Local Economic Strategies (CLES), 2002). Others stress the disjunction between the story portrayed through the narrative of renaissance and the operation on the ground of more fundamental processes and social relations that are hidden behind the discourse (Cooke, 2002; Brownill et al, 2003). Thus Lees (2003) argues that renaissance is a metaphor for 'state-led gentrification'; Cooke (2002) shows how the rhetoric of the devolution of power hides a centralization of control through budgets, law and managerial techniques such as performance indicators, and Edwards (2001) indicates that the language of community and inclusion fails to take account of the wide spectrum of stakeholders, noting particularly how people with disabilities are left out of the equation.

In this section I want to analyse the discourse and experience of renaissance from the point of view of gender. Are we seeing the same gap between rhetoric and reality, between the vision of a new inclusive urban environment and the operation of the 'dark side' of planning? Is the problematization of gender evident in previous rounds of urban policy recurring? This task is not made easier by the fragmentation of urban policy that is currently occurring. It is possible to distinguish three main strands, often referred to the three 'r's: 'regional, renewal and renaissance' (Brownill et al, 2003). 'Regional' refers to the activities of the Regional Development Agencies (RDAs) with their emphasis on economic development. 'Renaissance' is the name for the strand emerging from the Urban Task Force, the Urban White Paper (Department of Environment, Transport and the Regions (DETR), 2000a) and the more recent *Sustainable Communities* action plan (ODPM, 2003) concerned with promoting 'attractive' and 'liveable' towns and cities. 'Renewal' is the largely estate-based work aimed at 'closing the gap' between Britain's poorest places and the rest of the country and tackling social exclusion. Policies here primarily emanate from the Office of the Deputy Prime Minister (ODPM) and include New Deal for Communities (NDC), the Neighbourhood Renewal Fund, the *National Strategy for Neighbourhood Renewal* (SEU, 2001), and also the work of Social Exclusion Unit (SEU) with, for example, lone parents and young people. In what follows I concentrate on the last two 'r's. This is not to deny the importance of regional economic development for gender issues – indeed it is a major issue – but again confines of space and the recognition of a certain amount of overlap have intervened.

In looking at the discourse of renaissance I want to concentrate both on what is said explicitly about gender and also the implications of the policies for gender relations in the urban environment. In doing this I am going to focus on three main issues. Two of these are words and concepts that are essential to the whole notion of the renaissance – *inclusion* and *community*. The third issue is summed up by the phrase *gender, place and renaissance* and is a concern with the implications of the renaissance for the interaction of urban space and gender relations.

Exclusion, inclusion and gender

Unlike previous eras of urban policy where examining gender issues meant reviewing a silence (Brownill and Darke, 1998), the Urban White Paper (DETR, 2000a) represents one of the first major urban policy documents to refer to gender. Under the heading 'An Inclusive Society' it states:

> We want all who live in urban areas to have the opportunity to achieve their full potential – regardless of irrelevant factors such as race, age, gender, faith and disability. We also want all to have their say in policy development and implementation and to have equal access to services (p.36).

The story goes, therefore, that a government that is sensitive to difference, aware of social exclusion having undertaken extensive research into urban problems and past policy failures, has put together a coherent programme to make our cities both liveable and inclusive. But a closer examination reveals a different narrative. The use of the word irrelevant is particularly illustrative. Presumably used to imply that those formulating the policy do not think that the factors mentioned should be barriers to achieving opportunity, it also gives the impression that these are not significant enough issues to be addressed by policy. More to the point it suggests blindness to the operation of gender relations in the urban environment, which will be returned to later. Crucially this is the only reference to gender in the document. There is speculation that the design and physical-regeneration led vision set out in the Urban Task Force report (Urban Task Force, 1999), upon which the Urban White Paper was based, was adapted by the SEU to include references to social inclusion and exclusion. Indeed, an examination of the Task Force report reveals little connection with these issues. Likewise the *State of English Cities* report (DETR, 2000b), which provided the empirical base of much of the Urban White Paper, provides no discussion of gender. Gender is therefore marginalized within the 'renewal' and exclusion wing of urban policy rather than being integrated throughout the renaissance project. It is left to the eternal sticking plaster provided by 'joined-up government' to ensure the inclusivity that is intended.

Even if this marginalization is seen within the context of 'joining it all up', another reason for questioning whether this inclusive urban society will materialize is that the notion of social exclusion/inclusion employed by New Labour is itself gendered. While social exclusion is potentially seen as a more sophisticated concept than poverty, as it includes elements other than material deprivation, it still contains within it overtones of the deserving/undeserving poor dichotomy of previous generations. Zoe Morrison (2003), for example, has noted how when lines are drawn between who is included and who is excluded, single parents are regularly defined as excluded.

The assumptions about the 'general population' of cities that the Task Force discusses are themselves exclusionary (Lees, 2003). The language used is that of 'life-style choices', 'increased leisure time' and 'need for culture', but as Lees (2003, p.71) observes, 'where in this image of the general population are to be found the single parents, the unemployed, the immobile poor or those on low incomes?'. In a similar way, but this time in the context of the restructuring of city economies, the *State of English Cities* report (DETR, 2000b), turns women's success into a problem when it states: 'But problems remain since many of the jobs have been for women on a part-time basis, thereby leaving a large residue of unemployed men' (p.8). The more subtle and complex interactions between gender relations and the restructuring of local and regional economies is ignored. In this way the tendency to problematize gender, which occurred in previous eras of urban policy, is continuing under New Labour. Policy draws a neat boundary between who are the included and who are the excluded and the ways in which those boundaries are drawn are themselves gendered.

New Labour's approach to exclusion also prescribes routes to inclusion and regeneration, largely through work. But if the experience of living in urban areas and the experience of poverty and exclusion are different for men and women so too will routes to inclusion be different. Rose Gilroy (1996) notes the gendered aspects of routes to inclusion in an area of Newcastle. Jobs, their creation and their accessing through training schemes were seen very much as the strategy favoured by and directed towards men. Some women on the estate took a different route. For them the need for self-esteem and confidence was paramount. Starting with a group based at a local nursery school parents began meeting, sharing experiences, identifying needs and from this eventually grew community businesses and childcare projects.

The experiences of some of the projects within the ReGender group illustrate some further barriers to inclusion. A key contributory factor here was the absence of any real mechanisms for identifying and addressing gender inequalities within urban policy. For example, the Single Regeneration Budget (SRB), the main regeneration policy programme between 1995 and 2001 aimed at tackling exclusion, has no strategic objective relating to gender. Funding and monitoring arrangements do not specify the setting or meeting of gendered targets or outputs or the gathering of gender-disaggregated statistics. The WDS project, for example, had an original target to work with six partnerships on gender issues, but only three were found that gave enough priority to gender to become involved. The treatment of gender issues stands in marked contrast to that of those relating to race. To promote racial equality the SRB has strategic objectives that require regeneration projects to address the disadvantages faced by black and ethnic minorities, and also require partnerships to specify targets for black and ethnic minorities, for example for jobs created and pupils benefiting. This is not to argue that race should not get this treatment, but is shows that under a general heading such as exclusion or diversity, unless different dimensions are clearly identified and mechanisms put in place to ensure they are addressed they will fall off the agenda. While the SRB is rightly criticized for being target and output driven, there is no doubt that targets focus the minds of practitioners to deliver and open up opportunities for projects on the ground to secure funding.

Other policies tackling exclusion which will outlive the SRB, such as the NDC, are repeating this lack of attention to gender issues. Detailed Race Equality Guidance has been published for NDC projects but little or nothing on gender equality exists. The *National Strategy for Neighbourhood Renewal* (SEU, 2001) is based on a major review of information and policy carried out over two years by the SEU. In all, 18 Policy Action Team reports were published. In the initial consultation document there were two references to women. While questions were asked on every policy as to how they addressed ethnic minorities none were asked about gender. Alsop et al (2001, p.4) note that only one of these reports – that of the financial services PAT – contained a sub-section on gender issues.

At this point the observant reader who has examined Figures 13.1, 13.2 and 13.3 and looked at some of the projects under consideration may well say, 'But what about Objective One South Yorkshire?' It has a gender taskforce, a gender manager, has initiated projects to tackle gender disadvantage in the region and is looking to integrate gender issues within its programmes. The reason for this different experience is that South Yorkshire is in receipt of EU Structural Funds which between 2000 and 2006 require gender mainstreaming. Funding will not be released unless the programme can show that gender considerations are integrated into all aspects of the work. It is too early to say whether or not mainstreaming will deliver significant gender impacts in South Yorkshire, nevertheless the processes and structures established indicate what can be achieved when policy addresses gender issues.

Even in those areas not in receipt of EU funds, mainstreaming is being promoted as a way of incorporating gender issues into regeneration activity. For example, the West Midlands Gender and Regeneration Project, after trying unsuccessfully to raise awareness on gender issues in regeneration, shifted its strategy towards the development of a toolkit to be used by practitioners and grassroots organizations to embed gender issues within all stages of the regeneration process (Bennett et al, 2000b). The toolkit focuses on four key aspects of the regeneration process: programme planning, programme development, programme management, and monitoring and evaluation. For each of these phases guidelines and checklists are produced for practitioners and policymakers to follow to ensure a gendered approach. Thus as part of the background work to drawing up regeneration strategies the toolkit calls for a gender profile of the region to be drawn up, disaggregating data on employment, qualifications, etc. A similar process in South Yorkshire is showing great gaps between the economic strategy of high-tech employment being pursued and the educational qualifications particularly of young men in the region. The strategy stage would need to include a gender impact analysis of the proposed policies to ensure the gender needs identified in the first stage were being addressed and that the policies to be implemented did not exacerbate gender disadvantage. In the implementation stage, as well as an infrastructure of officers (such as that established in South Yorkshire) being put in place, all officers would need to adopt procedures for ensuring gender issues are included in project appraisal and monitoring systems. And finally, evaluation and monitoring should also have a gender dimension. This toolkit is now being progressed by the RDA in the region.

Other issues of strategy emerge from this discussion. New Labour's focus on exclusion covers a variety of dimensions, poverty, class, disability, race and gender. Some see this as an advantage. For example, the conclusion from many of those involved in the West Midlands project was that approaching gender through social exclusion was likely to meet with less resistance from policymakers and practitioners. The danger, though, is that gender becomes one voice among many and may not be prioritized. Therefore unless the statement in the Urban White Paper is backed up by clear policy guidance and greater moves towards mainstreaming gender it is likely to be a far from 'irrelevant' barrier to opportunity within cities.

Community

The second area of the discourse of renaissance of significance to gender is the notion of community. As Atkinson (1998 and 1999) and Imrie and Raco (2003) show, the community is placed at the forefront of regeneration policies[1]. This stems in part from the Communitarian roots of New Labour (see Johnstone, this volume) and is also seen as contributing to the restructuring of local government which is a further significant part of the New Labour project. The SEU (2000) for example, claims 'the most effective [policy] interventions are often where communities are actively involved in their design and delivery and, where possible, in the driving seat' (para.1.19). Through initiatives such as NDC, the government's commitment to bottom-up and community-led regeneration is evident and through the emphasis on capacity building the significance of community to the governance of urban policy is underlined. However, in practice this empowerment is firmly controlled and channelled through mechanisms of project approval and appraisal and bidding guidance (Edwards, 2001; Morgan, 2002; Brownill et al, 2003).

But community is also significant because of the way the concept itself serves to bring together an idea of place with gendered relations. I have argued elsewhere (Brownill, 1997) that the historical development of the term community was a reaction to the harsh realities of urbanized, capitalist society, portraying as it does an imagined, sheltered, warm and humanized place which rests on traditional ideas of the role of men and women. Community corresponds to the world of the home, the private sphere where relations are caring and attention is paid to those areas of life, such as housing, open space and collective activity linked to this. Community, therefore, comes to rest on the naturalization of the roles of men and women within society, and becomes part of its spatial manifestation. As we have already seen, it is usually only when men and women deviate from this role, through being single parents or turning against this refuge from the world, that policy intervenes.

It is against this backdrop that we must place the following statement from the Urban White Paper:

---

1 But note the increasing movement to 'mainstreaming' at present. That is not gender mainstreaming unfortunately, but the recognition that area-based initiatives need to be accompanied (or some would argue replaced) by ensuring mainstream budgets and service deliverers such as education, health etc work towards regeneration outcomes. The use of Public Service Agreements such as on educational achievement, which set minimum standards throughout the country, is evidence of this.

> Women are often the backbone of local community life – they make a huge contribution to improving the quality of life for their families and the wider community as mothers, volunteers, residents and workers (DETR, 2000a, p.37).

However, it is fair to say that the 'thereness of women' (Lofland, 1970) is not totally assumed. The next paragraphs of the White Paper go onto to explain how the government is working to widen opportunities for women through equal pay, family income credits and by providing services such as childcare, public transport and crime reduction. This reflects a welcome policy response to ways in which the urban environment disadvantages women outlined earlier in this chapter. Again however, these do not seem to find themselves embedded into the policies and proposals in the rest of the document. For instance, the section on creating employment provides an example of a women's enterprise centre in Glasgow in one of its vignettes of good practice, but there is no discussion in the rest of the chapter of how gender relates to economic development. As with exclusion we see recognition of the issue of gender but no systematic mechanisms to achieve this through policy.

There are other points to note here. One is the elision of gender and women. While the initial quote from the Urban White Paper noted gender as a barrier to achieving potential, the following pages of the document refer to women only. There is no section on men or gender issues in the urban environment from their perspective, underlining the fact that it is women's disadvantage in the urban environment as opposed to gender relations that are the focus. Yet this mirrors much practice on the ground. Of the three projects under consideration, only the one in South Yorkshire with its EU gender mainstreaming requirements is making a serious attempt to tackle both men's and women's issues rather than simply equating gender with the problems faced by women.

Community, power and decision-making

Within the New Labour lexicon, community is increasingly the site of governance and the place where the responsibility for achieving successful regeneration lies. Power is another area of the New Labour narrative where the underlying reality is at odds with the story being presented (Morgan, 2002; Brownill et al, 2003). Within regeneration it is the role of partnerships that is crucial in this respect and much has been written about the rise of partnerships in regeneration and their implications for local governance (see, for example, Hall and Mawson, 1999; Davies 2001). But it is the implications of this form of urban governance on the differential access to power afforded to different genders that is under consideration here.

Regeneration is not just a policy but also a process, and gender impacts occur in the everyday practice of regeneration and in the way decision-making processes are structured and carried out. Riseborough (1997), Brownill and Darke (1998) and Alsop et al (2001) all point out the contradictory potential for access to power by the gender most usually excluded – women – associated with community governance. While the numbers of women on regeneration partnerships far outstrip their involvement in local government and previous regeneration agencies such as Urban Development Corporations, exclusionary forces are also at work (Brownill and Darke, 1988). Skelcher et al (1996) noted that the conversion of pre-existing networks of local actors into regeneration partnership can serve to exclude women's and black and ethnic minority groups – it all depends on whom you know. May (1997) also notes the 'triple burden' of work, home and community involvement placed on women by the expectations that they will become involved in local activities. In addition, Gilroy (1996) observes that the culture of partnerships and the styles of power which characterize their ways of operating can be exclusionary – 'there's something about men in suits which makes me fall silent' – says one women from a local partnership quoted in her research. In her study of SRB projects in Sheffield, Appleton (1999, p.13) notes that 'women build, men take over'. She observes that while women may be morc active at the community level – this being seen as an extension of their responsibility for the home and children – when it came to partnerships and wider decision-making bodies it was often the men who represented local communities. The WDS (2002) and Alsop et al (2001) also maintain that consultation exercises and meetings are often run in ways which exclude women, particularly ethnic minority women, through being held at times which are difficult for parents to attend and being structured around familiarity with the language and jargon of regeneration speak. The WDS has developed some innovative ways of ensuring greater involvement of women in regeneration projects including using the storytelling traditions within the Somali community and training local women in research skills to undertake surveys of what people would like to see as a result of regeneration schemes within their communities (WDS, 2002).

In her account of regeneration in Bradford, Val Harris (1999) notes the 'ingrained male organizational culture' within regeneration initiatives. This affects both women regeneration officers and community participants. Here is one telling example:

> I'd get the kids to school and spend all day at the office. I would type all the papers and make all the phone calls...but when I got to the board meetings that same evening things we had talked about would be changed, they had all been to the pub in between and all the real talking and stuff went on there (p.17).

Regeneration is often linked to major strategic policies and building programmes. There is very much a culture within these projects which can only be described as macho – tough negotiations, moving quickly, taking the lead from the private sector partners and a 'can-do' mentality which sits uncomfortably with the ways of working of many women's organizations.

Mobilising women and men around gender issues in regeneration has also proved difficult for many projects on the ground. The West Midlands project (WMGRP, 2001) noted that regeneration and gender operate on a strategic level while grassroots organizations are motivated by immediate issues in their communities such as play space and places for people to meet. 'Gender' may be an issue that policymakers and some practitioners recognize, but it is not immediately accessible to groups on the ground. Projects faced a dilemma in that they needed to work around gender to push policy buttons but found that the same focus made grassroots work more difficult.

The discourse and process of renaissance therefore present some interesting challenges from the point of view of gender. Within the policy discourse we can see a progression from the silence on gender that has characterized most previous urban policies to the tentative introduction of gender to the regeneration agenda. However, the failure to follow up lip service to gender and, specifically, the role of women in urban communities with detailed policy requirements and mechanisms, ultimately undermines the inclusive rhetoric of the renaissance. Finally, one of the key issues identified in this section has been the way in which the renaissance leaves unchallenged the relationships between urban space and gender relations. It is to this that we now turn.

Gender, place and renaissance

While issues of exclusion and community are important to the vision put forward by the Urban White Paper, it is its designs on urban space which are surely crucial. That urban space interacts with relations of gender, simultaneously mirroring, transforming and entrenching them has been a central focus of feminist work on the city. The policies put forward and the processes implicit in the Urban White Paper inevitably enter into this dynamic relationship. Notions of liveability, of enterprising cities, of compact and sustainable urban forms need to be looked at through the lens of gender and it is important to reflect on the potential implications of these key aspects of the renaissance for the manifestation of gender in the urban environment. I want, to look at two aspects of the renaissance for some indications of this potential interaction between gender, place and renaissance: gentrification; and compact, sustainable urban form. In doing so I want to underline the complex and contradictory processes at work and to outline some political and theoretical approaches that could strengthen the positive aspects of these processes.

Emancipatory or unjust cities?

Inevitably, as we are talking about relatively new policy directions, there is little research or evidence on the ground to provide firm indications of the relationship between urban space and gender manifest in the renaissance. One area that it may be possible to draw some inferences from is the growing body of work on gender and gentrification (Bondi, 1999; Lees, 2000). As mentioned earlier, the renaissance and Urban White Paper have been called 'a manifesto for gentrification' (Lees, 2003). Many have commented on how the image of liveable cities is based on middle and upper class views of what desirable urban living is like. However, there are also gender issues within this process of gentrification.

The first point to note is its contradictory potential. In the same way that gentrification can be seen as revanchist or emancipatory, the renaissance may open up opportunities for the transformation of gender relations within urban space or the entrenchment of inequalities. Taking up Wilson's (1991) contention that cities are places of opportunity, Caulfield (1994) argues that, in some forms, gentrification can be subversive and can open up contradictions inherent in society that lead to the avoidance of the mono-class, mono-race spaces that potentially result from suburbanization. Some research has noted the connections between gentrification and changing gender relations and practices, at least within the middle classes. Thus Rose (1989) shows how households with large numbers of public-sector professionals dominated by women form a large proportion of gentrifiers. Warde (1991) even went as far as to assert that gentrification was a process driven by career-orientated women, though this has been refuted by later work (Butler 1997; Bondi, 1999) which looks at the interconnections between gender and class and gentrification. The recent publicity surrounding the BoHo index (Demos, 2003) which ranks innovative cities according to the percentage of gay households (among other indicators), and Manchester's place at the top of the UK index, is further evidence of both the emancipatory potential of regeneration and the positive role that restructured gender relations can contribute to the aims of regeneration in general.

But there is another side to this process that demands attention, what could be termed the dark side of the renaissance which we have already explored in relation to who is included and who is excluded. Smith (1996) calls this the revanchist city. This is not about emancipation but about recapturing the city for the middle and upper classes, about regaining control and about displacing those seen as the cause of urban problems – low-income households, single parents (if not gentrifying owner occupiers) and the unemployed. This work resonates with literature that sees the city as repressive to women, as entrenching inequalities, but it also highlights the divisions between women. As with gentrification, gender interacts here with class and race to determine who gets access to this revitalized urban landscape.

Amin and Thrift (2002) note how the process of gentrification excludes those on low incomes, and therefore potentially discriminates against women and women-headed households. The divisions within genders mean it is impossible to talk of an undifferentiated impact of the urban renaissance on women. Who will be employed on low incomes to enable the high earning men and women living in revitalized urban areas to participate in the renaissance lifestyle? The answer in all probability is other women and, depending on the city, more than likely ethnic minority women. The neo-liberal economic agenda identified by many as lying behind the renaissance (see, for example, Peck and Tickell, 2002) promotes polarization between sectors of the economy and population and equally interacts with gender relations. To date much of the literature concentrates on the middle-class owner-occupiers that the renaissance is attracting, but how, for example, the creation of mixed tenure developments on brownfield sites is interacting with relations of class, gender and race remains unexplored (Lees, 2003).

The compact city and the infrastructure of everyday life

Another critical aspect of the urban renaissance vision with implications for gender relations, largely unexplored by the Urban White paper, is the changes to the form, design and use of urban space it promotes. There is much emphasis within contemporary urban policy on concepts such as 'the compact city', 'sustainable urban form' and 'urban villages'. All of these aim to reduce the separation of spheres of life, especially work, home and school. Indeed, the White Paper claims that, already:

> In England we are starting to see people move back into city centres drawn by a life-style where home, work and leisure are interwoven within a single neighbourhood (DETR, 2000a, p.27).

For the government the reasoning behind these polices is to reduce travel and to reuse brownfield sites, but there is contradictory potential here for the restructuring of gender relations in the city.

The role of compact cities and other aspects of the renaissance agenda in providing part of the 'spatial backbone' for the transformation of everyday life mentioned by Horelli (2000) demands further exploration. The potential impact of the compact city idea, both on urban space and in the negotiation of roles and duties within households, is already beginning to be addressed. Work by Jarvis (2002) and McDowell (1997) looks at the relationship between spatial forms, economic development and changes in the way everyday lives are led. They discuss the spatial implication of the household management/ survival strategies within 'successful' and world cities. Typified by dual earner households and industries such as finance and media, with long hours and frequent travel, these economies impact on how households organize their daily routines and their sexual division of labour. As McDowell (1997) has shown, the choice of residential location of such households is heavily influenced by considerations of spatially integrating these roles, at least in the context of London. A crucial consideration here is the way in which gender, class and race interrelate. As with gentrification, there are also unanswered questions about who is going to live in sustainable places with the potential to spatially integrate the multiple roles of their lives and who is forced out to low income housing – potentially through the sustainable communities action plan, at some distance from the city, perpetuating the separation of spheres.

The utopian dream of the proponents of the infrastructure of everyday life, with the creation of self-governing units responsible for local resources and the integration of work, care and housing within these same spaces, is perhaps just that – a utopia. But there is definite resonance between the two debates which could be fruitfully explored. The discourse of the urban renaissance concentrates on the need to retain people in city centres, the implication being that once children come along households move out. However the evidence on the ground suggests some more complex dynamics between gender relations, divisions of labour within households, life courses and urban space are occurring which call for a widening of the policy response and the discourse of renaissance to encompass and enable these processes.

Conclusion

The urban renaissance therefore contains some contradictory messages about gender. Unlike previous rounds of policy, gender is recognized. But the failure to adequately theorize how the renaissance is itself gendered and to specify gendered policy objectives leaves a policy vacuum. More significantly this leaves unaddressed the ways in which renaissance can entrench unequal opportunities within cities. Similarly, the renaissance agenda opens up possibilities for breaking down the spatial separation of spheres (public and private, production and reproduction) and for transforming gender relations in the city, but the ways in which gender is conceptualized within current urban policy and the barriers to access to power and decision-making mean it is unlikely to happen in reality. While current policy presents the illusion of putting gender on the agenda, new practices looking at the infrastructure of everyday life and promoting the mainstreaming of gender within urban policy suggest more positive ways of maximising the potential of the renaissance for restructuring gender relations in the city and creating those inclusive cities that form part of the vision of renaissance.

References

Alsop, R., Clisby, S. and Craig, G. (2001), *Young, Urban and Female*, YWCA, Oxford.

Amin, A. and Thrift, N. (2002), *Cities: Reimagining the Urban*, Polity Press, Cambridge.

Appleton, Z. (1999), 'Women build: men take over', *The Regional Review*, vol. 9(2), pp. 13-15.

Atkinson, R. (1998), 'Countering urban social exclusion: the role of community participation and partnership', in R. Griffiths (ed), *Social Exclusion in Cities: The Urban Policy Challenge*, Occasional Paper No. 3, Faculty of the Built Environment, University of West of England, Bristol.

Atkinson, R. (1999), 'Discourses of partnership and empowerment in contemporary British urban regeneration', *Urban Studies*, vol. 36, pp. 59-73.

Bennett, C., Booth, C. and Yeandle, S. (2000a), *Gender and Regeneration Project: Developing Tools for Regeneration Partnerships: Review of Literature and Policy*, Centre for Regional Economic and Social Research, Sheffield Hallam University, Sheffield.

Bennett, C. Booth, C. and Yeandle, S. (2000b), *Gender and Regeneration Project: Developing Tools for Regeneration Partnerships*, Centre for Regional Economic and Social Research, Sheffield Hallam University, Sheffield.

Bondi, L. (1999), 'Gender, class and gentrification, enriching the debate', *Environment and Planning D*, vol. 17 pp. 261-82.

Braithwaite, M. (1998), *Manual for Integrating Gender Equality into Local and Regional Development*, INBAS, Brussels.

Brownill, S. (1997), 'Regen(d)eration; Women and Urban Policy in the UK', paper presented to *Women and the City Conferences*, Oxford Brookes University, Oxford, September.

Brownill, S. (2000), 'Regen(d)eration: women and urban policy in the UK', in J. Darke et al (eds), *Women and the City*, Palgrave, Basingstoke.

Brownill, S. (2003), 'Engendering Regeneration, paper presented to the Joint AESOP-ACSP Conference *Planning the Network Society*, Leuven, July 8th-12th

Brownill, S. and Darke, J. (1998), *Rich Mix: Strategies for Inclusive Regeneration*, The Policy Press, Bristol.

Brownill, S., Beasley, M. and MacInroy, N. (2003), 'Tales of the City: Some Reflections on Current Regeneration Policy and Practice', paper presented to *Planning Research Conference*, Oxford, April.

Butler, T. (1997), *Gentrification and the Middle Classes*, Ashgate, Aldershot.

Caulfield, J. (1994), *City Form and Everyday Life: Toronto's Gentrification and Critical Social Practice*, University of Toronto Press, Toronto.

CLES (2002), *The Language of Regeneration*, CLES , Manchester.

Darke, J., Woods, R. and Ledwith, S. (eds) (2000), *Women and the City: visibility and voice in urban space*, Palgrave, Basingstoke.

Davies, J. (2001), *Partnerships and Regimes*, Ashgate, Aldershot.

Demos (2003), *BoHo Britain Index*, Demos, London.

DETR (2000a), *Our Towns and Cities: The Future – Delivering an Urban Renaissance*, HMSO, London.

DETR (2000b), *The State of the English Cities*, HMSO, London.

Edwards, C. (2001), 'Inclusion in regeneration: a place for disabled people?', *Urban Studies*, vol. 38, pp. 267-86.

European Commission (1996), Council Resolution of 2nd December 1996 on *Mainstreaming Equal Opportunities for Women and Men in Structural Fund Programmes and Projects.*

Gilroy, R. (1996), 'Building routes to power', *Local Economy*, vol. 11(3), pp. 28-38.

Gilroy, R. and Booth, C. (1999), 'Building an infrastructure for everyday life', *European Planning Studies*, vol. 7(3), pp. 307-24.

Hall, S. and Mawson, J. (1999), *Challenge Funding, Contracts and Area Regeneration: a Decade of Innovation*, The Policy Press, Bristol.

Harris, V. (1999), 'Women and regeneration in Bradford', *The Regional Review*, vol. 9(2), pp. 16-17.

Hayden, D. (1981), 'What would a non-sexist city be like?', in C. Stimpson (eds), *Women and the American City*, University of Chicago Press, Chicago.

Horelli, L (2000), 'Creating the Infrastructure of Everyday Life in the Context of European Local and Regional Development', paper presented to *ESRC Seminar Series: The interface between Public Policy and Gender Equality*, Sheffield.

Imrie, R. and Raco, M. (eds) (2003), *Urban Renaissance? New Labour, Community and Urban Policy*, The Policy Press, Bristol.

Jarvis, H. (2002), 'Lunch is for wimps: what drives parents to work long hours in 'successful' British and US cities?', *Area*, vol. 34(3), pp. 340-52.

Lees, L. (2000), 'A reappraisal of gentrification: towards a 'geography of gentrification'', *Progress in Human Geography*, vol. 24(3), pp. 389-408.

Lees, L. (2003), 'Visions of 'urban renaissance': the Urban Task Force Report and the Urban White Paper', in R. Imrie and M. Raco (eds), *Urban Renaissance? New Labour, Community and Urban Policy*, The Policy Press, Bristol.

LGIU (1994), *Women and Regeneration*, LGIU, London.

Little, J., Peake, L. and Richardson, P. (eds) (1998), *Women in Cities: Gender and the Urban Environment*, Macmillan, Basingstoke.

Lofland, L. (1970), 'The thereness of women: a selective review of urban sociology', in M. Milman and D. Kanter (eds), *Another Voice*, Anchor, New York.

Mackenzie, S. (1989), 'Women in the city', in R. Peet and N. Thrift (eds), *New Models in Geography – Volume 2*, Unwin Hyman, London.

Massey, D. (1994), *Space, Place and Gender*, Polity Press, Cambridge.

May, N. (1997), *Challenging Assumptions*, YPS, York.

Morgan, K. (2002), 'The new regeneration narrative; local development in the multi-level polity', *Local Economy*, vol. 17(3), pp. 191-200.

Morrison, Z. (2003), 'Cultural justice and addressing 'social exclusion': a case study of an SRB project in Blackbird Leys, Oxford', in R. Imrie and M. Raco (eds), *Urban Renaissance? New Labour, Community and Urban Policy*, The Policy Press, Bristol.

McDowell, L. (1993a), 'Space, place and feminism: Part 1', *Progress in Human Geography*, vol. 17(2), pp. 157-79.

McDowell, L. (1993b), 'Space, place and feminism: Part 2', *Progress in Human Geography*, vol. 17(3), 305-18.

McDowell, L. (1997), 'The new service class: housing consumption and lifestyle among London bankers in the 1990s', *Environment and Planning A*, vol. 29, pp. 2061-78.

Objective One South Yorkshire (2003), *Celebrating Women's Contribution to Social and Economic Development in South Yorkshire*, Objective One South Yorkshire, Sheffield.

ODPM (2003), *Sustainable Communities*, HMSO, London.

Peck. J, and Tickell, A. (2002), 'Neoliberalising space', *Antipode*, vol. 34(3), pp. 380-404.

Riseborough, M. (1997), *The Gender Report: Women and Regional Regeneration in the West Midlands*, Centre for Urban and Regional Studies, University of Birmingham, Birmingham.

Rose, D. (1989), 'A feminist perspective of employment restructuring and gentrification: the case of Montreal', in J. Wolch and M. Dear (eds), *The Power of Geography*, Unwin Hyman, Boston, MA.

SEU (1998), *Bringing Britain Together*, Cabinet Office, London.

SEU (2000), *National Strategy for Neighbourhood Renewal: A Framework for Consultation*, Cabinet Office, London.

SEU (2001), *A New Commitment to Neighbourhood Renewal*, HMSO, London.

Skelcher, C., McCabe, A., Lowndes, V. and Nanton, P. (1996), *Community Networks in Urban Regeneration*, The Policy Press, Bristol.

Smith, N. (1996), *The New Urban Frontier*, Routledge, London.

Urban Task Force (1999), *Towards an Urban Renaissance* E & F N Spon, London.

Warde, A. (1991), 'Gentrification as consumption: issues of class and gender', *Environment and Planning D: Society and Space*, vol. 9, pp. 223-32.

West Midlands Gender and Regeneration Project (2001), *Putting the 'G' into Regeneration: Evaluation of the WMGRP*, RAWM, Birmingham.

Wilson, E. (1991), *The Sphinx in the City: Urban Life, the Control of Disorder and Women*, Virago, London.

Women's Design Service (2002), *Re-moving the Goalposts: Women and Regeneration in London*, WDS, London.

Chapter 14

The Cultural Impacts of Globalization and the Future of Urban Cultural Policies[1]

Franco Bianchini

A key aspect of New Labour's urban strategies is a desire to challenge growing patterns of urban homogenization and to create a more diverse and culturally invigorating urban experience. Indeed, at the heart of the Urban White Paper produced by New Labour is a vision of an urban society which embraces a wide range of racial, ethnic and faith communities (DETR, 2000, ch.3). This chapter considers some aspects of the cultural impacts of economic globalization on contemporary Western European cities, by concentrating on three trends: the dispersal of urban functions and the problem of the 'hypertrophic' city; the emergence of 'non-places' and of the 'experience economy', and the increasingly multi-ethnic and multi-cultural composition of cities in the UK and other European countries. The chapter then discusses some of the implications of these processes for the role of culture and cultural policies within future urban strategies.

The problem of urban hypertrophy

The debate on the cultural impacts of globalization on cities has intensified in recent years. During the 1990s there were widespread concerns about growing social divisions, fear of crime and alienation, the standardization of architecture and retail environments (with the decline of independent shops and the rise of multiple retailers), and the dispersal of urban services, residential and industrial functions over a larger area. The latter trend contributed to a crisis of local identity, and to making the provision of sustainable public transport systems more difficult (Bianchini and Ghilardi Santacatterina, 1997, pp.70-72).

---

1 This chapter has its foundations in a speech I delivered at the European Summer University in Birmingham in July 2002. The section entitled 'The rise of the multi-ethnic European city' is based on *Planning for the Cosmopolitan City*, an unpublished report I have written with Jude Bloomfield, commissioned by Comedia (2002).

Despite the revival of interest in the idea of the more environmentally sustainable, and less car-dependent, 'compact city' – advocated, among others, by Lord Rogers of Riverside, Chair of the UK government's Urban Task Force and reflected in the government's Urban White Paper – urban sprawl is arguably more visible today than a decade or so ago, especially in countries like Britain, which have adopted a market-driven model of urban development.

The hypertrophy of the city, sprawling into the countryside, in a sense goes hand-in-hand with the hypertrophy of the human body itself. Urban sprawl makes walking or cycling in the city often impractical, unpleasant and in some cases dangerous, and public transport often not viable, especially for many suburban and outer urban residential areas. This has the effect of massively reducing the number of pedestrians and cyclists in city streets and public spaces, and subsequently of contributing to fear of crime. As fewer people use the public realm, there is less public demand for it to be properly maintained and upgraded. There is also less demand for linking existing (and often pleasant) but disconnected parks, squares, cycleways and walkways so that they form legible and well-functioning public space networks. Dependence on the car, and the related lack of exercise, is one of the key reasons why growing numbers of people in Europe today are overweight or obese. According to research by Denmark's National Board of Health[2], 40 million EU citizens are overweight. This is particularly a problem for children (who constitute about six million of the 40 million overweight Europeans) due to factors including of course a preference for fast food, sugared drinks and sweets, but also sedentary leisure pursuits (like TV and computer games), the shortage of safe indoor and outdoor play areas, and the fact that their parents are often anxious about letting them walk to school or to their friends' homes, thus tending to ferry them everywhere by car.

Models of urban development conceived in countries like the US, Canada and Australia – which, largely because of the amount of space at their disposal, have a significantly different relationship between the city and the countryside from that characterising European history – have become established also in Europe. This can be seen in the mushrooming of out-of-town hypermarkets, shopping centres and 'citadels of entertainment' including multiplex cinemas, bowling alleys, fast food restaurants, and other leisure attractions. These places tend to be lacking in local distinctiveness, and resemble each other both in their design and their offer of retail and leisure activities, dominated by the large multiples. Despite this, they are increasingly significant as public spaces, although clearly not designed with that function in mind. For example, people, when visiting their out-of-town supermarket, multiplex cinema or leisure centre, often bump into or arrange to meet neighbours, friends and colleagues in the car park. This dull, pedestrian-unfriendly and 'placeless' expanse of tarmac, in many cases surrounded by badly designed sheds, is clearly not the most stimulating place for socialising and conviviality. The fact that these car parks have become significant components of

---

2 See www.eu2002.dk/news

the public realm is one of the curious and worrying aspects of the hypertrophic city.

The emergence of 'non-places' and of the 'experience economy'

Once you step inside the multiplex cinema, or the bowling alley, or the themed bar or restaurant, or the town centre or out of town shopping mall, you find that these places tend to lack the sense of discovery, unpredictability and of multiple possibilities which is a feature of traditional European city centres. 'Anywhere' places like most shopping malls and fast food restaurants are in many cases characterized by what American social theorist George Ritzer (1993) calls 'McDonaldization', a 'rational' model of organization which offers efficiency, speed and predictability of the quality of the product, but which can also be dehumanising both for the customers and for the people who provide the service. French anthropologist Marc Augé describes such places and others, such as airport lounges, supermarkets and cashpoints as 'non-places', typical of a world 'surrendered to solitary individuality, to the fleeting, the temporary and ephemeral' (1995, p.78).

The mushrooming of 'non-places' coexists with the growing currency of enthusiastic arguments for turning cities more and more into theme parks. The work of B. Joseph Pine II and James H. Gilmore (1998 and see also 1999) has been particularly influential in this regard. They write that, 'an experience occurs when a company intentionally uses services as the stage, and goods as props, to engage individual customers in a way that creates a memorable event' (1998, p.98). The two authors argue that as competition for the sale of services increases (for example, competition between the growing number of designer clothes shops, cafes, bars and restaurants in city centres) services have to be repackaged, themed and offered as 'experiences'. Moreover, 'an effective theme is concise and compelling...the theme must drive all of the design elements and staged events of the experience toward a unified story line that wholly captivates the customer' (1998, p.103). They add that, 'experience stagers...must eliminate anything that diminishes, contradicts, or distracts from the theme' (ibid.).

The argument made by Pine II and Gilmore is relevant to British cities because we are seeing here the emergence of new types of cultural attractions, inspired by American approaches to theming. Niketown in Oxford Circus, London, for example, is much more than a shop. It is an interactive museum of human performance in athletics and other sports. There are similarities here to the Sephora perfume stores in Paris, Nice and Barcelona, which offer overarching experiences, ranging from museum of scents, to bookshop, live event and space for meditation. This emerging 'experience economy' is not necessarily a negative phenomenon. As Marc Pachter and Charles Landry observe, it creates new types of institutions which blur 'the boundaries between shopping, learning and the experience of culture' (2001, p.46). These places can become successful visitor attractions and enrich a city's cultural landscape. However, new themed attractions often lack subtlety. Their effect can be to channel, control, simplify and 'banalize' our urban experiences.

The rise of the multi-ethnic European city

A third key factor of change concerns the increasingly multi-ethnic and multicultural character of European cities (Borja and Castells, 1997) that is the result of both increasing legal and illegal migration and the higher birth rate among populations of non-European descent. This trend could provide opportunities for artistic, cultural, social, economic, organizational and political innovation, rooted in genuine local distinctiveness. Very soon in many European cities the social groups still often referred to as 'ethnic minoritics' will not be minorities at all. These developments give rise to challenges for city governments, but also offer opportunities for counteracting the problem of the growing cultural standardization of European cities. There are lively debates in Europe as to which strategy would be the most effective.

Corporate multiculturalism

Since the 1980s, pragmatic, corporate multiculturalism has been the dominant urban policy response to the presence of ethnic minorities in Britain. This approach has worked in the main well in terms of securing relatively harmonious race relations (despite the incidents in 2001 in towns and cities in northern and central England, including Oldham, Bradford, Burnley, Leeds, Accrington and Stoke). It recognized former colonial subjects who settled in Britain as citizens, and came to address racial inequality and discrimination, both by legislative remedy and by accommodating ethnic minorities as communities, by negotiating with and channelling resources to group leaders. The weaknesses of multicultural policies in Britain have now become more apparent. By treating ethnic minorities as unified communities at the political – though not juridical – level, they often act as corporate groups, dominated by un-elected leaders or male elders who speak on behalf of the community, as though no individual rights or diversity of opinion operate within it. These features have been exacerbated by communitarian ideology, adopted by some local activists and politicians who close the door on dialogue and mediation, by fuelling head-on conflict over values between groups who are counter-posed as ethnic opposites. Corporate multiculturalism necessarily limits intercultural communication and understanding, and tries to protect community boundaries and traditional identities. This model has largely failed to build on the plurality of affiliations and the new kinds of identity that have emerged with subsequent generations born in the UK.

The British approach to multiculturalism is being re-examined in the light of the Macpherson Report (Macpherson, 1999) and, following the 2001 riots, the Cantle Report (Cantle, 2001). The ensuing debate is more open to consideration of different policy frameworks for cultural diversity. It would appear that such debates have an important role to play in shaping the cultural dynamics of urban policies in Britain over the next decade.

Civic cultural integration

France is characterized by a strong tradition of civic republicanism in which immigrants from the colonies have been integrated as citizens in a secular state with universal rights, which find their origin in the Revolution of 1789. However, until recently, this has happened within an assumption of the cultural uniformity of what it means to be French – whose symbols range from the French language as the embodiment of civilization, guarded against American contamination, to the distinctive flavours of regional cheeses and wines. While civic republicanism is secular, and religion considered a private matter, the personal display of symbols of religious faith by Catholics (and by Jews), has been tolerated in contrast to racist controversies about Muslim girls wearing headscarves to school. French institutions are now dealing with the problems of detaching universal citizenship rights from specific cultural norms – recognising the *de facto* pluralist character of French culture. This process has been helped by the success of the French national team in the football World Cup in 1998 and in the European Championships in 2000. The key role played in these victories by French footballers of diverse ethnic origins like Zidane, Henry, Vieira and Djorkaeff has enabled the Left in France to turn what could have been a traditional reassertion of national grandeur into a pluralistic redefinition of the nation.

Compared to Britain, the French civic tradition is better able to transcend neighbourhood-based class and ethnic identities, through a stronger sense of shared belonging to the city. Such civic identification is especially important today, in times of growing social fragmentation. In France the civic space is highly prized, as evidenced by the quality of design, maintenance and access to the public realm – for example, the successful upgrading of public transport systems and public spaces in cities like Lyons and Strasbourg. The high quality of urban spaces and services is visible also in schemes for improving peripheral housing estates (*banlieues*) where there are high concentrations of immigrants, such as the Banlieues '89 project, led by architect Roland Castro. At its most successful, it added a degree of civic urbanity to working-class dormitory areas, through the development of new squares, high quality housing, public art, cultural centres and festivals (Castro, 1994).

Interculturalism

This approach goes beyond equal opportunities and respect for existing cultural differences to the pluralist transformation of public space, civic culture and institutions. It does not recognize cultural boundaries as fixed but as in a state of flux and remaking. An intercultural approach aims to facilitate dialogue, exchange and reciprocal understanding between people of different cultural backgrounds. Urban cultural policies based on this approach, for example, would prioritize funding for projects where different cultures intersect, 'contaminate' each other and hybridize. This contrasts with the multicultural model, where funding is directed within the well-defined boundaries of recognized cultural communities. In other words, intercultural urban policies would be aimed at promoting cross-fertilization across all cultural boundaries, between 'majority' and 'minorities', 'dominant' and 'sub' cultures, localities, classes, faiths, disciplines and genres, as the source of cultural, social, political and economic innovation.

There are significant intercultural experiments at city level in many national contexts, including Canada, Denmark, France, Italy, the Netherlands and Portugal. For example, the regional authority in Tuscany (Regione Toscana) created 80 intercultural centres in public libraries in the region between 1999 and 2001. This initiative forms part of Regione Toscana's *Porto Franco* (Free Port) project, which seeks to change perceptions of cultural diversity and of visible minorities in the region by recasting Tuscan identity as diverse, and by reinterpreting the history of Tuscany as the product of intercultural influences from the Etruscans to the middle ages, when Tuscan society was influenced by Arab traditions of science, philosophy and the arts[3].

The new production of the built environment, in the centres of multi-ethnic cities in the UK, tends to be dominated by corporate international styles, with little consideration of cultural diversity and of how to draw on the skills and creativity of local citizens. The planning system in Britain appears to be too weak, or unconvinced about the merits of an intercultural strategy, and unwilling or unable to negotiate with developers to produce a greater diversity of styles, sources, contracts and uses. As a result, city centres fail to reflect the richness of local cultures. There is, for instance, virtually no involvement in new city centre-based developments of craftspeople from ethnic minority backgrounds, who work regularly in the production of religious buildings in many UK cities. While the Urban White Paper clearly envisages a greater role for cultural considerations within the planning system, it is less clear on the types of strategies and powers planners should use in order to create a more culturally diverse urban experience.

An experiment which showed some of the potential of intercultural urban design was carried out in the 'Balti zone' of the Ladypool Road, Sparkhill in 1998, (funded partly by the ERDF's URBAN programme) by Prasada – a Sanskrit term for a temple or palace which is also an acronym for Practice, Research and Advancement in South Asian Design and Architecture, an institute based at De Montfort University in Leicester. Prasada's aim is to bring together the study of traditional South Asian architectural forms, visual arts and crafts with contemporary South Asian cultural expression. The designs for the Balti zone are based on Moghul motifs and forms which add to and interact with the Victorian pavilions and church spires of the area[4].

The invention of new civic events can build on needs, desires and dreams,

---

3 See www.cultura.toscana.it/intercultura.htm and www.cultura.toscana.it/progetti/portofranco/home.htm

4 See www.lsa.dmu.ac.uk/Research/Prasada/projects.htm

creating not a false sense of jollity or togetherness (in some cases manufactured by tourist or place marketing agencies) but memorable festive occasions in which large swathes of the city participate in person, express their own ways of celebrating or commemorating, and share moments of conviviality. Such occasions express the French urban theorist, Henri Lefebvre's idea of the *fête* as a disruption of established routines that prefigures a possible alternative future (Lefebvre, 1996). One example of an attempt at enacting a new pluralistic civic identity is the annual Karnivale der Kulturen in Berlin – which is not a Carnival in the African Caribbean, Latin American or Mediterranean sense, which have their roots in Catholic culture. The Karnivale is held in the streets, with the participation of almost all the minority cultural organizations in the city, and has become hugely popular, attended last year by an estimated 600,000 Berliners. The structure of the event is not fully intercultural. Hybrid forms of music are presented in traditional terms, according to country of origin, on separate stages – Turkish dance, Russian disco, reggae, tabla, and food stands are separated according to national, geopolitical or ethnic definitions of the culture. So while it succeeds in creating a multicultural public space, the Karnivale does not fully exploit the potential of the cultural mixes that are a unique product of Berlin.

Intercultural place marketing strategies are being introduced at neighbourhood level in some cities, in some cases to counteract negative images which characterize urban areas where ethnic minority populations are concentrated. One example is Nottingham's Hyson Green district, where the Partnership Council – in collaboration with other local stakeholders – implemented a place marketing strategy to counter the stigmas of poverty, racism and crime, under the campaign slogan 'Life at the heart of the city'. It focused on the history and of the area and residents' perceptions of its tolerance, easy-going atmosphere and mix of cultures – reflected, for example, by the wide range of specialist shops, ethnic foods and fabrics – as well as its closeness to the city centre, to change its negative image. The media campaign used initiatives including adverts in the local press, posters on buses, a photographic competition and a website showcasing the area's cultural diversity. A series of highly publicised events, such as a public food tasting in the market square, a specially produced Hyson Green tea launched at a tea dance and a *Life at the Heart* CD featuring music tracks and lyrics by pupils in local schools were promoted as keys to experiencing the area differently. The project, also funded by the ERDF's URBAN Programme from 2000 to 2002 with an initial £100,000 budget, appears from independent evaluation work to have had a positive impact on the consciousness of residents and outsiders, attracting commercial investors and new homeowners to the area[5].

In short, intercultural approaches in urban policy can help deal with the dangers of cultural standardization and of the loss of distinctiveness which can be by-products of many entrepreneurial urban regeneration strategies.

---

5 See www.life-at-the-heart.co.uk/hyson.htm

Transculturalism

Cities that have developed an intercultural practice as part of mainstream urban strategies would be able to undertake transcultural projects, which transcend cultural differences, and focus on common humanity. Transculturalism aims to transcend cultural differences through values which define and unify us as a species, i.e. peace, solidarity, human rights and environmental sustainability. These values should find embodiment in the symbols of the city centre, flagship buildings, public art, education, transport, library and information services and social policies.

This approach is not new. It gained momentum after the Second World War with the development of peace memorials and gardens, and of the town twinning movement. In its more traditional forms, transculturalism can produce anodyne or banal solutions which unconsciously fall back on monocultural traditions which are assumed to be universal, but have not sufficiently engaged in an intercultural process.

The acceleration of globalization processes and the world environmental crisis have given new impetus to transcultural initiatives like the Local Agenda 21 movement, and global ethics and citizenship education programmes aimed at young people, such as the Birmingham Young People's Parliament project. Meanwhile, Barcelona City Council, in co-operation with the Catalan and Spanish governments and UNESCO, has launched the Universal Forum of Cultures initiative. First staged in 2004, this is a programme of exhibitions, performances, markets, games, conferences and debates focused on transcultural themes, involving most countries around the globe. The Forum is intended to be the first of a series of programmes, held every four years in different cities across the world[6].

There is a need in Britain for a debate on how the inclusion in future urban strategies of elements of the civic cultural integration, intercultural and transcultural approaches explored in this section could contribute to making the country's existing corporate multiculturalist model more open, democratic and creative.

'Cultural planning' strategies: learning from the processes of cultural production

The idea of 'cultural planning' is a possible response to the problematic cultural implications of globalization for cities. It is an attempt to challenge traditional approaches to urban development by recognising the value of local cultural resources. In many ways it is possible to detect traces of a cultural planning strategy within New Labour's urban renaissance programme, for example in the planning guidelines of the Urban White Paper, or in aspects of the policies of Neighbourhood Renewal Unit.

---

6 See www.barcelona2004.org

There is no doubt that the emphasis which was placed on the impact of cultural activities on consumer service industries, property development and place marketing in European urban cultural policies during the 1980s and the 1990s was an important addition to the battery of arguments for policy-making in this field. This perspective, however, is too narrow to provide a sound basis for sustainable urban development. 'Cultural planning', which has been discussed since the early 1990s in North America, Australia and Europe (Bianchini, 1990 and 1996; McNulty, 1991; Mercer, 1991 and 1996) is a possible alternative to both cultural policy-led urban regeneration strategies and traditional cultural policies. Unlike traditional cultural policies – which are still mainly based on aesthetic definitions of 'culture' as 'art' – cultural planning adopts as its basis a broad definition of 'cultural resources', which consists of the following elements:

- arts and media activities and institutions;
- the cultures of youth, ethnic minorities and other communities of interest;
- heritage, including archaeology, gastronomy, local dialects and rituals;
- local and external images and perceptions of a city, including the ways in which they change in the course of history and how they can be interpreted by different groups within the population – by, for example, children, particular ethnic communities, and the elderly;
- the natural and built environments, including public and open spaces;
- the diversity and quality of leisure, cultural, eating, drinking and entertainment facilities and activities;
- local milieu and institutions for intellectual and scientific innovation, including universities and private sector research centres;
- the repertoire of local products and skills in the crafts, manufacturing and services, including local food products, gastronomic and design traditions.

As of yet this appears to be a broader conceptualization of culture than that adopted by the New Labour government.

It is also significant that while traditional cultural policies tend to be sectorally focused – for example, policies for the development of theatre, dance, literature, the crafts and other specific forms of cultural activity – cultural planning adopts a territorial remit. Its purpose is to see how the pool of cultural resources identified above can contribute to the integrated development of a place, whether a neighbourhood, a city or a region. By placing cultural resources at the centre of the policy-making table, two-way relationships can be established between these resources and any type of public policy in fields ranging from economic development to housing, health, education, social services, tourism, urban planning, architecture, townscape design, and cultural policy itself. Cultural planning cuts across the divides between the public, private and voluntary sectors, different institutional concerns, types of knowledge and professional disciplines. In addition, cultural planning would encourage innovation in cultural production, for example through interculturalism, co-operation between artists and scientists, and crossovers between different cultural forms. It is also important to clarify that cultural planning is not intended as 'the planning of culture' – an impossible, undesirable and dangerous undertaking – but rather as a culturally sensitive approach to urban planning and policy. Once again, while contemporary urban planning under New Labour does address cultural issues, it does not as yet place culture at the centre of planning.

Crucially, in this context, advocates of the cultural planning approach argue that policy-makers in all fields should not simply be making an instrumental use of cultural resources as tools for achieving non-cultural goals, but should let their own mindsets and assumptions be transformed by contact with the richness and complexity of the often hidden and invisible assets of local cultural life. This can happen if policy-makers learn from the types of thinking characterising processes of cultural production.

Six main features of such processes can be identified. Firstly, the work of the best artists is, by nature, *interdisciplinary, lateral and holistic* and usually crosses disciplinary boundaries. By contrast, in the world of urban policy-making today, departmental and disciplinary divisions and rigidities remain among the most important blockages to innovation. Secondly, they tend to be *innovation-oriented, original*, and in some cases *experimental*. Unfortunately, in many of the practices surrounding physical planning and urban regeneration not enough space for experiment is allowed – there are perhaps not enough ideas competitions, research and development projects, and insufficient learning from examples of best practice from the private sector. There is also an excessive fear of risk, and often an inability to distinguish incompetent mistakes from 'competent' ones, which may contain the seeds of future success. Thirdly, artists are often renowned for asking awkward questions, for being *critical*, and for exploring contradictions and conflicts through their work and their public role. On the other hand, urban policies are in many cases well known for the opposite reasons – for pretending that there are no conflicts and contradictions, and that a public-private partnership consensus can be relatively easily achieved (often based on the 'common sense' idea that 'what is good for the business sector is good for the city'). There is in many cases a failure to understand that perhaps those conflicts and contradictions should be viewed positively, as policy resources to be explored, to develop more sophisticated, sustainable and democratic future urban strategies.

The fourth set of characteristics of cultural production is that it tends to be *people-centred, humanistic*, and healthily *suspicious of technological and economic determinism*. The influence of deterministic thinking on urban planning and policy is a continuing contributory factor to poor decision-making. Fifthly, it is a *'cultured'* approach, meaning that it is critically aware of history, and of traditions of cultural expression. One of the main critiques of physical planners, especially in Northern Europe, has been that they have not paid sufficient attention to aesthetic and historical considerations, and have made often fairly insensitive decisions, especially in the 1960s and early 1970s. One example is the legacy of urban motorways built especially in the 1960s, which have blighted and dismembered so many historic city centres in the UK and in other Northern European countries.

The final feature of cultural production is that artists insist typically on their work being *open-ended* and *non-instrumental* and on having a *non-judgmental* moment of creativity to try out new paths and ideas. This is, of course, often difficult to argue in urban policy-making, where there is tremendous pressure – from the media, opposition politicians, voters, pressure groups, as well as from central government, through extremely complex systems of auditing – to be very instrumental and achieve results quickly. However, urban strategies could be conceptualized, especially in their early stages, as more of a workshop process, with, for example, the use of temporary architecture to try out different ways of solving problems without committing oneself too early to a solution in bricks and mortar[7].

In cultural planning, the cultural policy-maker, the artist and/or the cultural manager can become the gatekeeper between the sphere of cultural production – the world of ideas and of the production of meaning – and any area of policy-making. In this sense the cultural planner's role is to improve the cultural skills of politicians and other policy-makers.

Researching local cultural resources

Today in the UK there is, at least in theory, an increasing recognition of the importance of local cultural resources. Every local authority in England was encouraged by the government to prepare a Local Cultural Strategy (LCS), by the end of 2002, aimed at integrating cultural resources into local economic, education, environmental, tourism, social and health policies. LCS development was not a statutory duty for local authorities, but it formed part of Best Value performance reviews. It is notable that in the research, on which these local cultural strategies are based, there is an overwhelming emphasis on needs analysis, and not enough on entrepreneurial opportunities and desires, on the dreams of individuals and groups in civil society. Local authorities and Local Strategic Partnerships could perform a useful brokerage function to bring to fruition these entrepreneurial opportunities. This process, however, would have to involve recognition of obstacles and constraints. In some cases, an excessive emphasis on auditing, monitoring and evaluation has become a constraint. It is diverting an excessive amount of resources and time away from the more creative task of identifying the cultural resources themselves, establishing the necessary partnerships and developing innovative strategies. There is also not enough emphasis in many places on the gatekeepers, gateways, networks and alliances linking the local cultural economy with national and international markets and opportunities. This is particularly important in cities which have large multi-ethnic

7 On the idea of the 'creative city' see Landry and Bianchini (1995) and Landry (2000).

populations. Often diasporic networks are not very visible because the gatekeepers are not particularly well integrated into the local policy network.

Equally, it is important for local authorities to learn from certain private sector industries, like the fashion and design sectors, to value people who can spot talent and identify creative and innovative milieu. These talent and trendspotters, sometimes described as 'coolhunters', can feed vital information into the local policy-making system. They can also design support services (ranging from access to venture capital, technology and cheap premises to advice on management, marketing and intellectual property) tailored for talented young people wishing to work in the creative industries. By doing this, they can help prevent the migration of talent from regional cities to London and the other global centres of the cultural economy.

Lastly, very few towns or cities have an adequate understanding of their image, not only now, but also historically. This is important because images of three or four centuries ago can still have a resonance and be 'used' to develop distinctive cultural initiatives and city promotion strategies. Researching local images means studying their multi-faceted components, from jokes and 'conventional wisdom' to songs, film, literary representations, mythology and media coverage. There are some worrying results from recent research by Chris Murray (2001). His analysis of tourism brochures and other place marketing literature produced by local authorities and tourism promotion agencies in 77 localities in England and Wales revealed 'a strong and persistent tendency...to focus on the past and be generally backward-looking; …[to] represent places as culturally uniform; and not to show diversity, but to promote a similar, bland mix of facilities and attractions for every area' (2001, p.9).

Specialists with a narrow training in rather formulaic approaches to product marketing – which is not appropriate for complex and multi-faceted entities such as cities – tend to dominate the place marketing discipline. Experts in product marketing need to work together with other disciplines possessing knowledge of the locality in historical, geographical, sociological, anthropological, economic and political terms. In other words, there is a need for a more interdisciplinary, team approach to city marketing, which would also involve artists and other people from the cultural sector.

Conclusions

In a speech to a conference in Dublin in 1994, the then Irish Minister of Culture, Michael D. Higgins, said:

> For too long...financial institutions have used their hegemony to set limits to policy in other areas, constantly diminishing the cultural space in which so much radical or innovative thinking is possible. One result has been a dire impoverishment of social philosophy: we no longer seem to be living in countries but in economies. It is not inappropriate to use the concept 'the depeopled economy' for such a development.

> Another consequence of the fracturing of intellectual life has been the devaluation of play as a creative activity, for a consumer society is so goal-oriented that it has little use for any goal-free activity. *Homo economicus* feels justified by his products, whereas play is concerned with means rather than ends, with the quality of an action rather than its results. Hence the major contradiction of our economic arrangements: that a society based on the negation of the play element presents itself as uniquely able to deliver play – but only as an experience of consumption. In the process play has been placed in the service of something which is not at all playful, being narrowed, some would say degraded to the level of specialized work. This degradation is only possible in a society which has lost an ancient wisdom which taught us that play, far from being a deviation from the workaday norm, is the basis of all culture (Higgins, 1994).

Higgins' argument about play is especially important in relation to the phenomenon, discussed earlier, of the danger of transforming cities more and more into theme parks. It would be more interesting and productive to try to, as Higgins suggests, recover a dimension of playfulness in cities, not primarily as an experience of consumption and carefully manufactured and staged commercial entertainment, but as a process of education and re-discovery.

Urban policy and the management and delivery of urban services, in short, should be infused with an understanding of the fine grain of the creative contents and of the cultural resources of a city. By drawing inspiration from the marvellous and ever changing detail of local culture, urban policy-makers should be better able to counteract the negative effects of globalization in their cities.

References

Augé, M. (1995), *Non-Places*, Verso, London.

Bianchini, F. (1990), 'Urban renaissance? The arts and the urban regeneration process', in S. MacGregor and B. Pimlott (eds) *Tackling the Inner Cities*, Clarendon, Oxford.

Bianchini, F. (1996), '"Cultural planning": an innovative approach to urban development', in J. Verwijnen and P. Lehtovuori (eds) *Managing Urban Change*, University of Art and Design, Helsinki.

Bianchini, F. and Ghilardi Santacatterina, L. (1997) *Culture and Neighbourhoods: A Comparative Report*, Council of Europe Press, Strasbourg.

Borja, J. and Castells, M. (1997), *Local and Global: The Management of Cities in the Information Age*, Earthscan, London.

Cantle, E. (2001), *Community Cohesion: A Report of the Independent Review Team Chaired by Ted Cantle*, Home Office, London.

Castro, R. (1994), *Civilisation Urbaine ou Barbarie*, Plon, Paris.

DETR (2000), *Our Towns and Cities: the Future – Delivering an Urban Renaissance*, HMSO, London.

Higgins, M. (1994), 'The Economy of the Arts: The Big Picture', unpublished paper presented at the conference *The Economy of the Arts*, Dublin, December.

Landry, C. and Bianchini, F. (1995), *The Creative City*, Demos, London.

Landry, C. (2000), *The Creative City: A Toolkit for Urban Innovators*, Earthscan, London.

Lefebvre, H. (1996), *Writings on Cities*, Blackwell, Oxford.

Macpherson, W. (1999), *The Stephen Lawrence Inquiry: Report of an Inquiry by Sir William Macpherson of Cluny*, HMSO, London.

McNulty, R. (1991), 'Cultural planning: a movement for civic progress', in *The Cultural Planning Conference*, EIT, Mornington, Victoria, Australia.

Mercer, C. (1991), 'What is cultural planning?', paper presented at the *Community Arts Network National Conference*, Sydney, Australia, 10th October.

Mercer, C. (1996), 'By accident or design. Can culture be planned?', in F. Matarasso and S. Halls (eds.), *The Art of Regeneration*, Nottingham City Council and Comedia, Bournes Green.

Murray, C. (2001), *Making Sense of Place*, Comedia, Bournes Green, in association with the International Cultural Planning and Policy Unit (ICPPU), De Montfort University, Leicester.

Pachter, M. and Landry, C. (2001), *Culture at the Crossroads*, Comedia, Bournes Green.

Pine II, B. J. and Gilmore, J. (1998), 'Welcome to the experience economy', *Harvard Business Review*, July-August.

Pine II, B. J. and Gilmore, J. (1999), *The Experience Economy*, Harvard Business School Press, Boston.

Ritzer, G. (1993), *The MacDonaldization of Society*, Pine Forge Press, Thousand Oaks, Ca.

Index